Diogo Gobira, Lucas Processi

**ALM Modeling and Balance Sheet Optimization**

# The Moorad Choudhry Global Banking Series

Series Editor
Professor Moorad Choudhry

Diogo Gobira, Lucas Processi

# ALM Modeling and Balance Sheet Optimization

A Mathematical Approach to Banking

DE GRUYTER

The views, thoughts and opinions expressed in this book represent those of the authors in their individual private capacities, and should not in any way be attributed to any employing institution, or to the authors as directors, representatives, officers, or employees of any affiliated institution. While every attempt is made to ensure accuracy, the authors or the publisher will not accept any liability for any errors or omissions herein. This book does not constitute investment advice and its contents should not be construed as such. Any opinion expressed does not constitute a recommendation for action to any reader. The contents should not be considered as a recommendation to deal in any financial market or instrument and the authors, the publisher, the editor, any named entity, affiliated body or academic institution will not accept liability for the impact of any actions arising from a reading of any material in this book.

ISBN 978-3-11-066422-5
e-ISBN (PDF) 978-3-11-066466-9
e-ISBN (EPUB) 978-3-11-066438-6
ISSN 2627-8847

**Library of Congress Control Number: 2023938222**

**Bibliographic information published by the Deutsche Nationalbibliothek**
The Deutsche Nationalbibliothek lists this publication in the Deutsche Nationalbibliografie; detailed bibliographic data are available on the Internet at http://dnb.dnb.de.


Cover image: Nikada/E+/Getty Images
Typesetting: VTeX UAB, Lithuania
Printing and binding: CPI books GmbH, Leck

www.degruyter.com

# Foreword

> A bank is a place that will lend you money, if you can prove that you don't need it.
>
> Bob Hope

At its core, the banking industry is as straightforward as the quote suggests: lending money to those who are able to repay the loan plus a fair amount of interest. However, for those tasked with managing a bank, there are numerous complexities that can keep them up at night.

As a banker, one must be equipped to handle a highly complex and multifaceted set of challenges, including managing interest rate and foreign exchange mismatches, preventing chaotic growth, combating fraud, reducing credit risk, managing reputational risk, retaining market share, and taming regulatory costs, among others. To address these issues, the banking industry and regulators have, as we all learned in school and in life, taken a fragmented approach, breaking down each problem and finding a separate solution for each one. It is the old saying attributed to Julius Caesar: "divide and conquer."

As a result, for each problem, a formula or specialized structure was developed to manage it effectively. This included different standards for dealing with credit risk, market risk, operational risk, and liquidity risk. Bankers then created separate teams to handle each type of risk, effectively putting each problem into its own box.

With time, regulations shifted their focus from ensuring the adequacy of current capital and liquidity to ensuring the long-term sustainability of financial institutions. This led to a need for testing the feasibility of institutions' plans in different scenarios and over the long-term. To do this, it was necessary to break down the silos and assess the interconnectivity between them.

The process of consolidation can either involve the straightforward (yet potentially flawed) approach of compiling projections from various units of a bank into a spreadsheet, or a more sophisticated method that involves the focused development of a single model. With the latter approach, each expert can bring their unique contribution within their domain of expertise and responsibility.

The second approach of consolidation comes with numerous benefits, such as reducing team effort, minimizing operational risk, and ensuring consistency across scenarios. However, it results in a complex model that encompasses the entire banking business, including treasury management, credit granting, compliance with banking regulations, managerial constraints, and pricing criteria that ultimately drive the profitability desired by shareholders. This book endeavors to unravel this complex web of rules and behaviors in a practical manner through the use of an optimization model under uncertainty.

The book comes from the perspective of someone who has dedicated substantial time to tackling this issue in real financial institutions. Thus, it offers valuable insights, particularly because its aim is not simply to describe an academic model. Instead, the

https://doi.org/10.1515/9783110664669-201

book shares observations on overcoming skepticism in institutions, the importance of simplification for practical use, troubleshooting strategies, and other tips. It is, therefore, a streamlined rocket science to efficient bank management for bankers who want to leave behind the traditional methods of the old banking era, forsaking once and for all the wagons of the old banking west.

Felipe Canedo
Head of Treasury Division at Brazilian National Development Bank (BNDES)

# Preface

The advent of linear programming has had a tremendous impact on the world. Developed by George Dantzig in 1947, linear programming has revolutionized decision-making in a variety of industries, like airlines, retail, power planning, shipping, telecommunications, consumer goods, and recently even artificial intelligence, which in its background makes intensive use of mathematical programming methods (Birge, 2022).

In today's competitive markets, having an optimization model is no longer a matter of choice, but a matter of survival. Without an optimization model, companies cannot effectively analyze and organize all the data, constraints, and targets they have, which will invariably lead to continued destruction of business value that could have been avoided. As a result, companies that do not have an optimization model in place are at a distinct disadvantage, since they just can't make the necessary adjustments to remain competitive.

In the context of banking, there can be numerous departmental use cases for optimization models. Asset management for sure is the most popular example of an optimization use case in finance, although applications in the area of funding, liquidity and settlement have become increasingly present since this area was inaugurated in 1952 by Markowitz's efficient portfolio model (Markowitz, 1952) which, by the way, was deeply rooted in Dantzig's accomplishments. However, at the end of the day, what really matters to shareholders and stakeholders in general is the financial health of the bank as a whole, not specific parts of it. Therefore, it makes sense to think that the main optimization use case in a bank should be the global optimization of the institution's balance sheet.

But, building a balance sheet optimization model is a challenging task due to the complexity of each of the parts that compose it and that affect its dynamics, such as financial instruments, accounting rules, business targets, risk limits, regulatory constraints, and the various scenarios that could arise in the future. Despite the individual difficulties inherent in each of the topics mentioned, it remains important to grasp their interconnections and how they affect the overall performance of the bank.

At a more conceptual level, it is possible to grasp the connection between these areas of knowledge and how a balance sheet changes over time. Many articles and books focus on the significance of integrated capital and risk management, and the need to connect business plans to various constraints under current and potential scenarios the institution may encounter in the future. Regulators also endorse this approach and highlight its importance through increasingly complex integrated stress testing exercises.

On a more technical level, the situation is quite different. As far as we know, there is no consensus on the most effective technical strategies for handling the goal and practical difficulties associated with creating an integrated balance sheet optimization model. These difficulties include the mathematical representation and computational technology required to develop a system of such scale and complexity while retaining ease of

https://doi.org/10.1515/9783110664669-202

readability, maintainability, and audibility. Additionally, it must also be able to run efficiently to be useful as a decision tool.

This is where this book comes in. We start with a brief overview of the essential terminology in accounting, financial instruments, financial statements, and mathematical modeling. This will help to get started and emphasize what will actually be the key components of a mathematical model. In this early stage, we will also share crucial modeling guidelines that can serve as guiding principles to aid the reader in organizing their work and focusing on what is most important in the various areas of knowledge involved in modeling the dynamics of a balance sheet.

However, the heart of our book lies in the later sections where we aim to provide what we consider to be most valuable: mathematical selections, programming technology choices, code examples, and our insights on each. Specifically, we will delve into the Julia programming language and its JuMP.jl and SDDP.jl packages that bring forth a very powerful mathematical programming method called *Stochastic Dual Dynamic Programming*. This technique was created to tackle large-scale optimization problems with multiple periods and uncertainties, which is a common requirement in financial planning and perfectly applicable to the optimization of a bank.

At the end of the journey, our goal is to provide a set of fully functional Julia code snippets that embody the essence of a multistage stochastic optimization mathematical model, along with a comprehensive examination of the choices, insights, and variables involved. This includes a discussion of the crucial decision variables, state variables, and constraints essential to the model's functioning, as well as a comprehensive array of optional business constraints that can be tailored to the reader's requirements.

While this book is primarily a technical guide aimed at individuals who wish to implement a balance sheet optimization model in practice, we believe that even non-technical professionals can benefit from its reading. We hope that this book help both groups broaden their perspectives and drive the technological advancement of integrated risk management and ALM in financial institutions.

# Contents

# 1 Introduction

Asset and Liability Management and Balance Sheet Optimization are classic topics that never lose relevance. However, their importance has been growing even more recently due to the increased complexity and competitiveness of markets, as well as stricter regulatory requirements following the 2008 financial crisis. The dangers of poor quality and insufficient capital in the banking sector were highlighted by this and other financial crises. During severe financial shocks, inefficiencies in capital management often come to light.

To enhance the resilience of financial institutions and the overall economy during stressful times, it is crucial for banks to enhance their stress testing and capital planning processes. This requires accurately identifying and assessing risks. As a result, regulators from various jurisdictions have started requiring financial institutions to participate in internal capital adequacy assessment processes (ICCAPs). These regulatory exercises entail institutions evaluating their health under various future scenarios and providing results through integrated accounting, capital, and risk forecasts. Integration means that all forecasts must be based on a shared set of assumptions, calculation rules, and rollover policies.

Furthermore, regulators expect the outcomes of such stress tests to be integrated into the financial institution's decision-making process, requiring not just systems but also efficient and timely execution. Ultimately, regulators expect that ICAAPs significantly contribute to the sustainability of the institution by ensuring its capital adequacy from both economic and regulatory perspectives, working in harmony. ICAAPs can also be viewed as a forward-looking evaluation of the institution's ability to meet all capital-related regulatory requirements and handle external financial constraints continuously. This evaluation encompasses not just a baseline scenario but also one or more adverse scenarios specific to the institution, in line with its planning objectives and risk tolerance.

To meet these objectives, we believe the only solution is to have an integrated balance sheet simulation system. This system must act as an efficient organizer of information on financial positions, market data, business assumptions, regulatory and financial constraints, and other necessary components to produce a realistic balance sheet simulation. The main aim of this book is to share our experience in solving this problem using mathematical programming techniques. We provide insights into the various challenges faced during each stage of system construction and include code examples that can serve as a starting point for implementation in the reader's work environment.

Specifically, we demonstrate how to formulate this problem mathematically as a multistage mathematical programming model using the Julia programming language and a method known as Stochastic Dual Dynamic Programming (SDDP). Ultimately, our aim is for readers to gain an understanding of the fundamental concepts of optimization theory, its relevance in finance, and how to implement a mathematical model that can forecast and optimize a bank balance sheet under uncertainty.

https://doi.org/10.1515/9783110664669-001

We believe this book will be valuable for individuals involved in integrated stress testing, capital adequacy, and general financial planning. Although it is primarily a technical book, filled with code examples and implementation strategies, we believe it will also benefit professionals in managerial roles by giving them a deeper understanding of the technologies that can assist in tackling banking issues.

## 1.1 What Is This Book About?

This book focuses on the methods and techniques required to construct an integrated asset and liability management model using mathematical optimization techniques, specifically dynamic programming techniques.

We delve into the advantages and difficulties of this approach, the necessary simplifications, and how we believe that once the learning process has been completed, it can not only speed up the preparation of financial statement projections in an integrated manner but also enhance the financial manager's understanding of bank operations. This book may bridge the gap between senior management and technical matters by incorporating a delicate blend of business and mathematical concepts and principles.

Interestingly, our experience shows that despite the distance between the board and technical matters, they quickly become familiar with concepts like decision variables, constraints, and objective functions. This often leads to a decrease in skepticism towards using mathematical models in decision-making, and their application expands beyond balance sheet projection, stress testing, and local portfolio optimizations. In essence, this book aims to encourage decision makers to adopt a comprehensive bank-wide portfolio view.

Furthermore, we believe that the process of identifying, mathematically describing, implementing, executing, and debugging a mathematical model can provide valuable insights into the banking problem. Through this journey, when considering the various relationships between different elements of a bank's balance sheet, it is not uncommon to be surprised by some model prescriptions. While in many cases the model will simply reinforce our existing assumptions, in others it will provide insightful solutions.

Throughout the book, especially in Chapter 2, we will sometimes put aside the technical aspects of our mission, focusing on other skills that we think are important to any practitioner who wants to lead the task of implementing an integrated balance sheet optimization model. As we hope to make clear, a good model can only be achieved with a good deal of entrepreneurship, negotiation, and patience.

In the technical part of the book, we will delve into the challenges surrounding financial and accounting modeling, decision representation, and uncertainty architecture. Then, we will explore the heart of mathematical modeling, covering topics such as coefficients, decision variables, constraints, and objective functions.

Our book focuses on specific aspects of building an integrated balance sheet optimization model, but it is important to note what we will not be covering.

To bring all these elements together and put them into action, strong programming skills are essential, particularly in scientific computing languages and in domain-specific languages focused on optimization. However, it is not the intention of this book to delve deep into these areas, not only because our knowledge in these areas is limited, but also because we do not have the space to do so. In other words, this book aims to provide a broad overview rather than an in-depth examination of these topics.

With millions of decision variables, constraints, and objective functions to consider, the process of solving the problem involves a combination of techniques at both the problem specification and mathematical problem-solving levels. These models can be incredibly complex and require a vast amount of computational power to solve, making it a challenging and intricate task for those involved.

We will concentrate on the modeling aspect of building a balance sheet optimization model and assume that there are adequate software tools available for solving the mathematical programming problems involved. We'll make use of commercial and open-source software that can handle mixed-integer linear programming problems using methods such as simplex, dual-simplex, barrier, and branch-and-bound and branch-or-cut. We'll also introduce the reader to the Stochastic Dual Dynamic Programming (SDDP) technique and its implementation in the Julia programming language using the SDDP package. Although we won't go into the theoretical details of the SDDP, we will provide enough information for the reader to become a proficient user of the package and method.

## 1.2 Assets and Liabilities Management

The acronym *ALM* stands for *assets and liabilities management* and, as the name suggests, it is such a broad area of knowledge. In fact, the roles and perimeter around ALM can vary significantly from one financial institution to another depending on the business model, on the enterprise organization, and on team skills. If we stick only to the case of banks, as highlighted in Bardaeva (2021), in retrospect it is also possible to see that over time ALM tasks in banks have been changing. Originally, even before the 1970s, the ALM team was primarily responsible for stabilizing interest margins. Over the years, this unit absorbed risk management functions related to other risk factors, with the mission of closing the most varied gaps. Subsequently, the ALM teams began to deal with liquidity risk as well, until today as a unit dedicated to solving multiparametric optimization tasks.

Therefore, instead of linking the acronym ALM to a specific type of risk, we prefer a more generic definition. And indeed, the bank's inability to meet its financial obligations on time can occur also due to market, credit operational, and refinancing risks, to name just a few, so it no longer seems to make sense to limit the scope of this unit to a single type of risk. That said, for us ALM is defined as the set of policies, processes, activities, and models a bank use to deal with the risks arising from the mismatch between its assets and liabilities.

This is consistent with Choudhry's *strategic ALM* concept (Choudhry, 2018) in which ALM is at the forefront of bank decision-making and plays a crucial role in determining a bank's profitability, capital, and liquidity, which are all key factors in its success, sustainability, and prosperity. Furthermore, Strategic ALM is an essential aspect of the ALM function in the post-crash Basel III era, as banks must efficiently manage their balance sheets. Banks must move away from the historically reactive and siloed approach to ALM and adopt a more integrated approach to balance sheet risk management.

In order to achieve this complex task, in our opinion, financial institutions need to resort to appropriate technological tools, such as *decision-support systems*. To be even more specific, asset and liability management cannot live without an integrated balance sheet optimization model that incorporates the bank's financial objectives, its risk appetite, the decisions it can takes, and the set of constraints that must be respected in order to create feasible decisions for the real world.

This model must work as a bank-level portfolio optimization tool, taking into account the institutional strategic objectives, and a series of financial and regulatory obligations. Among the decisions that such a bank-level portfolio optimization tool can help us to take are, for example, which assets to buy or sell at each moment in time, how to select fixed income and foreign exchange hedging transactions in order to comply with risk limits and targets, how to plan debt issuances in terms of time, volume, and characteristics, in order to maintain liquidity levels at acceptable levels, among other typical tasks related to day-to-day banking management.

Moreover, we believe that the solution to all the challenges mentioned must be derived from a single run of a single mathematical model. This ensures that the answers to various questions are in harmony and take into account the various trade-offs that exist. In summary, we think that *asset and liability management* and *balance sheet optimization*, while not necessarily having the same definition, are practically inseparable in their application.

## 1.3 The Banking Problem

A fundamental question a financial manager must be able to answer is if the bank is sustainable. But, what does it mean for a bank to be sustainable? A possible answer is to say that a bank is sustainable if it can comply with its business plan, generating returns compatible with incurred risks in the long-run, and abiding by regulatory limits all the time.

However, this definition of sustainability does not sound objective enough. It's not clear how to measure things. Managers, regulators, and investors need numbers. To do so, we must analyze the bank's balance sheet and financial statements under accounting, economic, and regulatory perspectives, on a projection basis, and, preferentially, under different scenarios, including stressed ones.

While traditional techniques such as duration gap analysis, combined with policies and risk limits, remain important tools, they are not sufficient to measure long-term bank sustainability, both because they are static tools and portfolio-oriented. Static because they do not consider the option that the financial manager has to make new decisions over time according to the state of nature, and portfolio-oriented because they do not consider the balance sheet as a whole. Therefore, such tools do not allow us to capture the opportunities for optimization that emanate from the interaction between the different parts of the balance sheet and the bank's operation over time.

Put in other words, suboptimal financial management is rarely the result of a single policy or decision, nor is it related to just one area of activity. In practice, suboptimal management manifests itself in different areas, but is amplified by the lack of interaction between them.

To avoid the pitfalls of a siloed approach, the only solution is to adopt a holistic strategy that encompasses different areas such as capital management, risk, liquidity and funding, to name just a few of the banking activities. We believe that such a holistic approach can be implemented quantitatively in an organized manner through a mathematical programming model, in which we can very transparently express the decisions that can be made, the constraints to be observed, and the bank's objectives.

In the banking sector, there exist varying levels of maturity when it comes to Asset Liability Management (ALM) and balance sheet modeling. To gain a deeper understanding of the advantages of having a balance sheet optimization model, it is helpful to outline at least three distinct stages.

In the *first stage* of maturity, institutions often utilize spreadsheet-based models, which are comprised of numerous balance sheet line items and a set of balance and cash flow generation rules under a single scenario that assumes a static rollover strategy.

This approach resembles modeling each balance sheet item with its own assumptions, and then incorporating a few fixed interconnection rules between them. This exercise offers a basic understanding of the issue and insight into data sources, among other things. However, the outcome is a single trajectory produced by a rudimentary strategy that does not reflect any risk representation.

In the second stage of maturity, institutions may choose to invest in developing Monte Carlo simulations that feature a clearer mapping of the connections between accounting records. This provides a number of valuable reports and risk analyses, including the probability of regulatory extrapolations at various time periods. However, rolling over rules are still fixed and explicitly-defined.

While the second stage of maturity provides a significant improvement in representing a bank's balance sheet dynamics when compared to the first stage, creating conditional decision rules in such a simulation system, with a large number of possible decisions and constraints, can be quite challenging. Due to the simplifications that must be made while programming such rollover rules, banks may end up with biased estimations of the future behavior of their balance sheet line items.

When considering simulations for extended time periods, the quality of the representation of rollover strategies and their relationship to the current bank position and economic conditions is crucial to the accuracy of the projections. Instead of simply programming rollover decisions, we may need to determine what these decisions should be, which leads us to the next stage of maturity.

In the third and final stage of maturity, a financial institution embarks on a *tour de force* as it shifts from simulating to optimizing its balance sheet through an optimization model. In this stage, the institution faces the crucial question: what is the objective of the bank? There may be multiple goals, but one of the most significant is to *maximize profits within a specified planning horizon while respecting a wide range of operational and regulatory constraints, while taking into account uncertainty and the possibility of rebalancing portfolios over time.*

The above concept can be mathematically represented as a multi-stage stochastic optimization problem. Our primary objective with this book is to demonstrate how we can specify and solve a mathematical programming model that accurately represents the banking problem.

## 1.4 Motivations to Optimize

Optimization models have been used to solve problems in many different industries and sectors, such as petroleum, chemical, manufacturing, transport and distribution, agriculture, health, mining, manpower planning, food, energy, pulp and paper, advertising, defense, and supply chain. We venture to say that, in most cases, the use of optimization models is a matter of survival, given the degree of competitiveness of such industries.

We observe the same trend in finance, where optimization models have been used extensively, especially in portfolio selection tasks, a theme that for many was inaugurated by Henry Markovitz in his seminal article (Markowitz, 1952). Optimization models have also been used to improve pricing, risk, funding and capital management, to list just a few examples. However, the importance of using optimization systems at the bank-level is a relatively recent discussion, primarily leveraged by the increasing regulation. In fact, it is relatively natural that those banks who have already entered this journey have done so in order to perform integrated stress tests faster.

For those directly engaged in building such a system, it is necessary to navigate through a range of knowledge domains such as strategic planning, accounting, contract modeling, pricing, scenario generation, mathematical modeling, model solving, reporting, and so on. By having to go through all these domains, professionals are led to meditate on the bank's operation in a very systematic manner, which may lead to new insights. We see this as a precious side effect of the modeling process.

In systems based on other paradigms, there would be specific code to express rollover rules. While these can be written in order to respect business rules, the actual rolling over will be only one of the possible courses of action the bank can take. However, there will not be any guarantee of optimality in those decisions.

On the other hand, in a mathematical programming model, business rules are explicitly stated as constraints. If the bank cannot sell a particular asset, there will be a constraint to represent this impediment. If the bank needs to respect a certain level of leverage, there will be another constraint, and so on. After that, the mathematical model will be responsible for producing the optimal rolling over decisions itself. Put in other words, we describe what we want done, not how it should be done.

Additionally, the declarative nature of a mathematical model specification leads to a very high level of transparency, which facilitates validation and audit processes.

Having a bank-level optimization system, however, may sound too ambitious, as if it were a single big hand dictating what should or should not be done. That's not the idea. A bank-level optimization system, in practice, will just be another decision support system to complement your arsenal. Obviously, there may be decisions already made, agreements between business units, internal cross-subsidies, legal impediments, and other objective constraints that conflict with an ideal single omniscient system.

In practice, an integrated balance management system can be fed with as many constraints as necessary for a given simulation exercise. Ultimately, we can completely limit how the rollover strategy should be executed, making the system basically a tool to organize data and simulation assumptions, as well as process them with the guarantees of coherence that are inherent to a mathematical programming model.

At the end of the day, the system will most likely act as a way of integrating all information, rules, and discretionary decisions, so that optimization will take place in the remaining degrees of freedom. Interestingly, we can calculate the impact of each prior discretionary decision on the bank's overall bottom line by disabling it, making the model a powerful hypothesis testing tool. By doing this, we may be able to unmask hidden opportunity costs, which can only be exploited by treating the balance sheet not as the only, but at least the most important, portfolio to be optimized in a bank.

## 1.5 Graphical Intuition

We have stated that banks aim to maximize profits within a planning horizon while considering a wide range of operational and regulatory constraints, as well as uncertainties. Technically, we seek to build a optimization model to help us make investment and funding decisions today and until a certain future date, at a given frequency and under multiple scenarios. Figure 1.1 graphically presents one of the possible architectures of the optimization model that we seek to build.

Since we are not sure about the future state of nature, we list the possibilities using a discrete set of scenarios organized as a graph. The root node $N_{0,0}$ represents today.

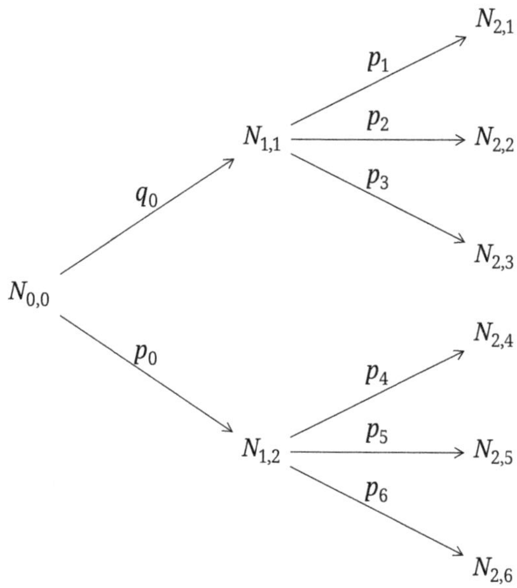


**Figure 1.1:** Graphical intuition of an ALM model.

The other nodes $N_{i,j}$ represent future moments and states at which we can make new decisions. In turn, each state is characterized by a probability of occurrence $p_i$, and by specific values for a set of state variables like prices and interest rates.

In addition, the directed nature of the graph imposes a non-anticipatory decision structure such that regardless of what state takes place in the future, we will have to bear the consequences of decisions taken in the previous node. The graph representation is therefore linked to the notion of non-arbitrage, a property that is desirable to avoid solutions built on the naive assumption of perfectly knowing the future.

For each graph node $N_{i,j}$, we want to build the corresponding balance sheet and other financial statements, consistent with the time, states, and decisions that led the bank to that point. Inspecting each of these future reports, we can assess its financial health on a projection basis, but with a probabilistic perspective, since we have a lot of different possible future versions of the bank. How large is the capitalization required to "completely" mitigate the risk of extrapolation of regulatory boundaries? And how much should we increase the spread to reach a given average ROE after 3 years? And so we can go on posing probabilistic questions about the bank's future. Setting up a model that supports us in seeking to answer these questions should be, in our opinion, one of the main goals of an ALM team.

## 1.6 Notations and Coding Considerations

Throughout this book we will discuss a lot the topic of mathematical modeling. The most natural decision would be to present example model equations in mathematical notation. At the same time, we want this book to be a computational implementation guide. Hence, it would be reasonable to present in the book both versions of the information – equations and the corresponding source code.

However, when the distance between the mathematical specification and the code is not so large, providing both versions may be a waste of pages, and the reader's time. In this situation, we soon had to decide whether to present model equations in mathematical notation or in programming language syntax. We have decided for the later option and, to justify our decision, we will make a brief digression.

Mathematical notation is certainly more stable than any programming language. In particular, the set of operators and mathematical equations that we will be dealing with throughout the construction of our balance sheet model is quite simple, being basically composed of linear equality and inequality expressions most of the time. Therefore, if we opted for the mathematical notation, we would be quite sure that such a representation would have a long life, remaining definitively valid.

When it comes to programming language, however, the story is quite different. To begin with, there are numerous programming languages. In addition, there are lots of versions of the same programming language, each one with slight differences in syntax and functionalities. Anyway, if someone knows what it means to program a computer, with some effort such a person will be able to read basic code in different programming languages. By basic codes we mean variables, arithmetic and logic operations, flow control commands, repetition commands, and function calls.

Nevertheless, to specify a mathematical programming model, it is inevitable to escape from using mathematical equations. Therefore, it is desirable that the selected programming language allows approximating mathematical and computational notations. This is precisely the purpose of so-called *domain specific languages*.

These are programming languages or programming language extensions designed for specific problem classes. For our mathematical programming problem, it is best to use a domain language that closely resembles mathematical language. The syntax should be similar to mathematical notation, allowing for easy coding and identification of crucial elements, such as decision variables, constraints, and objective functions, involved in mathematical programming.

Combining high-level syntax, performance, and integration with leading mathematical solver software, the Julia programming language (Bezanson et al., 2017), coupled with the Julia for Mathematical Programming (JuMP) (Dunning et al., 2017) package, has proven to be a good alternative in both university and industry. By analyzing a piece of code written in Julia and JuMP, one can almost immediately recognize the corresponding mathematical equation.

Additionally, by opting for clear names for decision variables and coefficients, we believe that the combination of Julia and JuMP will enable even non-experts to identify accounting and business rules within the model. This is the reason behind our choice for using those tools in our implementation examples.

As will be explained later in the book, we will utilize the SDDP technique to address the resource-intensive optimization problem associated with balance sheet modeling. To support this, we will also use the SDDP (Dowson and Kapelevich, 2021) package, which implements the stochastic dual dynamic programming algorithm in Julia.

For readers unfamiliar with these technologies, we suggest reading Appendix A before proceeding to the code examples in Chapters 6 and 7. Although brief, these appendices aim to provide a helpful introduction to working with Julia JuMP and SDDP code.

## 1.7 How to Read This Book

This section serves as a navigation guide for the book. While reading out of order from the table of contents is possible, it's not recommended. The parts of the model are presented in a specific sequence, not by chance, but due to conceptual dependencies. It's also worth mentioning that the different blocks of the system are interconnected, so understanding each one will likely enhance understanding of the others. However, this is just a suggestion. If you prefer, you can take a non-linear, more flexible approach to reading. We often ignore such suggestions ourselves.

The first part of this book lays the groundwork for creating a mathematical model of a financial institution. In Chapter 2, we offer a set of guidelines to assist you in developing a balance sheet model. Chapter 3 delves into the core accounting and balance sheet principles that must be considered when constructing an ALM model. Finally, Chapter 4 introduces mathematical programming and the key concepts that will be utilized throughout the book to develop a robust balance sheet model. This chapter also marks our initial encounter with the Julia, JuMP, and SDDP tools.

The second part of the book focuses on constructing and operating a balance sheet model using mathematical programming and stochastic dual dynamic programming. In Chapter 5, we outline the data required to build a balance sheet model and address the major challenges in obtaining and organizing this information. Chapter 6 establishes the minimum set of decision variables and constraints that a balance sheet model must have to work properly. By the end of this chapter, the model is able to accurately calculate current and projected balance sheets and income statements in accordance with accounting and financial principles. Chapter 7 builds upon the model by adding business rules in the form of mathematical constraints and objective functions. This allows the model to find optimal rolling over strategies that abide by various business assumptions, policies, and limits.

Chapter 8 showcases how to operate the model and create automated reports from its optimal decisions. Lastly, Chapter 9 introduces uncertainty into the balance sheet model, by using probabilistic and regime-switching scenarios to train and evaluate optimal policies.

The final part covers troubleshooting the most frequent errors, bugs, and challenges encountered in balance sheet modeling (Chapter 10). We then conclude (Chapter 11) with a discussion of the key insights, advancements, and state-of-the-art technologies in this area of research.

# 2 Modeling Guidelines

We cannot deny that a bank and the environment in which it operates is complex enough, making it natural that attempts to represent and optimize its operations are the object of questioning and skepticism.

We believe that by not constructing a formal and comprehensive balance sheet optimization model, we are making an implicit choice. At best, we will choose a formally defined but suboptimal decision framework. At worst, and most likely, we will rely on discretionary "blackbox" rules for making strategic decisions.

However, even if the modeler is confident that the new model accurately represents the bank and leads to improved performance, this may not be sufficient to alter the organization's way of doing things. To ensure that the model is actually utilized, the modeler must convince their colleagues, superiors, board members, and even regulators. To be successful in this crucial mission, we believe it is beneficial to adhere to certain modeling guidelines. This chapter lists the guidelines that we consider most crucial in ensuring that the final model is as useful and reliable as possible for the bank.

## 2.1 Read the Bank Business Plan

In traditional portfolio optimization or risk management models, we don't need to stick to the bank's long-term goals. Usually, what matters is maximizing return or minimizing risks in a typically short planning horizon. In addition, the budget for a given business unit is already given. In other words, such models are typically geared towards specific portfolios and do not explicitly take into account the bank's objectives for the coming quarters, or years. Such models are in a sense myopic in relation to time and in relation to other portfolios.

In a balance sheet optimization model, the bank's different portfolios, business, and regulatory constraints and long-term objectives must be taken into account in a coordinated manner. In order to provide the system with such rules and objectives, we need to know the bank's business plan for the coming years. But, as we know, business plans can be highly esoteric objects, with generic sentences that do not provide a quantitative guideline for capital and risk managers.

However, chances are that the business plan also contains important numbers, such as growth targets for different business lines, new product launches, cost reduction plans, among other objective information that can help us shape balance sheet evolution. Therefore, by knowing the business plan, we mean knowing which of its items may have implications for the bank's future in quantitative terms.

Such knowledge is what will allow the model to be equipped with mathematical constraints to guide the results in the direction designed by the business plan. The better and the more complete the representation of the business plan in the mathematical

https://doi.org/10.1515/9783110664669-002

model, the greater our ability to assess the consistency and feasibility of business goals, which is one of the first objectives of having a balance sheet optimization model.

Representing the business plan rules in the model can be a persuasive argument, as it derives legitimacy from the business plans and gives the model a democratic aspect, considering that business plans are typically the result of extensive collaboration by many different business units. Moreover, incorporating the organization's overarching business objectives can also foster closer alignment among key decision-makers, including the board, and make them more open to using mathematical modeling as a complementary tool for coordinating the vast amount and variety of information involved in the operation of a large financial institution, rather than as a replacement for human judgment.

## 2.2 Stick to Official Chart of Accounts

A chart of accounts is a list of names used to organize financial statements, especially balance sheet and income statement. Companies have some freedom to organize their chart of accounts, but in general it will likely be as large and as complex as the company itself. A company can also maintain different versions of charts of accounts, some of which are more useful for internal management while others are required by regulators or investors, for whom it is convenient to have some degree of uniformity to allow comparison between companies.

It's possible that none of the company's existing charts of accounts used for financial statements are suitable for building a balance sheet optimization model. This is because these charts are designed for accountants, not for modeling contracts and cash flows. Some balance sheet lines may not even relate to contracts, and some contracts could span multiple balance sheet items.

The modeler may be tempted to create a chart of accounts that is more conducive to modeling, which could speed up development. However, this new chart of accounts, designed specifically for modeling, may not be recognized by stakeholders. If the model results are presented in an unfamiliar format, they may have difficulty accepting and supporting them.

It's crucial to keep in mind that the official chart of accounts structure and numbers serve as a foundation for accountants and other stakeholders involved in the model. If they struggle to align the model results with the official financial statements, they may dismiss the model without hesitation.

Being able to communicate effectively with stakeholders by using their language is essential for the survival of a balance sheet model. That's why we advise you to adhere to the official chart of accounts, especially when presenting the model results. While it's okay to use alternative versions of the chart of accounts in the internal workings of the model, it's crucial to be mindful of the reconciliation between these versions.

## 2.3 Respect the Segregation of Duties

When constructing a balance sheet optimization model, it's important to understand the tasks and responsibilities of various bank units, such as planning, sales, credit, market and operational risks, funding, treasury, accounting, etc. This knowledge is crucial for accurately representing the decisions, calculation rules, and constraints each unit is subject to.

Our objective is to develop a centralized system that generates highly consistent balance sheet projections, eliminating the need for direct involvement from various divisions each time the system is run. This approach differs significantly from the traditional method, where the balance sheet projection task is divided among different divisions before a final consolidation step is performed.

It's clear that the siloed structure is inefficient and causes issues, resulting in excessive manual and repetitive tasks. Additionally, it's questionable whether it effectively addresses problems related to segregation of duties. From our perspective, a centralized approach is the better option, as long as the modeler takes the necessary steps to mitigate segregation of duties' concerns.

However, implementing a centralized model can be challenging because it inherently takes on some of the tasks previously divided among multiple divisions. If the responsibilities of each division in the overall process were not properly negotiated beforehand, tensions may arise.

Therefore, in the process of deploying a balance sheet model, the modeler's role is not just technical but also political. It's part of their job to clearly explain the purpose of the information requested from other divisions, the level of accuracy for the parts related to them, the workload it will create, and, most importantly, the workload it will save. In a time-consuming process such as regulatory stress testing or long-term financial projections, which require a vast amount and variety of information and assumptions from multiple divisions, the time savings can be substantial.

In conclusion, we believe that as the modeler and their team provide a platform for collaboration, validation, and preservation of authority over each of the key parts and assumptions of the model, tensions and misunderstandings tend to dissipate over time, especially when other divisions start to experience the time-saving benefits.

Finally, the modeler must foster a sense of ownership in individuals from different divisions by emphasizing and promoting the importance and authority of each of them in the overall process of financial projection elaboration.

## 2.4 Don't Wait for the Perfect Data

Modeling a bank's balance sheet involves modeling various types of financial contracts and accounting objects, whose information may be dispersed across different systems, databases, or even files. Some balance sheet lines will have data that is easier to obtain and manage, due to their standardized nature or their importance to the bank.

Some of the data may be stored in outdated spreadsheets or legacy systems with limited integration capabilities. Unless you work in a highly mature corporation, it's likely that you will not have immediate access to all of the necessary data to cover all balance sheet lines. This may be due to the lack of structure in the information or simply because it doesn't exist and has never been used in a financial projection in the manner you plan to use it.

However, it's also likely that you will have access to high-quality information regarding the most crucial parts of the balance sheet, such as loan, debt, and liquidity portfolios, and the income statement, like administrative costs and tax rates. If this data is critical to the bank's daily operations and monthly balance sheet consolidation, it will likely be well-organized and easily accessible.

On a positive note, the absence of complete data about balance sheet lines can help you focus on what truly drives the bank's financial stability in the long term. As a general recommendation, prioritize the essential information, develop reasonable "interpolation" rules for missing data, and ensure that your decisions accurately capture the bigger picture.

Finally, begin working with the available data, run a full cycle of model simulations, and the results will help validate your assumptions and guide your efforts to obtain more data or improve the existing data.

## 2.5 Be Careful With Basic Financial Calculations

The development of a balance sheet optimization model presents a variety of mathematical and computational challenges, ranging from simple to complex. Technical individuals may be easily sidetracked by the more complex aspects of the problem, such as mathematical modeling and computational strategies, at the expense of simple but important tasks like implementing loan and debt payment schedules, which rely on basic financial mathematics and interest calculation conventions.

However, it's important not to underestimate the importance of these basic tasks. The balance sheet optimization model is comprised of several building blocks, and one of the most critical is the model coefficients. These constants multiply the decision variables throughout the model and are present in every calculation, meaning even small deviations or errors can have a significant impact on the solver's optimal decision. This can undermine the trust of stakeholders and sponsors, which is essential for the success of a project like this.

Therefore, we advise the modeler to prioritize the accuracy of the building blocks that make up the model before diving into advanced mathematical specification and solution methods. Particular attention should be paid to the nuances of payment schedules for financial contracts, such as day counting and compounding conventions.

To ensure the reliability of the model, we suggest implementing automated tests as much as possible to minimize errors in the calculation of model coefficients. If existing systems can be used to calculate cash flows, market values, or interest accruals, it's worth exploring the possibility of integrating them, but additional testing layers should also be added. This is especially important if the existing systems are not frequently used for projections under multiple scenarios.

## 2.6 Don't Be Ashamed to Simplify

The operations of a bank are highly complex, characterized by non-linearities and uncertainty. These factors manifest in areas such as interest calculations, default probabilities, market fluctuations and liquidity, loan demand, withdrawal behavior, and many others. In reality, the workings of a bank are far from straightforward and there is no universally accepted method for modeling each of its aspects. However, certain models have become common across various financial organizations.

A prime example is the Black-Scholes option pricing model (Black and Scholes, 1973), which is still widely used by many market participants, not because it accurately reflects reality but because it allows for quick, relatively robust decision-making. Despite its naive assumptions about returns probability distribution and implied volatility dynamics, it remains useful and has proven to be beneficial in improving decision-making compared to a lack of a model.

More advanced models, such as Dupire's local volatility model (Dupire, 1994), Heston's stochastic volatility model (Heston, 1993), and the recent rough volatility models (Gatheral et al., 2018), are now available for derivatives pricing. However, despite their superiority, these models are often neglected due to their increased difficulty in implementation, understanding, and maintenance, highlighting the trade-off between complexity and practicality.

From a practical standpoint, the goal of the modeler should be to determine if a mathematical and computational model can improve the bank's decision-making, taking into account its limitations, the cost of creating and implementing the model, and the difficulty of interpreting the results. Sometimes the only way to answer this question is through trial and error.

In this case, simplification often means *linearization*, due to two main factors: efficiency and guarantees of optimality. If the banking problem can be expressed as a linear programming problem (or even a mixed-integer linear problem), there will be multiple solution methods with such guarantees that can be executed quickly with access to good computational resources and a good mathematical solver.

Other classes of mathematical programming problems, such as convex problems, may also offer these guarantees in certain cases, although it is important to note that the computational costs of solving these problems tend to be much higher compared to linear models.

Risk calculations for portfolios present a challenge for linearization in a balance sheet optimization model. Even with simple risk models like a Gaussian parametric model, the calculation of traditional risk measures such as Value at Risk is a non-linear function of the portfolio's exposures. One approach to simplify this calculation is to consider the portfolio risk as the sum of the individual risks of each position, disregarding the impact of diversification.

A more nuanced approach would be to factor in the average level of diversification in the portfolio by multiplying this sum by a constant. This method may work well if the portfolio composition remains stable. Another possibility is to have a multiplier that changes based on the scenario, considering lower diversification during stressed scenarios. These are just a few examples of ways to linearize the calculations to meet specific needs.

As a modeler, your role is to evaluate these simplifications and assess their accuracy, functionality, and limitations. Ultimately, you should strive to find a formulation that strikes a balance between improving the mathematical model's results, code readability, optimization speed, and result interpretability.

## 2.7 Get a Good Mathematical Solver

As we will explain in Chapter 6, balance sheet optimization models can have millions of decision variables and mathematical constraints, many of which are necessary to account for the number of contracts, time stages, and scenarios. However, some of these variables and constraints are redundant and simply exist to make the model easier to specify.

In cases where computational resources are limited, manual reduction of the model may reduce memory requirements. But, this also reduces model readability, increases the likelihood of specification errors, and makes maintenance more difficult.

In other words, attempts to save computational time in this manner are considered "premature optimization" in the sense described by Sir Tony Hoare and popularized by Knuth (Knuth, 1997). This kind of optimization can ultimately be more costly than using a high-end mathematical solver. Most mathematical solvers have pre-processing routines and heuristics that can automatically reduce the model, making it easier to handle in memory and solve.

Having a strong mathematical solver can greatly benefit the efficiency of a balance sheet optimization model in several ways. Good solvers have automatic strategies to handle numerical instability, which is a common issue in these types of models due to the wide range of values in the coefficients and constraints. While a good solver can't take care of all stability issues, it can certainly save time and effort.

Investing in a top-notch solver can be especially helpful during the development process, when the model needs to be run repeatedly for testing, debugging, performance evaluations, and corrections. A commercial solver not only speeds up execution but also provides more debugging tools.

Investing in a good commercial solver can be a wise choice, especially for complex mixed-integer problems, as these solvers often offer better quality solutions than free solvers. This is due to the investment made by commercial solver developers in developing and implementing advanced heuristics, pre-processing techniques, and cutting strategies that improve the performance and accuracy of the solver. By choosing a commercial solver with a proven track record of success, you can benefit from these improvements and achieve higher quality solutions.

To sum up, investing in a commercial solver can have significant benefits, especially when optimizing complex mixed-integer problems. These solvers tend to produce higher quality solutions due to their built-in heuristics, pre-processing and cutting strategies. Although the level of improvement is dependent on the model, even small gains can be significant when dealing with large balance sheets. Furthermore, a commercial solver with accompanying support service can be even more advantageous, as it gives you access to experts with high academic qualifications and practical experience in solving various specification, numerical stability, and integration problems.

# 3 Fundamental Concepts: Balance Sheet Model

Now that we have introduced the ALM modeler's commandments, it's time to study slightly more mundane artifacts. If we want to assess a bank's health, we need to measure its temperature, listen to its heartbeat and take its blood pressure. In this case, the measures are a series of reports that formally express the activities and positions of banks, known as *financial statements*. In this book, optimizing the bank's health corresponds to optimizing the numbers presented in such reports. We want to do it prospectively and consider different future scenarios. Therefore, we need to be able to forecast such statements under different states of nature. This chapter is dedicated to presenting the structure of key financial statements, contracts, and basic accounting rules. With such knowledge, we will be able to follow the money correctly and produce plausible forecasts for the bank's health indicators.

## 3.1 Balance Sheet

A balance sheet is the most fundamental financial statement reported by a financial institution. It summarizes financial balances of an organization (in our case, a bank). For a specific date, usually the end of a month, quarter or year, it lists all the assets, liabilities, and equity. Being related to a single point in time, it is analog to a snapshot of the institution. Table 3.1 shows the balance sheet of a hypothetical bank, which will be our reference for modeling purposes.

**Table 3.1:** Balance sheet example.

| | | | |
|---|---|---|---|
| **Assets** | 100 | **Liabilities** | 70 |
| Loans | 80 | Debts | 60 |
| Investments | 20 | Deposits | 10 |
| | | **Equity** | 30 |
| | | Capital | 25 |
| | | Retained Earnings | 5 |
| | 100 | | 100 |

Visually, balance sheets are usually organized as follows. On the left side we have assets. On the right side we have liabilities and equity. Then we have the so-called accounting equation, which states that the value of assets is always equivalent to the value of liabilities plus equity. Another relevant aspect about the balance sheet is that it presents the balances of assets and liabilities in aggregated levels such as loans, investments, deposits, debts etc. Each of these balance sheet lines is comprised of several contracts that may differ greatly in terms of currencies, asset class, rates, ratings, accounting method,

https://doi.org/10.1515/9783110664669-003

and so on. So to really understand how the value of a particular balance sheet will evolve, we need to look at the contracts that make it up.

In our model we will breakdown these fundamental records as much as needed in order to generate useful forecasts. This implies that sometimes our breakdown of a record can be different from the standard breakdown seen in our official financial statements. Imagine, for example, that our accounting team breaks "Loans" into two sub-accounts: "Loans – Short Term" and "Loans – Long Term." If we are interested in analyzing the optimal accounting classification of new loans, we could separate loans into "marked-to-market" and "amortized cost" instead. Or we could breakdown investments not by product type, but by strategy because it is relevant to assess the impact of each investment strategy in the balance sheet separately. We are free to create new breaks and/or drop the usual ones. The only caveat is that we need to produce initial balances for the chosen breaks, and they may not appear explicitly in our financial statements, even in the notes section. In that case you will need to calculate these initial balances yourself, either by resorting to more granular accounting data or to ad-hoc assumptions.

To create a mathematical model of balance sheet optimization, we need a stable balance sheet structure. The rationale behind the construction of the mathematical model will be independent of the input data. By rationale, we mean the format of the constraints. However, at least in our approach, the structure and names of balance sheet accounts will be reflected in various parts of the model, especially contract sets and decision variable names. Therefore, it is important to choose a balance format that is minimally stable and well known to people, specially the one used as model input. At the output layer, such considerations are still valid but it is easier to produce other balance versions, since at this stage there are no impacts on modeling. Producing different output balance sheets may even be desirable since different audiences may benefit from different aggregations or breakdowns of balances.

## 3.2 Income Statement

As we have seen, a balance sheet gives us a snapshot of the bank's situation on a given date. Although it gives us important information about the bank's portfolio, it tells us almost nothing about its performance. The most basic question we can ask about bank performance is: how much money did the bank make or lose in the period? A financial report that proposes to answer this is called an *income statement*. Such a report is also known as a profit or loss statement. Usually, the income statement is organized into sections, which in turn can be organized into subsections. Such organization may vary from business to business, but some separations always occur in all cases. The main one is the separation between revenues and expenses. A net income is then obtained after subtracting expenses from revenues. An example of an income statement can be seen on Table 3.2.

**Table 3.2:** Income statement example.

| | |
|---|---|
| **1 – Interest Income** | |
| 1.A – Loans | 100 |
| 1.B – Trading account assets | 80 |
| 1.C – Other Interest Income | 10 |
| Total Interest Income (= 1.A + 1.B + 1.C) | 190 |
| **2 – Interest Expenses** | |
| 2.A – Deposits | (15) |
| 2.B – Short-term Borrowings | (45) |
| 2.C – Long-term Debts | (100) |
| Total Interest Expenses (= 2.A + 2.B + 2.C) | (160) |
| **3 – Net Interest Income – NII** (= 1 + 2) | 30 |
| **4 – Non-Interest Income** | |
| 4.A – Service Fees | 60 |
| 4.B – Other Fees | 10 |
| 4.C – Trading Account Profits | 15 |
| 4.D – Gains on Sales of Debt Securities | 25 |
| 4.E – Other Non-Interest Income | 20 |
| Total Non-Interest Income (= 4.A + 4.B + 4.C + 4.D + 4.E) | 130 |
| **5 – Provision for Credit Losses** | (20) |
| **6 – Non-Interest Expenses** | |
| 6.A – Administrative Expenses | (30) |
| 6.B – Other Expenses | (10) |
| Total Non-Interest Expenses (= 6.A + 6.B) | (40) |
| **7 – Income Before Tax** (= 3 + 4 + 5 + 6) | 100 |
| **8 – Income Tax Expenses** | (25) |
| **9 – Net Income** (= 7 + 8) | 75 |

In bank balance sheets, in particular, there is a classic separation between interest and non-interest income. This makes complete sense, as charging interest represents the core business of most banks, although other fees and commissions are not negligible in a bank's results. Other rows of the income statement that deserve mention are securities gains or losses, change in provisions, and income tax. In the end, we have net income, which will be recognized in the balance sheet through equity. As we see, balance sheets and income statements are interconnected by definition. A good optimization model should take this link into consideration, and make this relationship fully transparent to users.

In a mathematical model, this is done through a series of auxiliary decision variables and constraints. As we will see in Section 6.8, we will need to define auxiliary decision variables for each row in our income statement, and their value will be calculated based on the performance of the contracts contained in one or more balance sheet rows. This is certainly the part of the model you will use most to validate whether your mathematical model respects the mechanics and hierarchy of constructing the statement of results. Accounting teams will be an important target audience in this process, and some of them may not have programming skills. Thus, the closer the nomenclature and hierarchy of accounts are to their common language, the less effort will be required during the validation of the model.

## 3.3 Cash Flow Statement

A cash flow statement is a financial report that tracks the inflows and outflows of cash (and equivalents) from a company during a time interval. It has a relationship with the balance sheet, as the sum of all inflows and outflows of cash must be equal to the variation of the balance of cash and cash equivalent rows. In a balance sheet model, we will see later that we have a special constraint to assure this. It does so by stating that no money can be created or destroyed within the model.

While an income statement report shows us the accounting view of gains and losses, a cash flow statement is concerned with the actual money that was earned and spent by the company during a quarter or a month.

If we have positions valued at amortized cost, for instance, an income statement report will show us the interest that was earned during that period, regardless of it being paid or not. A cash flow statement will, on the other hand, report only principal and interest that were actually paid (or received) in the exercise.

Other rows of the income statement that do not affect the company's cash positions are provision for credit losses and depreciation. Although they are expenses from an accounting standpoint, they do not imply disbursements of cash. Dividends will usually be out of an income statement report as they are not expenses, but they must of course appear in a cash flow statement as cash going out of the company.

An example of a cash flow statement can be seen on Table 3.3. Even though cash flow statements usually have a breakdown of operations, investing and financing activities, in a model the most important thing is to separate all variables that imply inflows or outflows of cash from the others, and make sure that they all appear in your report. The breakdown can assume other categories that are more fit for management, but we have to make sure that we create validation points that guarantee that there was no money creation or destruction during each time period.

**Table 3.3:** Cash flow statement example.

| | | |
|---|---|---|
| | **Investing Activities** | |
| | Loans Disbursement | (100) |
| | Loans Repayments | 120 |
| | Capital Expenditures | (10) |
| (=) | Net Cash from Investing Activities | 10 |
| | **Financing Activities** | |
| | Issuance of New Borrowings | 50 |
| | Borrowings Repayments | (60) |
| | Capital Transfers | 35 |
| | Cash Dividends Paid | (5) |
| (=) | Net Cash from Financing Activities | 20 |
| | **Operating Activities** | |
| | Interest Received | 3 |
| | Interest Paid | (2) |
| | Expenses Paid | (15) |
| | Income & Fees Received | 36 |
| | Taxes | (27) |
| (=) | Net Cash from Operating Activities | (7) |
| | **Change in Cash and Equivalents** | 23 |

## 3.4 Accounting Basis

The concept of accounting basis refers to the methodology under which revenues and expenses are recognized in the financial statements. The most important methodologies are *cash basis* and *accrual basis*. The latter is by far the most widely used in banks. However, as the notion of accounting basis will appear in central parts of a balance sheet model, such as coefficients and decision variables, it is worth exploring in more detail the differences between these two methodologies.

Under the cash basis, a bank recognizes revenue only when cash is received, and expenses when their obligations are paid. The recognition is directly related to the existence of a positive or negative cash flow. It is the simplest recognition method, but it is not always best suited to represent the true financial condition of a bank. Suppose a bank has lent 1 billion dollars to a company, which is due to be repaid after three years at a rate of 5% per annum. If revenues are recognized under the cash basis approach, we will have a large concentration of revenue at the end, while in the meantime we will not have complete visibility of the true value of the bank's assets.

However, as such a loan agreement specifies the conventions for calculating interest over time, we are able to calculate the outstanding balance at any given time. We may use the result of this calculation to recognize revenues periodically, for example quarterly, giving greater clarity to the true value of the bank's financial positions. This approach is known as accrual basis. Under this basis, a bank recognizes revenue when earned and expenses when expenditures are consumed. Recognition is linked to earning that quantity rather than receiving it.

Accrual basis approach requires greater knowledge of accounting principles, contract features, interest rate, and date conventions than is required by its counterpart. It is important to notice that when a cash flow occurs in a contract (an interest payment or amortization, for example), it is always accompanied by a corresponding decrease in the outstanding balance. Thus, roughly speaking, the effect of cash flows on the recognition of bank revenues or expenses working under the accrual methodology is neutral.

In practice, a company uses both base to evaluate its financial performance. For example, while cash basis is the concept behind the construction of a cash flow statement, a company can also use accrual basis to evaluate gains or losses in its income statement.

## 3.5 Accounting Classification

The accounting classification of a financial asset determines how it should be stated in the balance sheet, and how its changes in value should be recognized. Account classifications are defined by the so-called GAAP, which stands for generally accepted accounting principles (GAAP). They refer to a common set of accepted accounting principles and procedures that companies must follow to prepare their financial statements. The purpose for using such principles is to improve the clarity of the communication of financial information. Although different jurisdictions adopt slightly different principles, their essence remains the same.

In essence, there are three fundamental classes of financial assets: held to maturity, trading securities, and available for sale. Any other is just an combination of those three, and we expect the modeler to extrapolate their definition if necessary. *Held to maturity (HTM)* securities are financial assets and liabilities which the company has the intent and ability to hold until it matures. These are reported at amortized cost, which corresponds to the accrual basis methodology. *Trading* securities are financial assets and liabilities held mainly for trading in the short term. These positions are reported at *fair value*[1] on the balance sheet. The fair value is evaluated according to its current supply and demand or, in the absence of market data, the supply and demand for similar securities. The variation of fair value from period to period (also called unrealized gains or losses) will appear as profits or losses in the income statement.

Finally, *available for sale* securities include all other securities, and are an intermediate case between the first two. Financial assets and liabilities that are classified in this category are usually reported at fair value but their unrealized gains and losses are not

1 In this book we will use *fair value* and *market value* interchangeably, although their definitions can differ in the literature.

included in earnings, rather being accumulated in a specific sub-account of shareholders' equity. Only when the security is traded is the resulting gain or loss realized as profit or loss in the income statement.

In practice, a company is not entirely free to choose the accounting classification of a financial asset, as the choice must be coherent with the intention and ability to sell it. Nonetheless, one can use a mathematical balance sheet model to test and optimize this choice, considering its effects in an integrated manner with other investment choices. As we will see later, accounting classification is not a decision variable in the strict sense. However, it is an attribute of the contract. Therefore, the system can optimize this choice indirectly, provided that in the list of new contracts we have the same contract available with different classifications.

## 3.6 Financial Contracts

Financial contracts are all the agreements that an institution can close with its counterparts that involve certain or contingent exchange of financial quantities. Some of the most important categories of financial contracts are: fixed income securities, stocks, funds, derivatives, currencies, and commodities.

These contracts usually compose different portfolios that gather agreements that are similar in nature or purpose. For example, a loans portfolio would normally be composed of similar fixed income securities that differ one another at least by maturity, amortization schedule, and rate. It could also include related derivatives, like swaps and futures, used to hedge or mitigate some of the risks that come from those fixed income securities. A liquid assets portfolio could have securities that can be similar in nature to those deals included in a loans portfolio, but of course they would have a very different purpose, i. e., a rather distinct role to play in a financial institution's operation.

From a balance sheet model standpoint, we need to make sure we map the main characteristics of each type of financial contract. Some of the characteristics may be pertinent to all financial contracts, like the currency in which the financial quantities involved in the agreement are denominated. Some may be applied only to specific types of contracts. Typically, fixed income securities will be classified according to their rate type: fixed rate or floating rate securities. “Floaters” can then be segregated by index: LIBOR deals, SOFR deals, etc. LIBOR deals can have different tenors, like 1-month LIBOR or 3-months LIBOR, etc.

This classification of contracts is important because some of the model constraints will involve only contracts of a specific characteristic. For example, we can write a constraint to limit the acquisition of new fixed rate loans in order to model a corporate policy of prioritizing floating rate deals over fixed ones, or a constraint that imposes back-to-back hedging of fixed rate deals by buying swaps and futures.

Finally, you will have to feed your mathematical model with lots of numbers coming from valuing your financial contracts in different points of time and under multiple scenarios. These numbers can be produced by current corporate solutions or you can gather the information about all contracts and use a specific library to feed your model. Either way, the metrics required by a mathematical model will include for each unit of a contract under each different scenario and in all projection dates:

- **price**: marked-to-market (fair value) valuation of all future cash flows;
- **accrual**: amortized cost valuation, consisting of principal and accrued interest;
- **cash flow projection**: date, currency, amount and type of each future cash flow;
- **risk metrics**: risk evaluation of a contract, like DV01, duration, expected shortfall, repricing gap, greeks, etc.

Those metrics will be paramount in creating our mathematical model coefficients, as we will discuss in Chapter 6.

## 3.7 Financial Positions

Although a financial contract entity has all the information necessary to price it and project its cash flows, it says nothing about where this contract should be allocated in a balance sheet. We can have, for example, two fixed rate deals, but one is an asset allocated at the loans portfolio, the other a liability allocated to borrowings. Or two identical future contracts, but one hedges a loan and the other a debt security, which could make those two sit in different places in our balance sheet. Or even two identical fixed rate bonds, but one held to maturity and the other classified as trading.

A *financial position* is a concept we will use throughout this book to store accounting information about a financial contract. This information is can include:

- **Financial Contract**: the contract itself or a pointer to it;
- **Balance Sheet Path**: location where this contract should appear in the balance sheet;
- **Type**: Asset, Liability, Equity, etc;
- **Accounting Classification**: held to maturity, available for sale, trading, etc;
- **Accounting Method**: fair value or amortized cost;
- **New Position**: is it a current contract or a new contract created for the model to roll over portfolios?

In our opinion, all data that impacts projected cash flows or the price of a contract should be stored in a financial contract. This is the information that would appear in a contract document signed with a counterpart (if applicable for that deal). This contract instance could be of course reused in multiple positions. All other information, that will typically link that contract to the balance sheet or to the mathematical model, should be stored in an instance of a financial position.

Then, from a modeling standpoint, when you see a balance sheet account like "Loans" or "Borrowings" you should think of it as a collection of financial positions that contain (or refer to) a collection of financial contracts.

## 3.8 Non-Contract Accounting Records

In the previous section we have seen that a financial position is a concept that contains (or refers to) a financial contract. But in a balance sheet we have also accounts that are not composed of financial contracts. A classic example of this type of accounting record is provision for credit losses. Such records appear as an asset, and correspond to a reserve for credit losses, expressed in aggregate form as the sum of loan portfolio provisions.

For a coherent balance sheet simulation, these relationships must be represented, and the model must be able to increase or decrease the balance of the provisions account considering that this is a function of the balance of loan accounts.

In the abstraction we are going to use, such accounting records that do not directly correspond to financial contracts will be treated as non-financial contracts, or *pseudo-contracts* that can be bought or sold to emulate the change in balance of such accounts. Obviously, purchases or sales in the case of provisions do not have cash effects, representing only an accounting operation.

Other important examples of pseudo-contracts are equity accounts, such as retained earnings accounts, and the par value of capital account. The case of retained earnings is similar to that of provisions, as the purchases and sales of this pseudo-contract represent the accounting process without cash effects.

If we want to represent the capitalization of the bank, we need to allow the model to buy pseudo-contracts of the capital type, and unlike the retained earnings contract, this will have a cash effect.

To account for those different cases, a pseudo-contract instance would have to store at least:

- **Buy Cash Flow**: buying one unit of this contract should imply disbursing (or receiving) cash?
- **Sell Cash Flow**: selling one unit of this contract should imply receiving (or disbursing) cash?
- **Currency**: currency in which this contract should be represented

For example, a "provision for credit losses" pseudo-contract would not imply buy cash flow when being provisioned, nor sell cash flow when being released. On the other hand, a par value capital pseudo-contract would imply inflow of cash when a capital transfer is executed, or an outflow of cash when dividends are paid.

# 4 Fundamental Concepts: Mathematical Programming

In this chapter, we will present the general concepts of mathematical programming that will be used in the construction of our balance sheet optimization models. We will start by discussing what a model is and what its uses are in the decision-making process. Then, we will discuss in a little more detail a specific class of models, the so-called mathematical programming models and their main variants, covering the notions of decision variables, constraints and objective functions. We will emphasize some precautions necessary when building mathematical programming models, with special emphasis on the readability of the models and on the ease of debugging. We will introduce the basic anatomy of linear programming, integer programming, and nonlinear programming models. Finally, we will introduce the concept of dynamic programming, emphasizing its applicability in solving multi-stage optimization problems. In particular, we will present the main concepts associated with the dynamic programming method called Stochastic Dual Dynamic Programming (SDDP), which will be used in solving the balance optimization models built throughout the book. It is worth noting that it is not the purpose of the chapter to explore the details of each of the methods and technologies associated in the construction of mathematical programming models, but only to equip the reader with the necessary concepts to navigate through the book and use the technologies in a conscious and safe way.

## 4.1 What Is a Model?

The word model is commonly used to refer to a structure created to represent part, but not all, of the characteristics and functionality of a given object. The set of characteristics and functionalities represented by the model depend on the purpose that is sought for the model. In some situations, the models are concrete, such as models of buildings, prototypes of airplanes or ships, etc.

However, in the field of operational research, most of the time the models of interest are abstract entities constituted in the form of mathematical equations that seek to replicate the internal relationships of the modeled object. In our case, such an object will be a financial institution whose "operation" will be expressed through the evolution of its financial statements over time and under different economic scenarios and assumptions.

For such a model to be useful for the purpose of optimizing, say, the bank's profitability, it needs to be able to represent the main relationships involved in calculating profit. Among them should be, for example, the relationships between the macroe-

https://doi.org/10.1515/9783110664669-004

conomic variable values and the value of the contracts, the relationships between the value of the contracts and the lines of the income statement, etc.

Notwithstanding the fact that our main motivation for building a model to represent the functioning of a bank is profit optimization, let's say that there are numerous other, slightly more general motivations for building models, which will be discussed in the next section.

## 4.2 Motivations for Having a Model

A first motivation for building a model is that the simple exercise of building the model could end up revealing a series of relationships and links that were not apparent at first sight. Therefore, a positive side effect of the model building process is a better understanding of the modeled object.

In turn, a better understanding of the modeled object can lead us to changes in direction and timely decision-making that would never have been achieved without the help of mathematics. Additionally, a model allows us to carry out experiments that are impossible or very complicated to be carried out with the real object.

In the case of banks, we may be talking about testing, for example, the reduction of net intermediation margins or the taking of different financial positions from those that the bank is used to. Such decisions, if wrong, can lead the bank into complicated situations, so simulating their possible effects through a model is quite desirable, if not a prerequisite in some institutions.

Even in the face of such very legitimate motivations to have a model from which we can simulate the operation of the real object under certain conditions, it is still common to find a lot of criticism around the idea of trying a complex object through a model, which by definition it is just a simplification of reality. Much of the criticism centers on the quality of the data used to build the model.

The basic argument is that if much of the data used in the modeling is not accurate enough, how can we believe the answers provided by the model? However, the absence of the model invariably implies quantifications and implicit calculations, which use the same data that would be used to build a model. However, in the absence of a model, the process of searching for answers becomes much less impersonal, structured, reproducible, and auditable. Therefore, it seems to us a mistake not to invest in building a model whenever possible.

In contrast to the critics, there are those who believe almost religiously in mathematical models, which also seems to us to be a failure to understand the usefulness of models. Naturally, models are subject to errors and limitations, whether due to the absence or inaccuracy of data or failures in the definitions of the internal relations of the modeled object.

With this in mind, we argue that a model should be just one of the tools used in the decision-making process, and its results should be validated before being put into practice. If the answers offered by the model prove to be impractical, the reasons for this impracticality should be, as far as possible, incorporated into the model.

By repeating this process successively, those involved will certainly end up knowing more about the functioning of the modeled object and the model itself will become increasingly acceptable and useful.

## 4.3 Mathematical Programing Models

The first common feature among mathematical programming models is that they are defined through a series of mathematical relationships. The second characteristic that mathematical programming models have is that they almost always involve the maximization or minimization of some objective.

In other words, mathematical programming models are often associated with optimization. However, mathematical programming can also be applied to problems that do not have optimization objectives, in which the objective is basically to test the combined feasibility of a set of constraints.

The basic anatomy of a mathematical programming model is shown in Equation 4.1. At the top of the description, we have our objective, which in this example is to maximize the value of the $f$ function, which in turn is defined in terms of the variables $x_i$. The $g_j$ and $h_k$ functions are used to express a set of constraints that must be obeyed by the optimal solution.

$$\begin{aligned} \min_{x} \quad & f(x) \\ \text{s.t.} \quad & g_j(x) \leq b, \quad \forall j \in J \\ & h_k(x) = d, \quad \forall k \in K \end{aligned} \tag{4.1}$$

Such constraints are expressed in the form of equality or inequality relations with respect to the constant values $b_j$ and $d_k$, which appear on the right side of the equations. The $g_j$ and $h_k$ functions are also defined on the same set of variables $x$. Such variables express the decisions that can be made by the model user, and therefore are known as decision variables.

According to the domain of allowed values for the decision variables $x$ and the form of the functions $f$ and $g_j$ and $h_k$, we have different classes of mathematical programming models. As far as decision variables are concerned, we have two basic types of problems. In continuous problems, the decision variables can assume real values. In integer problems, the decision variables can only assume integer values, as the name suggests.

The shape of the $f$, $g_j$, and $h_k$ functions is also decisive in the classification of problems. When such functions are linear, we say we have a linear programming (LP) problem. When they are nonlinear, we say we have a nonlinear programming (NLP) problem.

Within the nonlinear problems, there is a specific subclass of quadratic problems, which appear recurrently in finance in the field of portfolio optimization.

A very important class of problems are the so-called mixed integer linear problems (MILP). These are linear programming problems in which part of the decision variables are integers and another part is continuous. The main types of mathematical programming models that we are interested in are listed bellow:
- Linear programming (LP)
- Mixed-integer linear programming (MILP)
- Quadratic programming (QP)
- Mixed-integer quadratic programming (MIQP)
- Quadratically-constrained programming (QCP)
- Mixed-integer quadratically-constrained programming (MIQCP)

In this list, models are presented in order of complexity of the representative mathematical relationships. However, the greater capacity to represent the more complex classes is accompanied by a greater difficulty in resolution, requiring greater algorithms and computational power.

For an excellent introduction to mathematical programming, readers should refer to Williams (2013), which discusses the general principles of model building and how they can be applied to various types of problems, emphasizing the importance of the building and interpreting of models rather than the solution process. For those who wish to explore the algorithmic aspects further, see Bertsimas and Tsitsiklis (1997) and Nemhauser and Wolsey (1988) are excellent resources providing an introduction and survey on linear programming, integer, and combinatorial optimization.

## 4.4 Solution Methods

Although it is not the purpose of this book to explore these algorithms and their variations in detail, we consider it appropriate to present the essence of each one of them so that the reader gains some intuition on the subject and can navigate reasonably well through the options available in mathematical solvers.

The most classic algorithms for solving mathematical programming problems are the simplex method for continuous linear problems and the Branch-and-Bound method for integer problems. Such methods date back to the 40s and 60s respectively, and naturally have been modernized and improved by a variety of mathematical strategies, some exact and others heuristic.

First, let's talk a little about linear programming problems and the simplex method. In geometric terms, the feasible region of an LP model is defined by all values of decision variables that respect the restrictions and form the convex polytope. An extreme point or vertex of this polytope is known as the basic feasible solution.

It can be shown that for a linear program, if the objective function has a maximum value on the feasible region, then it has this value on at least one of the extreme computation points, what reduces the problem to a finite since there is a finite computation number of extreme points. However, the number of extreme points can be incredibly large, preventing the search for the global optimum from a brute force approach.

Luckily for us, it can also be shown that, if an extreme point is not a maximum point of the objective function, then there is an edge containing the point so that the value of the objective function is strictly increasing on the edge moving away from the point. Hence, if the edge is finite, then the edge connects to another extreme point where the objective function has a greater value. Otherwise the objective function is unbounded above on the edge and the linear program has no feasible solution.

What simplex in fact does is apply this insight by walking along the edges of the polytope to extreme points with greater objective values, until the maximum value is reached, or an unbounded edge is visited. The algorithm is mathematically guaranteed to terminate because the number of vertices in the polytope is finite.

However, what really makes Simplex a useful method is its practical computational complexity. In mathematical terms, simplex has exponential complexity. However, for practical problems, it usually exhibits a polynomial performance. Interestingly, the so-called interior point methods for solving linear problems, which, contrary to the simplex method, reaches the best solution by traversing the interior of the feasible region, although formally having polynomial algorithmic complexity, very commonly tend to perform worse than the simplex method.

In summary, what we want to emphasize is that the performance of the solution methods is highly dependent on the problems, and it is desirable that the user tests the different methods and the different parameterizations allowed for each one of them.

Now, let's move our attention to Branch and Bound methods, intended for solving integer optimization problems. A branch-and-bound algorithm consists of a systematic enumeration of candidate solutions that is thought of as forming a rooted tree. The method explores branches of this tree, which represent subsets of the solution set. Before enumerating the candidate solutions of a branch, the branch is checked against upper and lower estimated bounds on the optimal solution, and is discarded if it cannot produce a better solution than the best one found so far.

Being a little more precise, we say that the pruning process can be due to quality due to infeasibility. In quality elimination, if the solution of a given node is worse than a solution of the original problem obtained previously, its branch can be discarded. In the case of infeasibility elimination, if a node presents infeasibility, its children will also present it, and then the branch can be discarded in the search process.

Efficient estimation of the lower and upper bounds of candidate solutions within branches is critical to the performance of the algorithm. In general terms, such estimates are made by solving the relaxed optimization problem associated with the node, that is, the optimization problem without integrality constraints. When solving an integer minimization problem, a relaxation gives us a lower bound, while any feasible solution gives us an upper bound. Such bounds are called dual and primal bounds, respectively. The same reasoning can be applied to maximization problems.

When solving integer optimization problems through a solver, we usually have control over the type of method used by Branch and Bound to solve relaxed problems, so the same considerations made earlier about the importance of testing the different options are valid in this case.

## 4.5 Modeling Languages

In theoretical terms, mathematical programming is not linked to computer programming. The "programming" part of the expression is much more related to the idea of planning, so the term mathematical planning would be just as suitable as mathematical programming. However, even for small mathematical programming problems, with less than a dozen decision variables, the use of computers is already necessary. In other words, for real problems, mathematical programming invariably implies computer programming.

The task of programming a computer to solve a mathematical programming problem, to some extent, resembles the task of writing a system of equations. Without loss of generality, let us consider the particular case of a linear programming problem. For such a problem, the system of equality and inequality equations that compose the model's constraints can be expressed in what we call a matrix format.

Because of this, the first efforts to facilitate the task of coding a linear programming model focused on facilitating the generation of such matrices and vectors that form the model. Programs designed to do this sometimes used to be called matrix generators. These systems can also be thought of as special-purpose languages or, simply, modeling languages.

In general, such languages seek to offer a more natural input format for the computer, reducing the distance between the mathematical specification and the source code. By increasing the readability of the source code, maintenance and debugging are made easier, which is especially useful in view of the almost monolithic nature with which the final specification of the model is treated in the resolution phase, preventing conventional debugging strategies such as including breakpoints and inspecting variable values in memory. Such challenges became a little clearer in Chapter 6.

Modeling languages also increase productivity and decrease the chances of error by providing ease of repetition of variables, constraints, etc. Such features are useful since, in most cases, large models arise from the combination or repetition of smaller models. In our case, for example, we will be interested in optimizing a bank at various future times and under a number of different economic scenarios. However, the specification of the different problems associated with each of these optimizations is practically the same.

The modeling language we will use will be JuMP. To be more precise, it is an extension of the Julia programming language, JuMP being an abbreviation for Julia for Mathematical Programming. An introduction to JuMP can be found in Appendix A.

## 4.6 A Simple LP Model Example

Imagine we have four different stocks available for an investor to buy. This person has a total capital of 100 dollars and wants to maximize expected dividends coming from those stocks at the end of a certain period.

While stocks A and B are highly risky and pay a high expected dividend, stock D has low risk and a low expected dividend payment. Stock C is an intermediate case, with medium dividends and risk. Table 4.1 shows us the risk profile and expected dividends for each stock.

**Table 4.1:** Stock characteristics example.

| Stock | Risk | Expected Dividends |
|---|---|---:|
| A | High | 6% |
| B | High | 8% |
| C | Medium | 4% |
| D | Low | 2% |

Suppose that this investor does not want to have more than 20% of their portfolio invested in high-risk stocks. Imagine now that they also do not want to have more than 60% of their portfolio invested in high or medium-risk assets. In order to avoid asset-specific risk, they do not want to have more than 40% invested in a single asset, and no short-selling is allowed.

Using the structure of an LP problem stated in Equation 4.1 and assuming that $x_A$, $x_B$, $x_C$, and $x_D$ are the dollar amount invested in each stock, we can formulate this linear programming problem as:

$$\max \quad 0.06x_A + 0.08x_B + 0.04x_C + 0.02x_D \tag{4.2}$$

$$\text{s.t.} \quad x_A + x_B + x_C + x_D = 100 \tag{4.3}$$

$$x_A + x_B \le 20 \tag{4.4}$$

$$x_A + x_B + x_C \le 60 \tag{4.5}$$

$$0 \le x_k \le 40, \quad \forall k \in \{A, B, C, D\} \tag{4.6}$$

In this formulation we see that the objective function shown in Equation 4.2 is to maximize the mulplication of allocated dollars by expected dividends for each asset.

Constraint 4.3 limits the total budget to be invested in all stocks. Inequalities 4.4 and 4.5 limit, respectively, the amount allocated in high-risk assets and high-or-medium-risk stocks. Finally, Equation 4.6 implements short-selling restrictions and per-asset allocation limits for each one of the four stocks.

We can then use JuMP and Clp to solve this linear problem in Julia, as we can see implemented in the script shown in Code Snippet 4.1.

**Code Snippet 4.1:** LP Stock Allocation Example.

```
1   using JuMP
2   using Clp
3
4   m = JuMP.Model(Clp.Optimizer)
5   STOCKS = [:A, :B, :C, :D]
6   HIGH_RISK = [:A, :B]
7   MEDIUM_RISK = [:C]
8   YIELDS = Dict(:A => 0.06, :B => 0.08, :C => 0.04, :D => 0.02)
9
10  # variables
11  @variable(m, 0 <= x[s in STOCKS] <= 40)
12
13  # constraints
14  @constraint(m, sum(x[k] for k in STOCKS) == 100)
15  @constraint(m, sum(x[k] for k in HIGH_RISK) <= 20)
16  @constraint(m, sum(x[k] for k in union(HIGH_RISK, MEDIUM_RISK)) <= 60)
17
18  # objective function
19  @objective(m, Max, sum(x[k] * YIELDS[k] for k in STOCKS))
20
21  optimize!(m)
22  println(solution_summary(m))
23  for v in all_variables(m)
24      println(v, ":", value(v))
25  end
```

From lines 1–4 we are instantiating all required packages and creating an empty JuMP model that uses Clp optimizer as its solver engine. In lines 5–8 we are declaring variables that hold the information related to the mathematical optimization problem. We use vectors to hold all stock symbols and also to mark high and medium-risk assets. We also use a dictionary to hold the relationship between stock symbols and their expected dividend yields.

In line 11 we declare all four decision variables while enforcing short-selling and per-asset constraints. Total budget and per-risk-class limits are defined later in lines 14–16. The objective function and its sense are then created in line 19.

After that, we can run the optimization routine and print a solution summary and optimal values for each model variable. The output of this script is shown as comments in Code Snippet 4.2.

**Code Snippet 4.2:** LP Stock Allocation Example Results.

```
1  # Coin0506I Presolve 0 (-3) rows, 0 (-4) columns and 0 (-9) elements
2  # Clp3002W Empty problem - 0 rows, 0 columns and 0 elements
3  # Clp0000I Optimal - objective value 4
4  # Coin0511I After Postsolve, objective 4,
5  # infeasibilities - dual 0 (0), primal 0 (0)
6  # Clp0032I Optimal objective 4 - 0 iterations time 0.012, Presolve 0.00
7  # * Solver : Clp
8  #
9  # * Status
10 # Termination status : OPTIMAL
11 # Primal status : FEASIBLE_POINT
12 # Dual status : FEASIBLE_POINT
13 # Message from the solver:
14 # "0 - optimal"
15 #
16 # * Candidate solution
17 # Objective value : 4.00000e+00
18 #
19 # * Work counters
20 # Solve time (sec) : 1.20001e-02
21 #
22 # x[A]:0.0
23 # x[B]:20.0
24 # x[C]:40.0
25 # x[D]:40.0
```

From lines 1–20 we can see that an optimal solution was found by Clp in less than a second. The optimal objective function value was 4, which is the expected dividends this investor will receive by holding this optimal portfolio.

Optimal allocations are printed in lines 22–25. The investor should allocate the whole 20% of high-risk budget in stock B, which has the highest expected dividend. The remaining 40% that could be allocated to high-or-medium risk should invested in C, while the remaining budget ought to be used in purchasing low-risk stock D.

## 4.7 A Simple MILP Model Example

Now imagine an investor is about to purchase a total of 150 over-the-counter contracts, and has three different counterparts that can supply them with a portion of those exotic contracts. Each counterpart has different transaction costs, that are composed of both: a transaction fee that is charged regardless of the number of contracts bought, and a per-contract brokerage cost. All counterparts require a minimum of 30 contracts to close a deal.

Table 4.2 summarizes transaction fees and brokerage costs for each market agent, while also showing the maximum amount of contracts that can be purchased from each one of them.

**Table 4.2:** Transaction costs and limits example.

| Counterpart | Transaction Fee | Brokerage Cost | Maximum Contracts |
|---|---|---|---|
| A | 4,500 | 450 | 110 |
| B | 2,300 | 300 | 80 |
| C | 5,600 | 420 | 65 |

So, to calculate optimal values for $x_A$, $x_B$ and $x_c$, the number of contracts to be purchased from each counterpart, we can declare the following mixed-integer linear problem:

$$\begin{aligned}
\min \quad & 450x_A + 4500i_A + 300x_B + 2300i_B + 420x_C + 5600i_C && (4.7)\\
\text{s.t.} \quad & x_A + x_B + x_C = 150 && (4.8)\\
& 30i_A \leq x_A \leq 110i_A && (4.9)\\
& 30i_B \leq x_B \leq 80i_B && (4.10)\\
& 30i_C \leq x_C \leq 65i_C && (4.11)\\
& i_k \in \{0,1\}, \quad \forall k \in \{A,B,C\} && (4.12)
\end{aligned}$$

Notice that variable $i_A$ is a binary indicator variable, that is set to 1 when there is a deal closed with counterpart A, or set to 0 otherwise. Similarly, $i_B$ and $i_C$ follow the same rule with their relationship to counterparts B and C.

The objective function shown in Equation 4.7 shows us that we want to minimize total transaction cost, represented by the sum of brokerage cost times the amount of contracts purchased plus a transaction fee times the indicator variable $i_k$ for each counterpart. In Equation 4.8 we define the total number of contracts to be purchased.

In Equation 4.9 we define the dynamics that set indicator variable A while implementing lower and upper purchase limits for counterpart A. Imagine that variable $x_A$ is set to zero, meaning no contract will be purchased from counterpart A. In this case, the first part of the inequality would force $i_A$ to zero, otherwise we would have an infeasible inequality $30 \times 1 \leq 0$. On the other hand, if the solver decides for buying a non-zero quantity of A, the second part of the inequality would force $i_A$ to be one, or we would have $x_A \leq 110 \times 0$ for a positive $x_A$. And in case $i_A$ equals to one, lower and upper limits for $x_A$ are activated, due to the resulting inequalities $30 \times 1 \leq x_A \leq 110 \times 1$. Similar arguments apply to counterparts B and C represented in Equation 4.10 and Equation 4.11.

In Code Snippet 4.3 we use JuMP and Cbc to define and solve this mixed-integer optimization problem.

**Code Snippet 4.3:** Over-the-Counter Operation Example.

```
using JuMP
using Cbc
```

```
3
4    m = JuMP.Model(Cbc.Optimizer)
5    COUNTERPARTS = [:A, :B, :C]
6    FEES = Dict(:A => 4500, :B => 2300, :C => 5600)
7    BROKERAGE = Dict(:A => 450, :B => 300, :C => 420)
8    CONTRACTS_LIMIT = Dict(:A => 110, :B => 80, :C => 65)
9
10   # variables
11   @variable(m, x[k in COUNTERPARTS])
12   @variable(m, i[k in COUNTERPARTS], Bin)
13
14   # constraints
15   @constraint(m, sum(x[k] for k in COUNTERPARTS) == 150)
16   for k in COUNTERPARTS
17       @constraint(m, x[k] >= 30 * i[k])
18       @constraint(m, x[k] <= CONTRACTS_LIMIT[k] * i[k])
19   end
20
21   # objective function
22   @objective(
23       m,
24       Min,
25       sum(BROKERAGE[k] * x[k] + FEES[k] * i[k] for k in COUNTERPARTS)
26   )
27
28   optimize!(m)
29   println(solution_summary(m))
30   for v in all_variables(m)
31       println(v, ":", value(v))
32   end
```

In lines 1–5, we set up all packages and a JuMP model that uses Cbc as its solver. From lines 5–8 we define problem data as a series of vectors and dictionaries. The definition of variables is taken care of in lines 11 and 12. Notice that, whereas $x$ variables are continuous, indicator variables $i$ are defined as binary, by using the `Bin` keyword at the end of their declaration.

In lines 15 we define the total contracts constraint. From lines 16–19, for each counterpart, we define the inequalities that set indicator constraint values and trading limits. The `@objective` macro sets the problem to minimize transaction costs. After that, we run the optimization and print results that can be seen on Code Snippet 4.4 as comments.

**Code Snippet 4.4:** Over-the-Counter Operation Example Solution.

```
# Welcome to the CBC MILP Solver
# Version: 2.10.5
# Build Date: Jan 1 1970
#
# (truncated ...)
#
# Result - Optimal solution found
#
# Objective value: 62300.00000000
# Enumerated nodes: 0
```

```
11 # Total iterations: 0
12 # Time (CPU seconds): 0.06
13 # Time (Wallclock seconds): 0.06
14 #
15 # Total time (CPU seconds): 0.08
16 # (Wallclock seconds): 0.08
17 #
18 # * Solver : COIN Branch-and-Cut (Cbc)
19 #
20 # * Status
21 # Termination status : OPTIMAL
22 # Primal status : FEASIBLE_POINT
23 # Dual status : NO_SOLUTION
24 #
25 # (truncated...)
26 #
27 # x[A]:69.99999999999999
28 # x[B]:80.0
29 # x[C]:0.0
30 # i[A]:1.0
31 # i[B]:1.0
32 # i[C]:0.0
```

From Code Snippet 4.4, we can see Cbc found an optimal solution for the MIP problem, with an associated minimal transaction cost of 62,300. This involves buying 70 contracts from counterpart A and 80 units from B. To counterpart A there would be a payment of 4,500 due to transaction fees and $450 \times 70 = 31{,}500$ as brokerage costs, summing to a transaction cost of 36,000. B would receive $2{,}300 + 300 \times 80 = 26{,}300$.

Notice from lines 30–32 of Code Snippet 4.4 that indicator variables are correctly set to one for A and B, and marked as zero for counterpart C.

## 4.8 Dynamic Programming

Dynamic programming is a method for solving complex problems by breaking them down into smaller, simpler subproblems. The key idea behind dynamic programming is to store the solutions to subproblems so that they can be reused, rather than recalculated each time they are needed. In finance, dynamic programming is used to solve a wide range of problems, including portfolio optimization, option pricing, and risk management. This session will introduce the basic concepts of dynamic programming and show how they can be applied to a financial problem.

In a dynamic programming problem we are often interested in maximizing or minimizing an *objective function*, like in the other mathematical programming we have been discussing in previous sections. But, because we are representing the action to be taken as a sequence of decisions over time, we have to make sure to keep a way of storing and transmitting information between different time steps. We use the term *state* to refer to the set of *state variables* that are responsible for passing values from two sequential instants of decision.

At each point of time, a model will take decisions through *control variables*. The values of such variables will exist only inside a time step and they will, with the help of the incoming state, modify the values of state variables, so they can be passed to the next time step. This process is often represented by a *state transformation function*.

The dynamic programming algorithm is intended to produce a *policy function*, which is the representation of a decision rule that sets the values of control variables as a function of an income state. Finally, we can construct a *value function*, which represents the objective function evaluation of the optimal policy.

One of the most important tools one can use in order to solve dynamic programming problems is Bellman's principle of optimality. This principle is referred to as "an optimal policy [that] has the property that whatever the initial state and initial decision are, the remaining decisions must constitute an optimal policy with regard to the state resulting from the first decision." (Bellman, 1957) It is also translated into a recursive equation, which is frequently referred to as Bellman's equation:

$$V(x) = \max_{a \in \Gamma(x)} \{F(x,a) + \beta V(T(x,a))\} \tag{4.13}$$

If $x$ is an income state and $a \in \Gamma(x)$ is the set of possible decisions to be taken at that time step, in Equation 4.13, we can see that the value function $V(x)$ is the maximum value of the payoff function $F(x,a)$ plus a discount factor times the value function evaluated at a next step, whose incoming state is a new state generated by the state-transformation function $T(x,a)$.

In other words, given an income state $x$ we have to choose a decision $a$ that gives us the maximum objective function value for this period and assume that we will always take optimal decisions from then on. This ideia is represented in the recursiveness of Equation 4.13. So instead of finding an optimal decision for the whole model altogether, we can use this formula to solve it step-by-step, and transmit optimal decisions from one step to another.

Let's illustrate this principle with a discrete optimization example. Imagine we managing a hydroelectric reservoir, and want to decide how much water we should release in order to maximize profit. Imagine that we are planning two months ahead, then we will have two sequential places of decision, or model steps.

The reservoir has a maximum capacity of four units and we know for sure that rain volume will be three and two units over the next two months. For simplicity, consider that there is no water evaporation. Suppose that the reservoir starts with one unit.

So, we can derive a transformation function $T$ given by an incoming state reservoir level $S$, a control variable of water inflow $q$, and a water release decision variable $r$. The function is represented in Equation 4.14:

$$T(S,q,r) = S + q - r \tag{4.14}$$

It is important to notice that this state variable $S$ is only defined in the interval between zero and the reservoir capacity.

We will assume that we have a discrete function that maps each release level to a benefit value, which is constant for all periods. From Table 4.3 we can conclude that a release of zero units generates a negative benefit of 100, while a release of two units generates a positive benefit of 320.

**Table 4.3:** Water release benefits function.

| Release | Benefit |
|---|---|
| 0 | –100 |
| 1 | 250 |
| 2 | 320 |
| 3 | 480 |
| 4 | 520 |
| 5 | 520 |
| 6 | 410 |
| 7 | 120 |

We want to define how much we should release ($r$) in each period in order to obtain the maximum benefit over the next three months. Let's start by solving each step separately, from the last to the first, using Bellman's principle of optimality.

In the last month, we know that we will have an inflow of two units. So, for each possible incoming reservoir level $S$ we will have an optimal release to be done, as shown in Table 4.4.

If the initial level, coming from the end of the first period, is equal to zero we will have three possibilities: release nothing and get a benefit of –100, release the two units of inflow and get a benefit of 320, or do a partial release of one unit to get a benefit of 250. Of course, the optimal release $r^*$, conditional to a zero incoming level, is to do a full release and achieve a benefit of 320. Additionally, if we had an initial level of 1, we could release three units of water and get a benefit of 480. In the case of three units for example, we could choose between releasing four or five units and get the same benefit of 520. The value function is then illustrated by the first and fourth columns of Table 4.4, meaning that for each incoming level $S$, we can calculate a maximum benefit $V_2(r)$ that can be achieved. A policy function $r^*$ can also be derived from the first and last columns of the same table. It states that for each incoming level $S$ we can derive an associated decision of how much water we should release ($r^*$) in order to maximize benefits.

Now we will use Bellman's principle to calculate the value function at the first period, assuming that we already have an optimal policy for the last period. In this case,

**Table 4.4:** Value function in the last period.

| Incoming Level (S) | Release (r) | Benefit ($F(r)$) | Maximum Benefit ($V_2(S)$) | Optimal Release ($r^*$) |
|---|---|---|---|---|
| | 0 | −100 | | |
| 0 | 1 | 250 | 320 | 2 |
| | 2 | 320 | | |
| | 0 | −100 | | |
| | 1 | 250 | | |
| 1 | 2 | 320 | 480 | 3 |
| | 3 | 480 | | |
| | 0 | −100 | | |
| | 1 | 250 | | |
| 2 | 2 | 320 | 520 | 4 |
| | 3 | 480 | | |
| | 4 | 520 | | |
| | 0 | −100 | | |
| | 1 | 250 | | |
| | 2 | 320 | | |
| 3 | 3 | 480 | 520 | 4 or 5 |
| | 4 | 520 | | |
| | 5 | 520 | | |
| | 0 | −100 | | |
| | 1 | 250 | | |
| | 2 | 320 | | |
| 4 | 3 | 480 | 520 | 4 or 5 |
| | 4 | 520 | | |
| | 5 | 520 | | |
| | 6 | 410 | | |

Equation 4.13 can be rewritten as:

$$V_1(r) = \max_{r\in\Gamma(S)}\{F(r) + \beta V_2(T(S,q,r)))\} \tag{4.15}$$

Table 4.5 illustrates the mechanics of this equation. We know that we have an initial level of one unit and that the inflows in the first period sum to three units. So, if we decide for releasing nothing in the first period ($r = 0$), we would have an imediate benefit of −100. Then four units would be passed as the initial state for the second period. By looking up at the value function for the last period ($V_2(S)$) in Table 4.4, we would see that this level would lead to a 520 benefit in the second period. Using Equation 4.15 and assuming no discount factor ($\beta = 1$), we would end up with a total benefit of $-100 + 520 = 420$.

If we decide for releasing three units in the first period, we would achieve an immediate benefit of 480, leaving one unit of water in the reservoir. To that unit we would

**Table 4.5:** Value function in the first period.

| Release ($r$) | Benefit ($F(r)$) | Outgoing State ($T(S, q, r)$) | Recursive Term ($V_2(S)$) | Value Function ($V_1(r)$) |
|---:|---:|---:|---:|---:|
| 0 | −100 | 4 | 520 | 420 |
| 1 | 250 | 3 | 520 | 770 |
| 2 | 320 | 2 | 520 | 840 |
| 3 | 480 | 1 | 480 | 960 |
| 4 | 520 | 0 | 320 | 840 |

add an inflow of two units in the second period, and would decide optimally for a full release of three units, resulting in an additional benefit of 480 in the second period. That would be the optimal policy, resulting in a total benefit of 960, as we can see in the last column of Table 4.5.

In summary, we've broken down a multi-stage decision problem into two separate subproblems and used Bellman's principle of optimization to find the optimal global decision rule by using the value function of each subproblem.

While this approach can be applied to problems with more stages and variables, it does have a drawback: the curse of dimensionality. As we add more steps and variables, the computational and memory requirements increase rapidly, making the model difficult to solve.

For this reason, other methods have been developed to solve these types of problems. In the next session, we'll discuss one such method called *Stochastic Dual Dynamic programming* (SDDP), which utilizes machine learning and optimization theory to approximate the second term of Bellman's equation, eliminating its recursive nature.

## 4.9 Stochastic Dual Dynamic Programming

*Stochastic Dual Dynamic Programming* – known as SDDP (Pereira and Pinto (1991) and Pereira (1989)) – is a powerful optimization technique that is used to solve multi-stage decision problems. These problems involve making a series of decisions over time, where the future states and costs are uncertain. SDDP is particularly useful for problems with large numbers of stages and variables, where other methods may struggle due to the "curse of dimensionality."

The SDDP method combines elements of dynamic programming, stochastic optimization, and machine learning. It works by approximating the solution to the problem through a series of dual problems. Each iteration of the method provides a better approximation of the true solution. This allows for faster convergence and more efficient computation compared to traditional dynamic programming methods.

SDDP has a wide range of applications in different fields such as finance, energy, and transportation. It has been used to solve problems such as portfolio optimization, hydroelectric power plant scheduling, and transportation network design. The method has proven to be very effective in these fields, providing optimal solutions to complex problems.

The architecture of an SDDP model is defined with the help of a few concepts:

A *node* or (*stage*) represents a point in time at which a decision must be made. The decision made at each node will affect the future states and costs of the problem. Each stage will have its own objective function, also referred to as *stage objective*.

Beside state and control variables, an SDDP problem can also contain *random variables*. These are represented by a set of possible values and associated probabilities that are going to be used in a stochastic setup of SDDP. The ideia is that in each simulation we will draw a specific realization of that random variable using its specific probability distribution.

Finally, a *policy graph* is a visual representation of the SDDP problem that shows the relationship between the nodes. It is used to track the progress of the algorithm and to visualize the solution of the problem. There are many different types of policy graphs that can be used depending on the nature of the model.

The *linear policy graph* is a graph where decisions are taken sequentially, and each node represents a model step. It is the most simple graph, and it represents well deterministic problems, or stochastic models without regime switching.

In Figure 4.1 we can see a visual representation of a linear policy graph in a stochastic setup with three sequential decisions nodes. Full arrows represent the passing of states between subsequent nodes. The probability distributions $\Omega_1$, $\Omega_2$, and $\Omega_3$ are used to draw values for random variables in each node.

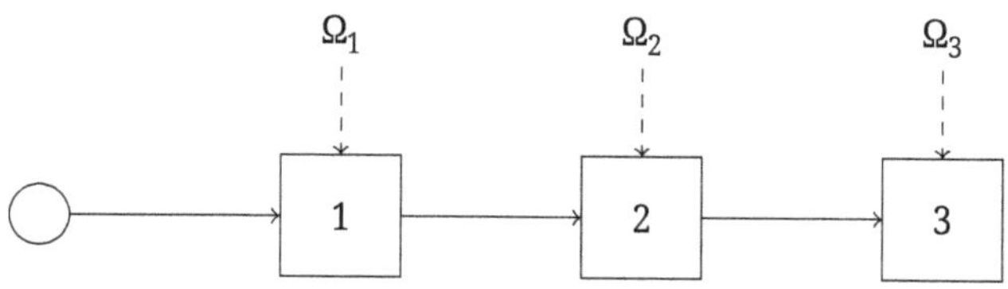


**Figure 4.1:** Linear policy graph example with three stages.

The process of a forward pass in a graph representation of a dynamic programming problem can be described as follows:

1. Start by initializing state variables in the initial node and passing their values as the incoming state of the first node.
2. Draw values for all random variables using the appropriate stage probability distribution $\Omega$.
3. Make optimal decisions based on the appropriate stage objective.

4. Use the state-transformation function to update the outgoing values of all state variables. These values will become the incoming state for the next stage.
5. Repeat steps 2–4 for each subsequent stage, updating the state and making optimal decisions at each node.

In a stochastic environment, Equation 4.13 can be restated by replacing the second term of Bellman's equation with an expectancy of the value function in the next period. This expectation is calculated over all different scenarios considering their respective probabilities.

$$V(x) = \max_{a \in \Gamma(x)} \{F(x,a) + \mathbb{E}[V(T(x,a))]\} \tag{4.16}$$

SDDP then uses *Kelley's cutting plane algorithm* to iteratively approximate these expectancies. This is referref to as the *training phase* of SDDP. During this phase, the algorithm begins by creating an initial feasible solution and then performs a forward pass. With the help of results from the dual problems that are generated from the forward pass, it adds new constraints to each subproblem, known as "cutting planes", to improve the solution of each stage and better approximate its value function until it is accurate enough. After that, a new forward pass is performed using the recently-cut subproblems. This leads to an approximation of the true value function that can be utilized in the decision-making process of the SDDP method. Once this process is completed, the policy is considered to be trained.

After the policy is trained, we move on to evaluating the policy rules against different simulated scenarios. This is commonly referred to as the *simulation phase*. This is typically done by running forward passes over the trained policy. Sometimes it can be helpful to use different probability distribution (samplers) for training and simulation, which allows for out-of-sample assessment of the quality of a policy function.

It's important to note that the performance of a policy can change depending on the set of scenarios used for the simulation. To get a more robust evaluation of the policy, it's recommended to use a large number of scenarios and to use a representative sample of the possible future states and costs of the problem.

In a purely deterministic SDDP model, there will be no random variables and no sampling will be required. In this scenario, we only need to simulate once to evaluate the deterministic policy obtained.

Other types of policy graphs can help the practitioner to better represent uncertainty in a stochastic SDDP model. For example, Figure 4.2, shows us a Markovian policy graph with two Markovian states: good (G) or bad (B). In this setup we would have to supply SDDP with three *transition matrices*, containing probabilities of switching between those two states before entering each of the three model stages. The main difference between the states is the probability distribution $\Omega$. In this example, we could have a $\Omega_1^B$ distribution attributing higher probability to realizations of random variables that

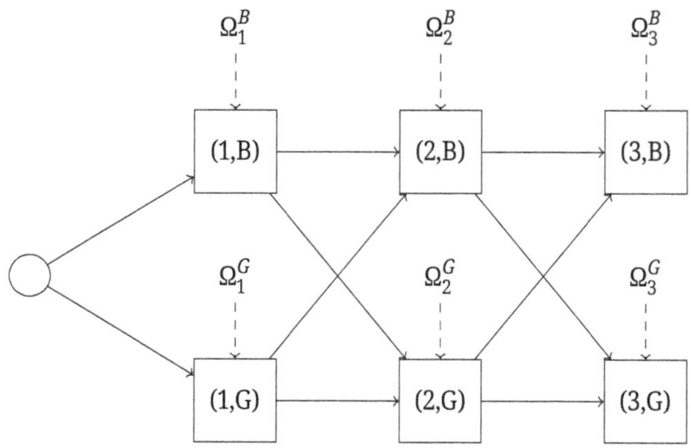


**Figure 4.2:** Markovian policy graph example with three stages and two states.

are considered bad in the context of the problem. On the other hand, $\Omega_1^G$ would have a tendency toward good outcomes.

The algorithm for a forward pass in a Markovian policy graph is as follows:

1. Begin by initializing the state variables in the initial node and passing their values as the incoming state for the first node.
2. Sample from the first transition matrix to evaluate the initial Markovian state of the problem.
3. Draw values for all random variables using the appropriate probability distribution based on the current stage and Markovian state.
4. Make optimal decisions based on the appropriate stage objective.
5. Use the state-transformation function to update the outgoing values of all state variables. These values will become the incoming state for the next stage.
6. Sample from the next stage transition matrix to evaluate the Markovian state at the next node.
7. Repeat steps 3–6 for each subsequent stage, updating the state and making optimal decisions at each node.

In conclusion, SDDP is a powerful optimization technique that can be used to solve complex, large-scale, and multi-stage decision-making problems. Its ability to handle uncertainty and randomness through the use of duality theory and Markovian assumptions makes it well-suited for applications in various fields such as energy, finance, and transportation. The SDDP algorithm is a combination of forward and backward passes, which allows for the efficient computation of the value function and the optimal policy.

Overall, SDDP is a valuable tool for decision-makers and researchers facing problems with uncertainty and stochasticity. With the growing need for robust and efficient decision-making in the face of uncertain and dynamic environments, the use of SDDP is likely to become increasingly important in the future.

Throughout this book, we will be utilizing SDDP to address the challenge of balance sheet optimization. To do this, we will be utilizing the Julia programming language and two powerful packages that work seamlessly with it: `JuMP.jl`, a domain-specific modeling language for mathematical optimization, and `SDDP.jl`, a Julia implementation of the SDDP algorithm. In Appendix A you will find a brief overview of these tools. Additionally, you will find an example of how to use SDDP to solve both deterministic and stochastic production planning problems, providing a hands-on understanding of the capabilities of these powerful packages.

# 5 Data Preparation Pipeline

In this chapter, our focus will be on gathering the necessary data to construct a balance sheet optimization model effectively. We will examine the crucial considerations to keep in mind when working with various data types, such as the chart of accounts, balances, financial positions, contract specifications, historical and projected market scenarios, and business assumptions. The goal is to familiarize you with the key data elements that must be processed while creating a data preparation pipeline for a balance sheet optimization model.

## 5.1 Chart of Accounts

The main objective of this book is to construct a balance sheet optimization model, and the first step in doing so is to obtain a balance sheet template. This financial statement serves as the foundation for our data preparation pipeline and provides the names, structure, and official balances of the ledger accounts.

It is crucial to choose the appropriate balance sheet template as the mathematical model will frequently refer to these ledger accounts, especially in the constraints. The chosen template should accurately reflect all relevant business constraints in a detailed manner.

However, institutions usually have multiple versions of charts of accounts to cater to different stakeholders, so the modeler must choose the version to base the model on, particularly in the input layer. Although a flexible data preparation process that accommodates an unpredictable balance sheet format may have benefits, it also comes with a high cost in the mathematical modeling layer.

We prefer to use a fixed balance sheet template instead of adjusting the mathematical model equations to accommodate an unpredictable format, as this can lead to decreased code readability, increased error points, and difficulties in maintenance. When changes are needed, we make the necessary modifications to other parts of the system, such as the decision variables and constraints.

It may be advantageous for the modeler to create a new balance sheet template that aligns with your programming needs. This is especially important for the reconciliation of balances against the financial position databases, which is guided by the chosen balance sheet template.

For example, in the management of interest rate and foreign exchange risk in bank portfolios, a reorganization of official ledger accounts may be useful when dealing with derivative contracts such as swaps and futures.

The value of such contracts may change sign over time, sometimes representing an asset and sometimes a liability. As an example, an accounting convention could be to record the contract value in an asset account if it is positive and in a liabilities account

https://doi.org/10.1515/9783110664669-005

if it is negative. From an accounting perspective, this rationale is understandable, however, it is of little use to the risk manager. For the latter, it may be more beneficial to organize derivatives on the balance sheet according to their purpose rather than their current value. To facilitate this, it would be useful to provide a balance sheet template with ledger accounts that have more descriptive names, indicating, for example, the portfolios being hedged by the derivatives in that record.

Deviating from official formats may be sensible in certain situations, and these should be evaluated by the modeler. Generally, it is less troublesome to add more lines to the balance sheet than to combine two or more lines into one, since it provides more clarity and detail. Such divisions can be beneficial, for instance, in order to facilitate the definition of business constraints, as well as to make input validation and output reporting more straightforward.

To sum up, while using alternative balance sheet templates is a valid and legitimate approach, we suggest exercising caution when doing so. A template that strays too far from the official versions can make an independent validation a harder process, as well as making the reconciliation against official financial statement balances difficult.

## 5.2 Outstanding Balances and Runoff Positions

As previously mentioned, the balance sheet template serves as a guide for constructing our data preparation pipeline. For each line on the balance sheet, we query financial position databases to retrieve the contracts that make up the ledger accounts. These contracts are the ones already booked in the portfolios an institution holds. The positions related to them are referred to as *runoff positions*.

To ensure that these queries were executed correctly, we must compare the book value of each ledger account with the sum of the book values of the associated financial positions. The outstanding balances for each ledger account, along with the balance sheet template, are the second essential pieces of information in our pipeline.

It's crucial to be mindful of the units of measure used in accounting during this stage. In the ideal scenario, ledger account balances and individual financial position balances should all be expressed in the base currency (e. g. dollars) and not in thousands or millions. However, it's common for information to be available in different units of measurement across different databases. Careful mapping of these conventions is crucial to ensure proper reconciliation.

It's important to keep in mind that balance sheets have a hierarchical structure, meaning the balances of the top-level accounts are always the total of the balances of the lower-level accounts immediately below them. To ensure the accuracy of the data, a vital verification that should be done is to confirm that this relationship holds true for all ledger accounts in the balance sheet.

Although this type of discrepancy is rare in a bank's financial statements, it can easily be introduced during the various programming steps involved in automating the model-building phase. Thus, it's advisable to perform this basic test at the source of the information as well as after transforming the information into the internal structures of the balance sheet model.

## 5.3 Reconciliation Rules

In an ideal scenario, the official book value of each ledger account that forms the financial statement would match the sum of the book values of the corresponding financial positions recorded in financial position control systems.

However, it is possible that these values may differ from each other. In such cases, we have to determine how to reconcile them. Typically, we believe that the ledger accounts' balances should take precedence due to their more official status.

Another reason to use financial statements as the authoritative source of balance information is that these numbers have likely undergone reviews, validations, and independent audits. With this in mind, let's examine the most common reconciliation methods that a modeler can adopt.

The first and most frequently used reconciliation strategy is called *scaling*. This involves multiplying the book values of financial positions by a constant so that the sum of the scaled positions equals the book value of the ledger account.

The benefit of this approach is that it maintains the relative contributions of the financial positions that make up a particular ledger account. However, the scaling process doesn't take into account other ledger accounts, which could lead to artificial currency or interest rate mismatches that don't actually exist in reality.

The second reconciliation strategy involves adding a dummy financial position to reconcile the balances. This strategy is referred to as *shifting*. The dummy position should not affect the risk and return configuration of the balance sheet.

While neither the scaling nor the shifting strategy is perfect, they are both necessary to ensure that the model starts from the official balances reported in the financial statements.

A particular case where a reconciliation strategy is needed refers to lines whose balances do not correspond directly to financial contracts, such as the "allowance for credit losses" line. The balance of this line relates to an aggregate estimate of expected credit loss for one or more credit portfolios.

In such a case, we need to adopt a reconciliation strategy that involves creating one or more pseudo-contracts to represent the change in the balance of the line in question. For example, in the case of the "allowance for credit losses" line, we would create a pseudo-contract that can be bought or sold to represent the increase or decrease in the balance of this line. This approach is useful not just for asset and liability accounts but also for equity accounts like unrealized gains and losses and par-value capital. By creating these pseudo-contracts, we can capture the dynamics of the balance and its cash flow, if applicable.

The data preparation pipeline for the model has a parameter that involves mapping the reconciliation rules to be used for each balance sheet line. Additionally, there is a designated safety threshold, beyond which differences between ledger accounts and position databases are deemed unacceptable.

This threshold can be expressed in absolute or relative terms, and can be customized to suit the requirements of the modeler, taking into consideration the nature of the financial positions and the accuracy of the financial position databases. The thresholds can also be set specifically for individual ledger accounts.

## 5.4 New Positions

According to Homer Simpson, you can have all the money in the world, but there is one thing you will never have: a dinosaur. And the reason you cannot have a dinosaur is simple: there is none for sale as far as we know. Therefore, you need to plan your life without this possibility, which certainly will not be a serious problem.

The balance sheet optimization model we aim to build is designed to assist us in making decisions, including entering new financial positions on both sides of the balance sheet. Unlike the runoff positions, these new financial positions have not yet been booked in any portfolio. However, it is the responsibility of the modeler to provide the model with a set of new financial positions that the bank can enter today and in the future, under certain price and rate conditions.

The solution of the model will be limited if the set of new positions is limited, no matter how accurate the model's constraints and objective function may be. Thus, it is crucial to list a wide range of new positions, including those that form the bank's strategy as well as positions with different characteristics in terms of currencies, rates, maturities, sectors, and ratings, among others.

Imagine we have established a constraint that requires us to increase the portfolio duration. If we don't offer new contracts with long maturities, the model might struggle to meet this constraint, and, in the worst scenario, we can end up with an unfeasibility. Likewise, if we aim to have a specific exposure to a currency, we need to provide the model with contracts denominated in that currency so that it can find a suitable rollover strategy to fulfill that requirement. This highlights the importance of having a wide range of new contracts with varying characteristics.

This approach is necessary to determine the optimal investment, funding, hedging, and diversification opportunities. Even if it does not make sense for the bank to change its current strategy, being prepared to test new strategies quickly and efficiently is valuable. This flexibility in simulating new strategies, particularly investing in new products or market segments, can reinforce the importance and applicability of the model for strategic planning, not just for stress and risk testing exercises for which many balance sheet simulation systems were originally created.

It's important to note that the conditions of the new positions must be in line with the scenarios being used in the projection. To illustrate this, consider an example where a 5% fixed-rate transaction is made available for purchase in a scenario where the current market rate is 3%. In this case, the model must ensure that the contract is valued at its fair value, without creating any unrealistic arbitrage opportunities that would distort the solution. Every transaction must occur at a fair value, considering the scenario at hand.

## 5.5 Contract Aggregation Strategies

A bank's portfolio can consist of a vast number of financial contracts, including debts, stocks, bonds, derivatives, loans, and deposits, which in total can number in the tens of thousands or even millions.

Although each contract is negotiated individually in reality, the financial planning problem of interest may be approached at a more aggregate level, so a detailed representation at the contract level is not necessary. Aggregating contracts and financial positions serves two purposes: to reduce the dimensionality of the mathematical problem, making it easier and faster to solve, and to represent risk and business constraints accurately while preserving the quality and implementability of optimal decisions.

The level of aggregation should be determined based on the tradeoff between reducing problem size and maintaining the correct representation of risk and business constraints. Practical examples of aggregation criteria can provide guidance in making this determination.

The first example and most important criterion for aggregation is based on the balance sheet line. This criterion ensures that financial positions that are originally recorded in different balance sheet lines are never aggregated together. This helps preserve the conventional representation of the institution's balance sheet, both in terms of input and output for the model.

This approach to aggregation makes the model results easier to understand for those who are familiar with the traditional balance sheet representation, as the model's output will have the same lines, ordering, and breakdown structure as what they are used to.

Another example of aggregation criteria is contract risk factors, such as currency, index, and floating rates. When aggregating contracts with different risk factors, it can lead to a type of basis risk, as the aggregated risk factors are not the same in reality. To maintain the model's ability to reflect foreign exchange, interest rate, and other risks accurately, it is important to carefully design the aggregation between different risk factors, considering the bank's level of exposure to each and the potential outcomes if our aggregation assumptions prove to be incorrect in the future.

The use of balance sheet line, risk factor, and risk book aggregation criteria is likely to be universal among banks, even those subject to low regulation. Other criteria may be necessary depending on the modeler's objectives. To give the reader some further insight, let's consider some examples.

Ratings refer to the level of risk involved in a particular transaction, especially with loans. In theory, the ratings are linked to the interest rates charged. Loans to companies with lower ratings will result in a higher-interest portfolio, but also a higher exposure to default losses. If the model aims to simulate rollover strategies targeting specific rating profiles, then operations with different ratings cannot be aggregated. A similar scenario is a bank seeking better allocation by economic sector, in which case the sector must be used as an aggregation criteria alongside rating aggregation criteria.

Another interesting situation to consider is a bank with a trading desk that uses complex strategies and operates in multiple markets with a wide range of financial instruments. In a model focused on representing the overall balance sheet dynamics and long-term perspectives, accurately representing this type of balance sheet line may be challenging. However, it can be modeled based on its return, risk, and capital consumption profiles, while obscuring the details of intra-portfolio management. Before making such simplification, it is crucial to thoroughly analyze the significance of these desks to the bank's balance sheet.

In a more flexible framework, data preparation routines can be designed to accommodate different levels of aggregation to meet the goals of specific simulation or optimization exercises. This way, to enhance performance in longer-term simulations, we can opt for more aggregation, while in more tactical or operational simulations, we can choose to aggregate less.

## 5.6 Market Data

A bank's balance sheet is primarily composed of financial contracts, which means that in order to project the balance sheet and other financial statements, we need to estimate the values of these contracts and their cash flows over time. To do so, we need to estimate numerous variables, such as currency quotes, stock prices, interest rates, and other information that affects the values and cash flows of the contracts. For simplicity, we can refer to all of these variables as "indexers."

Our first step in the data preparation process is to compile a list of indexers present in the bank's portfolio, as well as any indexers that may appear in the future. The set of indexers in the future balance sheet may differ from the current set for various reasons, such as the bank's expansion into new markets or countries, or the discontinuation of a specific market rate.

Once the inventory is complete, we need to identify the sources of market data for these indexers. For historical data, we may be able to obtain it from external providers or centralized internal databases. For projections, the information may be more decentralized, as it may be generated by different business units and through various models.

However, our ultimate goal is to produce a consolidated balance sheet simulation, so it's important to make sure that the projections for the various market variables are consistent. A common strategy to try to ensure some level of consistency between the numbers generated by these different "satellite models" is to run them conditionally on a set of shared economic variables.

While the pros and cons of different scenario generation architectures and models are not the focus of this book or the modeler's primary responsibility, the modeler should understand the requirements for a good integrated simulation and the risks of using uncoordinated and unrealistic scenarios for different variables.

As such, the modeler must act as a mediator in the scenario-generating model building process, trying to reuse as much as possible and preserving the responsibilities for each of the numerous variables that may be necessary for projecting financial statements.

It is crucial to pay close attention to the conventions used by each of the satellite models, to avoid errors when integrating the projections. Some models may use averages, while others use beginning-of-period or end-of-period values. Some may rely on specific day count and interest rate conventions, while others may use entirely different ones. The modeler must identify and address these differences before incorporating future market scenarios into the balance sheet model.

Another relevant issue concerns the computational performance while storing and accessing such data throughout the projection process. That is because, in the balance sheet simulation process, each of the contracts will need to have their values calculated on a projection basis for a large number of scenarios.

Given that the volume of contracts, periods, and scenarios can be substantial, the time required to perform these evaluations can become prohibitive if the system, data structures, and data access methods are not highly efficient. These inefficiencies can be exacerbated in cases where coefficients depend on sensitivities or Monte Carlo simulations, which is common in risk analysis or derivatives pricing.

In our experience, the time required to instantiate a balance sheet model can be much longer compared to other applications of mathematical programming. This is due to the need to evaluate all financial contracts based on projections for a large number of scenarios. To speed up the process, it is necessary to use cache mechanisms, or other calculation acceleration techniques. The organization of market data and the efficiency of data access methods are critical factors that must be carefully considered to prevent a bottleneck in the model's performance.

## 5.7 Business Assumptions

Running a balance sheet simulation over the long term involves a multitude of business assumptions, including the volume and segmentation of investments, funding strategy, transaction costs, capitalization schedules, tax rates, dividend payment policies, and more.

Compared to other types of data used to construct the model, like balance templates and financial positions information, business assumptions can be more diverse and challenging to fit into a single or rigid data structure. This responsibility is often shared among different areas within the institution.

Furthermore, these assumptions often already exist and are structured differently across various departments. The original format of this information may not be directly compatible with the balance sheet model, leading to the need for adaptation.

Consequently, the modeler should work with relevant stakeholders to make sure that the business assumptions are provided in a format as close as possible to the balance sheet model's requirements. This involves considerations such as the level of detail, the segmentation of investments into economic sectors, product types, currencies, and rates, among others.

The aim of this collaboration should be to minimize the need for adjustments to the original assumptions, avoiding the need for the modeler to create additional assumptions to make them suitable for use in the mathematical model. For instance, consider a business unit that uses an econometric model to forecast semi-annual disbursements. If the volume of these disbursements is a crucial premise for the mathematical model, then it is a good start. However, if the balance sheet model operates on a monthly basis, the semi-annual disbursement forecasts will need to be adapted to be used in the model.

It may not be adequate to simply consider all disbursements will happen at the end or beginning of a period. Although distributing them evenly over the months may seem like a better solution, it may not accurately reflect reality, especially in cases where there's a clear seasonality within the semi-annual periods. Making a poor choice could have significant effects on the results of the mathematical model and decisions related to managing liquidity targets.

The ideal solution would be to see if the original forecast model can be modified to provide monthly results, as this could improve planning and ultimately lead to lower internal transfer costs, making the business unit more competitive.

Timing assumptions are crucial for a balance sheet optimization model, as it all ultimately comes down to liquidity issues. The modeler should not overlook the potential problems that could arise from additional assumptions regarding the timing of cash flows from programmed investments and disinvestments, as well as from non-financial contracts such as fees, commissions, and taxes.

In summary, when building a balance sheet optimization model, there are many business assumptions to consider and many departments responsible for defining them, leaving ample opportunity for errors, particularly related to incorrect interpretation of information such as value units and rate conventions.

It's important to carefully and comprehensively catalog the assumptions and desired level of detail for the model, map out responsibilities, and outline a clear strategy for obtaining, processing, and adapting each assumption, as well as a plan for obtaining missing assumptions that are necessary for the model.

# 6 Building the Model: Foundations

Model formulation is by far the most central phase of solving a real problem, since there is no point in solving an optimization model that does not accurately represent reality or does not provide solutions that are implementable in the real world. In any case, however accurate the model, it will remain just a model, and will always be subject to criticism. On the other hand, skepticism tends to decrease as the model is equipped with more decision variables and constraints, allowing users to recognize the real problem when analyzing the mathematical specification. Given the importance of this mission, we dedicate the following chapters entirely to it. We will dive into the identification and implementation of each of the building blocks of a bank ALM model, with special emphasis on the preparation of the model coefficients, on the definition of decision and state variables, and on the elaboration of a large inventory of constraints that appear recurrently in the formulation of balance sheet optimization models.

## 6.1 Initial Considerations

In the following sections, we will present a handful of code snippets in order to illustrate how a balance sheet mathematical model is built using `Julia` language along with `JuMP` and `SDDP` packages. If you are not familiar with them, please refer to the introduction to those tools available in Appendix A.

The main goal of this chapter is to show how we usually organize and represent the different concepts related to balance sheet simulation and optimization. As we have seen in Chapter 5, the amount and variety of data required to build such a model is often substantial. Recalling this, we will need data on runoff positions, new potencial future positions, historical market data, future scenarios, and a large array of institution-dependent assumptions.

As to make that data available during the build process, which is the task we will look into during this chapter, we should have executed our data pipeline as described in Chapter 5.

The output of such a pipeline should be a collection of data that is stored in data structures that correspond to each of the various types we have mentioned. These structures will be referred to along most of the model's equations, therefore we need an organized way to access them from inside our model builder functions.

So, we will use *getter functions* to symbolize a function that returns specific subsets of such data along the code. The concrete implementation of those getter functions is solution-dependent and it is up to the modeler to design the best way to acquire, transform, store, and retrieve all pieces of data the model will need.

For example, one getter function could be `get_positions(balance_sheet_path::String)`, which should receive a balance sheet path string (like `"Assets/Loans"`) and return all positions associated with that balance sheet account. Notice that in practice

https://doi.org/10.1515/9783110664669-006

there will be more parameters required by this getter function. For example, we could need one parameter that holds or points to the place where all positions are stored. Because these parameters are also implentation-dependent, we will omit them in our examples.

In the code snippets that will be presented in the following chapters, we will assume that those getter functions exist and are correctly implemented, and focus on the usage of the information provided by them. Some of those functions will be explained during our flight but, before taking off, it is important to highlight the ones that will recurrently appear in the model specification, like positions getters and scenarios getters, among others.

## 6.2 Key Data Structures

A *contract* is a data structure that embodies the specific details of financial instruments. In a fixed income contract, for instance, the contract instance would hold at least: the maturity as a date; notional and coupon rate as floating point numbers; and an amortization scheme that could have a vector-like structure of principal repayments. Of course, each type of financial contract requires a unique structure to accommodate its unique characteristics.

A *position* always comprises of a contract and its corresponding financial statement information. This information may include a balance sheet reference (such as a string “ASSETS/LOANS”), accounting classifications, pricing methodologies, and the relationship to a particular strategy or portfolio, among other details.

To assist in building a mathematical model, the following set of minimum position-related functions should be implemented:

- `ids(v::Vector{Position})::Vector{String}`: receives a vector of positions and returns the correspondent vector of position identifiers as strings.
- `get_all_positions()::Vector{Position}`: returns all positions that are registered in a model.
- `get_positions_by_balance_sheet_path(path::String)::Vector{Position}`: returns the subset of positions that are associated to a balance sheet item `path`.
- `get_position_by_id(a::String)::Position`: returns a specific position by its identifier.
- `is_new(p::Position)::Bool`: checks if a position is part of the current portfolios or if it is a new position that can be acquired by the model in future dates.
- `get_accounting_method(p::Position)::String`: returns the accounting method associated to a position.
- `model_sign(p::Position)::Int64`: returns +1 for asset and asset-like positions, and –1 otherwise. This is used to sign model constraints later in the building of the model.

A *scenario* is a potential future state of reality, represented as a collection of economic and financial data. These variables may include GDP, inflation, interest rates, yield curves, stock prices, exchange rates, credit demand, prepayment and withdrawal levels, and more. They can be represented as decimal values or more complex structures such as yield or forward curves.

When constructing the model, it's necessary to access various scenarios. A basic interface would include:

- `get_scenario_at_open(t::Int64)::Scenario`: get the deterministic scenario on the opening date of a model step.
- `get_scenario_at_close(t::Int64)::Scenario`: get the deterministic scenario on the closing date of a model step.

Other data and their unique data structures are required when implementing a balance sheet model. Some of these will be covered with code examples throughout the book. It's worth noting that the more organized your data structures are, through the use of Julia's object definitions and multi-dispatch capabilities, the easier it will be to manage the large volume of data necessary to model a financial institution altogether.

## 6.3 Contract Sets

A set can be defined informally as a selection of elements that share common attributes. For example, we can think of Arsenal's fans, Asian countries, French-speaking population, etc. In our context, we use the notion of sets to group contracts around one or more characteristics that are required to specify the mathematical model. It is the sets of contracts that will delimit the scope of the summation that form the model equations. In other words, if we need to compute the total asset balance, we need to group assets into one set. If we need to write a constraint to limit the bank's exposure in foreign currencies, we need a new set, and so on. Of course, the universe of sets we will need is model dependent, especially the constraints that need to be represented, but typically we will need to separate sets around attributes such as currency, indexer, rating, portfolio, rating, etc.

Sets related to the contract currency may be useful in constraints to limit risk exposures. Portfolio-related sets may be useful in constraints related to strategic planning, while accounting-related sets are critical for correctly calculating profit by the prevailing accounting standard. The greater the number and granularity of constraints, the greater the number of sets required to represent them. Although the idea of organizing contracts into sets may sounds trivial, this part of the modeling process can become a real nightmare if a particular contract is mistakenly included in two sets that are supposed to be mutually exclusive, leading to duplication of its contribution to the total balance, triggering a series of potentially difficult to track errors. On the other hand, if a contract is not mapped in a particular portfolio, its risk can be evaded, which consequently will affect the regulatory and managerial restrictions of risk and capital adequacy.

To avoid this kind of problem, we should pay particular attention to the coverage and coherence of sets, and whenever possible create new sets by joining, intersecting, and differing existing ones. By following this rule, we establish a kind of set hierarchy, in which we have primary sets and derived sets. For example, we may have two primary sets to separate assets and liabilities, and two sets to separate fixed rate and floating rate contracts. We can then use intersection operations to create, for example, the set of floating rate active contracts. Although it is not possible in advance to identify all types of sets that will be required for modeling, especially because constraints evolve with bank policy and regulation changes, it is valuable to invest a lot of time in the sets architecture and, as far as possible, try to anticipate needs. Among all the mathematical model layers, the contract sets is perhaps the part where implementing automated test routines is most cost effective, and is a highly recommended practice.

Ultimately, we emphasize that we should not underestimate this part of the modeling process. Poorly specified sets can cause the model solution process to be unfeasible, creating false clues that can lead you to spend a lot of time actually analyzing constraints that may be correct but underfed. As a consolation, when we fall into such a trap, we often end up with interesting insights by looking at the "point of view" of the mathematical solver, who will always do their best to solve the model, even if it means solutions that are meaningless or even illegal from the accounting perspective. If you come across this, I strongly recommend that you do not use the model solution.

## 6.4 Model Initialization

After we have prepared our programming environment with all the packages of interest, in particular the packages `JuMP.jl` and `SDDP.jl`, the first step to start building our balance optimization model using the Julia language is to instantiate an empty model, which will be filled throughout the chapter with the definitions of decision variables, constraints, etc.

The code snippets below show how this can be done. As we are going to express the model as an SDDP problem, the first step is to create a policy graph. Furthermore, our first formulation will be a deterministic balance optimization model, but with multiple stages. So, in terms of the SDDP package, we can use a linear policy graph. This can be done using the code snippet in Code Snippet 6.1, which we will analyze in detail in this section.

**Code Snippet 6.1:** Creating a Linear Policy Graph.

```
model = SDDP.LinearPolicyGraph(
    subproblem_builder;
    stages = 12,
```

```
        sense = :Min,
        upper_bound = 0.0,
        optimizer = Clp.Optimizer
    )
```

The first parameter of the function we are using is, in itself, the name of the function responsible for building the JuMP subproblems that make up the balance sheet optimization model. So far, this function does not yet exist. It is just a placeholder for the functions that will actually build the model by creating decision and state variables, constraints, and objective functions for each of the subproblems.

The stages parameter is the number of stages the model will have. For example, if the model horizon is one year and we want to represent decisions in monthly steps, then the number of stages should be 12. The sense parameter, in turn, indicates that the subproblems will be minimization or maximization problems, while the upper_bound parameter (or lower_bound) indicates maximum or minimum values for the objective function of the subproblems.

Finally, we have the optimizer parameter, which is used to define the solver that will be used in the process of building and solving the model. It is worth noting that there are different signatures[1] for the functions of building the SDDP model, but we believe that this is the most compact for the version that we will build at first.

## 6.5 Core Decision Variables

Decision variables are the cornerstone of mathematical programming models, as all model equations are expressed as a function of them. In the model we are building, the key variables are those that express optimal decisions at the most granular level possible, indicating what should be done with each contract, at each time point, in each scenario. They can be of four distinct types: Buy, Sell, Prepayment, and WriteOff. Although their own names already give us hint of their functions in the model, we will detail below how are they used for different types of contracts and balance sheet accounts.

### 6.5.1 Buy Variables

Buy variables represent the addition of any quantity of a position in a portfolio, both in Assets and Liabilities. On the Assets side, buy transactions represent purchases, while on the Liabilities side, they represent fund-raising.

1 Signatures are a combination of parameter types. For instance, the two versions `sqrt(x::Int64)` and `sqrt(x::Float64)` are two different signatures of the same square root function `sqrt`.

Throughout the construction of the model, we will use buy variables not just to represent financial contract transactions, but also accounting operations, like profits and provisions calculations, tax payments etc. When we have a profit of 1,000, for example, we can buy from a pseudo-contract called Profit to represent such a result. This abstraction will become clearer when preparing the coefficients of the mathematical model.

Buy variables are defined for each particular position of the model. In Code Snippet 6.2, we can see the definition of all buy variables in a sub-problem `sp` (lines 1–4). The `a` dimension of this variable receives each element of a vector of strings returned by the function `ids(v::Vector{Position})::Vector{String}`. The input for that function is a vector of positions, returned by `get_all_positions()::Vector{Position}`, that contains all positions registered in the model.

The second dimension is `h`, which stands for the stage in which the position was bought. It is important to keep track of this dimension because the book value of a contract will typically depend on the rates prevailing at the time in which the position was acquired, especially for positions that are valued in an accrual basis. The getter function `get_all_stages()` returns identifiers for all stages of the problem. If we are modeling a three-step model, this could return a vector with the integers 1, 2, and 3.

But now, we need to set that whenever there is a decision to buy from a position, the proper value for the `h` dimension is set. In lines 6–11, the group of constraints defined states that when we are in time `stage`, positive values for buy can only happen when dimension `h` equals to `stage`. All buy variables with different `h`s are set to zero. Imagine there is a position with ID “L1” in a three-stage problem. If the model decide to buy 10 units of this position in stage 2, the only possible combination of variables would be:

$$\begin{aligned} \text{Buy}[L1,1] &= 0 \\ \text{Buy}[L1,2] &= 10 \\ \text{Buy}[L1,3] &= 0 \end{aligned} \tag{6.1}$$

And that is the mechanism our model would use to track that 10 units of position “L1” were acquired at time 2.

Notice that buy variables are not state variables, because they are decisions that take place only inside a decision node. Nonetheless, the result of buy operations will accumulate from node to node through quantity state variables, as we will see in more details in Section 6.6. With that said, it is important to emphasize that buys are dimensionless and related to quantity rather than to dollar value. This means that when a buy variable assumes the number 3.0, we are buying three units of a contract, rather than 3.0 dollars worth of it.

**Code Snippet 6.2:** Buy Variable Declaration.

```
1 @variable(
2     sp,
```

```
    Buy[a in ids(get_all_positions()), h in get_all_stages()] >= 0.0
)

# only populate indexes associated with current stage
for a in ids(get_all_positions()), h in get_all_stages()
    if stage != h
        @constraint(sp, Buy[a,h] == 0)
    end
end
```

Buying a liability causes new cash flow to enter into the institution and therefore imply a positive buy cash flow. On the other hand, in order to buy an asset the institution must invest existing cash flow, so it is a convention to represent an asset buy cash flow with a non-positive number.

Some derivative contracts, like swaps and futures, which can be bought with no upfront costs, will be represented with a zero buy cash flow, meaning that the model can buy those contracts without needing to use cash.

Other types of contract that have no cash flow expenditure/generation during a buy event are, as discussed in Section 3.8, positions associated with some non-contract accounting records like provision for credit losses and retained earnings.

### 6.5.2 Sell Variables

Variables of type *sell* are used to represent positions fully or partially exiting from a portfolio. For example, if you need to sell five units of a bonds to pay taxes, we will use the Sell variable to represent such an operation.

In terms of cash flow sign, selling an asset implies inflow of cash to the model and therefore this operation is represented with a positive sell cash flow. The amount of cash generated in a sell operation is usually determined by its unit price (fair value), because we are assuming that we are handling the contract to a counterpart in a secondary market. This agent would in exchange pay us back the fair market price for that position.

Selling a liability would, on the other hand, imply outflow of cash and a negative sell cash flow. But, for a number of reasons, the use of sell variables is more restricted than the use of buy variables. This restriction is usually associated with the accounting classification of the position, the institution's allocation policies, or the absence of market liquidity. The most usual setup is that the sell variables are defined only for asset positions and some special pseudo-contracts in "shareholder's equity".

In Code Snippet 6.3 we can see the definition of sell variables. As buy variables, they are also defined for all positions and all hs. The difference is that we can only sell positions that were bought in a previous stage. This consistency rule is implemented through the constraints defined in lines 3–7. Additionally, the equality part in the comparison established in line 5 assures that the model cannot simultaneously buy and sell from the same position within a node.

In our example model, although we define sell variable for all contracts, we use the constraints specified in lines 4–6 to disallow the model from selling liabilities.

**Code Snippet 6.3:** Sell Variable Declaration.

```
1   @variable(
2       sp,
3       Sell[a in ids(get_all_positions()), h in get_all_stages()] >= 0.0
4   )
5
6   # only sell what was previously bought
7   for a in ids(get_all_positions()), h in get_all_stages()
8       if h >= stage
9           @constraint(sp, Sell[a,h] == 0)
10      end
11  end
12
13  # disable selling of liabilities
14  for a in ids(get_positions_by_balance_sheet_path("LIABILITIES"))
15      for h in get_all_stages()
16          @constraint(sp, Sell[a,h] == 0.0)
17      end
18  end
```

In fact, one way to see the selling of a borrowings position, for example, is as a prepayment of that debt. Nevertheless, it is common to separate those operations in a dedicated prepayment variable in order to facilitate the reporting of debt re-structuring decisions. These dedicated variables will be the subject of the next section.

### 6.5.3 Prepayment Variables

Like sell variables, prepayment variables represent the departure of positions from portfolios. But, in particular, these variables are used to track settlements of debts that occur before their official due dates.

Differently from selling, the amount of cash involved in such operations are usually written in a contract and are a function of its accrual value (for example, it could include prepayment penalties).

One interesting aspect of prepayments is that the logic the model will use to determine its values while solving the problem will be different for assets and liabilities.

On the liability side, the institution often has the option to prepay some or all of its debts. This may be the optimal decision in a wide variety of cases, such as when the contractual rate has become too expensive in the face of current funding possibilities, or simply because the maturity structure of assets has changed substantially, justifying partial replacement debt for another with a new term. That is, on the liability side, prepayment variables are in fact decision variables, and can be used wherever possible so that their values are actually optimized.

However, in the particular case of non-maturity deposits, the decision to prepay is not in the hands of the bank. In these situations, prepayment values should be fixed and determined by exogenous statistical models rather than being optimized. Even so, the model may protect us in other ways, by offsetting the risks arising from it through other allocation decisions.

On the assets side, the situation is similar to that of deposits, where the decision to prepay is not in the hands of the institution but rather in the hand of its counterpart. Similarly, the value of these variables will be set using appropriate statistical models.

In Code Snippet 6.4, we can see the definition of all prepayment variables. We then create a set of all non-liability positions by using Julia's `setdiff` function, and use it to disallow the prepayment of all positions that are not liabilities. We could even be more specific and only allow prepayment in specific balance sheet accounts, like `"LIABILITIES/BORROWINGS"` or `"LIABILITIES/NON-MATURITY DEPOSITS."`

**Code Snippet 6.4:** Prepayment Variable Declaration.

```
@variable(
    sp,
    Prepayment[a in ids(get_all_positions()), h in get_all_stages()] >= 0.0
)

# disable prepayment of non-liabilities
non_liabilities = setdiff(
    ids(get_all_positions()),
    ids(get_positions_by_balance_sheet_path("LIABILITIES"))
)
for a in non_liabilities, h in get_all_stages()
    @constraint(sp, Prepayment[a,h] == 0.0)
end
```

### 6.5.4 Write-Off Variables

Write-off variables are used to denote the reduction of book value of an asset due to unreceived payments that are assumed to be uncollectable.

A counterpart default and its implications are not a decision that can be taken by the lender institution. These variables are by no means subject to optimization within our model, but rather variables whose values are set with the help of credit risk models.

However, we still treat `WriteOff` as a decision variable for modeling convenience, as the quantities bought, sold, prepaid, and written off will affect balances in a very similar way, although multiplied by different coefficients.

All `WriteOff` variables are defined in Code Snippet 6.5. Because of their definition, these variables are disabled for positions not classified as assets.

**Code Snippet 6.5:** WriteOff Variable Declaration.

```
@variable(
    sp,
    WriteOff[a in ids(get_all_positions()), h in get_all_stages()] >= 0.0
)

# disable write-off of non-asset
non_asset = setdiff(
    ids(get_all_positions()),
    ids(get_positions_by_balance_sheet_path("ASSETS"))
)
for a in non_asset, h in get_all_stages()
    @constraint(sp, WriteOff[a,h] == 0.0)
end
```

## 6.6 Core State Variables

In the SDDP framework, as we have stated in Chapter 4, we have control and state variables. While the former live inside a specific node, state variables are responsible for sharing data between subsequent nodes. They do so by setting the outgoing state of a variable in one node equal to its incoming state in the next node.

The decision variables we saw in Section 6.5 are control variables as those decisions are taken only in the scope of a time step (node). Now we will see some of the state variables that accumulate the output of those decisions throughout the whole projected horizon, connecting all the sub-problems into a large and coherent balance sheet multi-stage model.

### 6.6.1 Quantity Variables

Quantity is the most basic state variable of a balance sheet mathematical model. It accounts, of course, for the quantity held of each financial position at any simulated node. It is the main state variable because almost all other state variables are defined as the quantity state variable multiplied by a constant (coefficient). For example, if someone wants to fair value a position at a node, one should just multiply its unit price coefficient by its quantity state. In Code Snippet 6.6, we can see a definition of the quantity variable implemented.

**Code Snippet 6.6:** Quantity State Variable Declaration.

```
@variable(
    sp,
    Quantity[a in ids(get_all_positions()), h in get_all_stages()],
    SDDP.State,
    initial_value=get_initial_quantity(a,h)
)

```

```
8   # initial value: incoming state of stage 1
9   function get_initial_quantity(a,h)
10      if h > 1
11          return 0.0
12      end
13      pos = get_position_by_id(a)
14      if !is_new(pos)
15          return 1.0
16      else
17          return 0.0
18      end
19  end
```

Quantity will typically be defined for all positions: both runoff and new, but also positions containing financial contracts and pseudo-contracts. That is why, in line 3, we have an a dimension populated with the "all positions" getter. These variables are also indexed by the stage h in which that particular quantity of a was acquired.

In line 5, we have to initialize the quantity of a position, given its identifiers a and h. The auxiliary function `get_initial_quantity`, implemented in lines 8–19, states that at the incoming state of node 1 we have one unit of each runoff contract and no unit of new contracts. That is precisely how the model assembles all runoff positions in their respective portfolios at the beginning of root node. The first stage is assumed to be the node where initial quantities were bought, and that is why we return 0 for all indexes where h is greater than 1.

Re-balancing decisions will take place at node 1 and potentially a new quantity of position a will be allocated to the outgoing state of node 1. This new quantity will, of course, be passed to the next stage as the incoming state for the same variable quantity, and will help assemble a new incoming portfolio at node 2.

The dynamics equations for quantity state variables are implemented in Code Snippet 6.7. They state that for each position a the final quantity will be the initial state plus the units bought in that node, discounting sellings, prepayments, and writeoffs. It is important to remind that all these control variables were defined to all positions, and disabled to a subset of them when applicable. Had we not defined those variables to all contracts in the first place, some of those dynamics constraints would raise errors on their creation in SDDP.

**Code Snippet 6.7:** Quantity State Variable Dynamics.

```
for a in ids(get_all_positions()), h in get_all_stages()
    @constraint(
        sp,
        Quantity[a,h].out =
            Quantity[a,h].in
            + Buy[a,h]
            - Sell[a,h]
            - Prepayment[a,h]
            - WriteOff[a,h]
    )
end
```

### 6.6.2 Valuation Variables

Valuation variables are a collection of state variables that store the value of a position in a node. They come in different flavors depending on characteristics of the position, and ultimately sets the evolution of the balances that appear in financial statements.

`FairValue` is the variable that holds the marked-to-market value of a position in a node. It is, of course, a function of the quantity held of that position at the time and its unit price. This price is usually a function of a scenario of market conditions observed at that node. For example, if a position is related to a liquid stock, usually a scenario would hold the price of one unit of that stock in that particular point of time. If a position holds a bond, its fair value could be a function of risk free yield curves and spread curves as seen from that node.

Either way, we assume that a function `price(p::Position, s::Scenario)::Float64` that receives at least a position and a scenario and returns its fair price as a floating-point number is available and implemented for all positions and underlying contracts.

In Code Snippet 6.8 we define fair value state variables for all positions. In lines 8–12 we implement a function that prices a position at the beginning of the first node, by passing the scenario available at the opening of the first node to the `price` function times the initial quantity held of that position.

We should also implement a `model_sign(p::Position)::Int64` function which returns the sign a position's projected cash flows should have in the model. This function should usually return `1` for asset positions and `-1` for liabilities and shareholder's equity items, for example. In this way, we could model all liabilities' financial contracts without worrying about signs, like they were all assets, because of their cash flow and price signs.

By using the model sign `w` variable in line 10, we assure that liabilities like borrowings always have negative prices, and that positive prices are assigned to assets like loans.

**Code Snippet 6.8:** FairValue State Variable Declaration.

```
1   @variable(
2       sp,
3       FairValue[a in ids(get_all_positions()), h in get_all_stages()],
4       SDDP.State,
5       initial_value=get_initial_price(a, h)
6   )
7
8   function get_initial_price(a, h)
9       pos = get_position_by_id(a)
10      w = model_sign(pos)
11      scenario = get_scenario_at_open(1) # root scenario
12      return w * get_initial_quantity(a) * price(pos, scenario)
13  end
```

The state dynamics associated with this variable is simply the product of the quantity times the unit price calculated by that same price function at the end of each stage, as we can see in Code Snippet 6.9. In this equation, `price(pos, s)` is a constant and so `FairValue` is just a linear function of the state variable `Quantity`. One thing that we should notice is that we need not define the incoming state of the fair value variable. There are two reasons for that: for the first node, we have already defined the incoming state of the variable using `get_initial_price` in Code Snippet 6.8. Also, for the remaining nodes, the incoming state of fair value will be exactly equal to the outcome state of the previous node, so we do not need to define it again.

**Code Snippet 6.9:** FairValue State Variable Dynamics.

```
s = get_scenario_at_close(stage)
for a in ids(get_all_positions()), h in get_all_stages()
    pos = get_position_by_id(a)
    w = model_sign(pos)
    @constraint(
        sp,
        FairValue[a,h].out = w * Quantity[a,h].out * price(pos, s)
    )
end
```

`AccrualValue` is a variable we use to valuate a position using the accrual basis of accounting, like described in Section 3.4. Instead of using current market conditions to find a fair price, we use acquisition prices to account for an amortized cost over the time. In a bond, for example, we could use the premium or discount observed at the time in which the contract was bought and amortize it over time until the contract matures.

The definition of these variables is very similar to the definition of fair value variables, but we must use an `accrual(p::Position, as_of::Date, acquisition::Date)::Float64` function instead of the `price` used in the latter. The assumption is that this new function receives at least a position and a date `as_of` and knows how to calculate the accrual price (as a floating point number) of an underlying contract that was bought at date `acquisiton`.

In Code Snippet 6.10 we can see the implementation of accrual value variables. Notice that the variable `stage` is a parameter of the sub-problem builder function and is an integer (1 for the first node, 2 for the second, and so on). The function `get_open_date(stage::Int64)::Date` returns the open date of a stage.

**Code Snippet 6.10:** AccrualValue State Variable Declaration.

```
@variable(
sp,
    AccrualValue[a in ids(get_all_positions()), h in get_all_stages()],
    SDDP.State,
    initial_value=get_initial_accrual(a,h)
)

function get_initial_accrual(a,h)
    pos = get_position_by_id(a)
```

```
        w = model_sign(pos)
        dt = get_open_date(1) # model root date
        acquisition = get_open_date(h) # decision date at node h
        return w * get_initial_quantity(a) * accrual(pos, dt, acquisition)
    end
```

The dynamics of accrual variables are also very close to their marked-to-market counterparts. In Code Snippet 6.11, we see that the closing accrual value is the quantity times a constant that is given by an accrual function. The date `dt` is the closing date of that stage, which is returned by the `get_close_date(stage::Int64)::Date` function.

**Code Snippet 6.11:** AccrualValue State Variable Dynamics.

```
dt = get_close_date(stage)
for a in ids(get_all_positions()), h in get_all_stages()
    pos = get_position_by_id(a)
    w = model_sign(pos)
    acquisition = get_open_date(h)
    unit_accrual = (pos, dt, acquisition)
    @constraint(
        sp,
        AccrualValue[a,h].out = w * Quantity[a,h].out * unit_accrual
    )
end
```

In financial statements, the accounting method used to valuate a position is usually linked to its accounting classification, as discussed in Section 3.5. For example, trading positions are commonly marked-to-market while held-to-maturity positions are reported using accrual prices. To account for the actual value that should go into financial statements' books, we define a variable called `BookValue` in Code Snippet 6.12.

In lines 8–18 we implement a getter of the initial book value of a position. Function `get_accounting_method(p::Position)::String` returns strings that are either `"FairValue"` or `"AmortizedCost."` We use this information to dispatch the execution to the appropriate initialization function, and throw errors whenever invalid accounting methods are retrieved (just to be sure).

**Code Snippet 6.12:** BookValue State Variable Declaration.

```
1   @variable(
2       sp,
3       AccrualValue[a in ids(get_all_positions()), h in get_all_stages()],
4       SDDP.State,
5       initial_value=get_initial_book_value(a,h)
6   )
7
8   function get_initial_book_value(a)
9       pos = get_position_by_id(a)
10      am = get_accounting_method(pos)
11      if am == "FairValue"
12          return get_initial_price(a,h)
13      elseif am == "AmortizedCost"
14          return get_initial_accrual(a,h)
15      else
```

```
            error("invalid accounting method: $am")
        end
    end
```

In Code Snippet 6.13, the dynamics of the book value variable implements conditional constraints in the model. These constraints populate the variable with either fair value or accrual value depending on the accounting method. We should also notice that we do not need to use model signs to define book values because fair values and accrual values are already signed amounts.

**Code Snippet 6.13:** BookValue State Variable Dynamics.

```
    for a in ids(get_all_positions()), h in get_all_stages()
        pos = get_position_by_id(a)
        am = get_accounting_method(pos)
        if am == "FairValue"
            @constraint(sp, BookValue[a,h].out = FairValue[a,h].out)
        elseif am == "AmortizedCost"
            @constraint(sp, BookValue[a,h].out = AccrualValue[a,h].out)
        else
            error("invalid accounting method: $am")
        end
    end
```

One could argue that book value variables are unnecessary, because they just conditionally store information that is already written in other variables of the model. It is a fair concern, but we think that such variables help us be more clear in the formulation of the model and more precise in assessing its results and producing reports from them. For example, to produce the book value of all loans and populate a projection of a balance sheet record called "Loans" throughout time, we would just need to sum all book value variables of all loans positions for each model projected date.

## 6.7 Cash Flow Variables

Cash flow variables are another very important group of model variables that record the amount of cash generated or required by a position at a given node. They are usually a function of the quantity state variable, multiplied by special cash flow constants.

### 6.7.1 Decision Cash Flows Variables

This type of variables is created to hold the amount of cash flow involved in decisions taken by the model, such as buy, sell, and prepay.

We call `CashFlowsBuy` the amount of cash required (or generated) in the decision for increasing the quantity of a position in a given node. It is of course very related to `Buy` variables discussed in Section 6.5. Whenever we buy a new bond, we have to invest an amount of cash in that buy operation. If we issue new debt, the increase in the quantity of the borrowing's positions will generate cash that will be allocated by the model to other portfolios or used to pay expenses.

In Code Snippet 6.14 we define and populate all buy cash flow variables.

It is assumed that we have implemented a function called `get_unit_buy_cashflow (p::Position, stage::Int64)::Float64` that returns the amount of cash involved in the buying of one unit of a position. Here we assume that all decisions are taken at the beginning of the node by observing the impact of such decisions at the end of the node. With such an assumption, we could define one implementation of this function as the price of that position in the beginning of the node.

Notice that the `w` variable is responsible for givings signs to cash flows. Because buying assets involves expenditure of cash, it is a convention to represent the buy cash flow of an asset position as a negative quantity. That is why we have to use `-w` as a multiplier of the unit buy cash flow. A liability would have a `-1` model sign and thus a positive buy cash flow, meaning that the increase in liabilities adds cash to the system.

**Code Snippet 6.14:** CashFlowsBuy Variable Declaration.

```
@variable(
    sp,
    CashFlowsBuy[a in ids(get_all_positions()), h in get_all_stages()]
)

for a in ids(get_all_positions()), h in get_all_stages()
    # grab position
    pos = get_position_by_id(a)
    # cash flow sign
    w = model_sign(pos)
    # amount of money required to buy one unit
    unit_buy_cf = get_unit_buy_cashflow(pos, stage)

    @constraint(sp, CashFlowsBuy[a,h] == (-w) * unit_buy_cf * Buy[a,h])
end
```

In Section 6.5, beside buy decisions, we also have sell, prepayment, and write-off choices to be taken. The latter is an accounting event that does not imply any cash flow. Sell and prepayment, on the other hand, have to have their respective cash flows mapped in the model. We do so by resorting to, respectively, `CashFlowsSell` and `CashFlowsPrepayment` variables.

The definitions are very analogous to that of buy cash flows variables, and can be seen on Code Snippets 6.15 and 6.16. Notice that the model sign variable, differently from buy cash flow dynamics, is not multiplied by `-1` in sell or prepayment. That is because if we sell an asset we expect inflow of cash, and if we prepay a debt we expend money to anticipate the end of the deal.

**Code Snippet 6.15:** CashFlowsSell Variable Declaration.

```
@variable(
    sp,
    CashFlowsSell[a in ids(get_all_positions()), h in get_all_stages()]
```

```
)

for a in ids(get_all_positions()), h in get_all_stages()
    # grab position
    pos = get_position_by_id(a)
    # cash flow sign
    w = model_sign(pos)
    # amount of money required to sell one unit
    unit_sell_cf = get_unit_sell_cashflow(pos, stage)

    @constraint(sp, CashFlowsSell[a,h] == w * unit_sell_cf * Sell[a,h])
end
```

One should also think that the unit cash flows to buy, sell, and prepay a position could be the same and equal to its fair value price. That is not always the case. Buying and selling a same financial contract could have different deal prices because of bid-ask spreads and other execution costs like brokerage fees. Also, prepayment costs are usually a function of the amortized cost of a financial contract and could also include fines and penalties for ending a deal prematurely. It is up to the modeler to identify and account for those particularities for each type of event.

**Code Snippet 6.16:** CashFlowsPrepayment Variable Declaration.

```
@variable(
    sp,
    CashFlowsPrepayment[a in ids(get_all_positions()), h in get_all_stages()]
)

for a in ids(get_all_positions()), h in get_all_stages()
    # grab position
    pos = get_position_by_id(a)
    # cash flow sign
    w = model_sign(pos)
    # amount of money required to prepay one unit
    unit_prepayment_cf = get_unit_prepayment_cashflow(pos, stage, h)

    @constraint(
        sp,
        CashFlowsPrepayment[a,h] == w * unit_prepayment_cf * Prepayment[a,h]
    )
end
```

### 6.7.2 Contractual Cash Flows Variables

Even when we are not trading a position in a given node, we can incur in contractual cash flows due to the fact that we hold a quantity of that contract in our portfolios. These cash flows could be certain like interest and amortization payments, uncertain like cash dividends or contingent like options' payoffs.

We will focus on the two certain cash flows that come from fixed income contracts, but the approach should be analogous for other types of contractual cash flows. To account for amortization and interest payments, we will define respectively two variables: `CashFlowsAmortization` and `CashFlowsInterest`. The definitions can be seen on Code Snippets 6.17 and 6.18. We should notice that assets usually yield positive cash flows because we are receiving the contractual payments we are entitled for. Conversely, borrowings should have negative cash flows as we are fulfilling contractual obligations with our lenders.

**Code Snippet 6.17:** CashFlowsAmortization Variable Declaration.

```
@variable(
    sp,
    CashFlowsAmortization[a in ids(get_all_positions()), h in get_all_stages()]
)

for a in ids(get_all_positions()), h in get_all_stages()
    # grab position
    pos = get_position_by_id(a)
    # cash flow sign
    w = model_sign(pos)
    # amount of amortization during this stage
    unit_amort_cf = get_unit_amortization_cashflow(pos, stage)

    @constraint(
        sp,
        CashFlowsAmortization[a,h] == w * unit_amort_cf * Quantity[a,h].out
    )
end
```

There are also a few details one should be careful about while implementing the helper functions `get_unit_amortization_cashflow` and `get_unit_interest_cashflow`.

These quantities are always the sum of a subset of the projected cash flow payments of a contract. These payments, although they may happen in foreign currencies, should be converted to the balance sheet model's base currency and unit (for example, thousands of US dollars) using FX rates available in a node's scenario. Even for cash flows denominated in model's base currency, some cash flow projection may also depend on scenario data, like the ones coming from floating-rate bonds. Fixed-rate bonds are, on the other hand, scenario-independent. That said, you have to make sure that these helper functions have access to the market data scenario that is being considered in that node.

Suppose now that the model decides to buy a quantity of a position in a node `t`, and the underlying contract pays interest during the time span of the very node `t`. Should we consider this interest cash flow in the calculation of `CashFlowsInterest`? Because we assume that all decisions are being taken at the beginning of model nodes, the answer is yes. That is why in line 16 of Code Snippet 6.18 we write this variable as a function of `Quantity[a].out`, which has already incorporated the decisions taken at node `t`. If we chose an assumption of end-of-node decisions, we had to write it as a function of `Quantity[a].in`. Assumptions of decisions being taken in the middle of a node would be more tricky, as we should consider the actual dates of the cash flows and compare them to the date of acquisition.

Suppose now that we have a model with monthly steps. The first node starts on June 30 and the second node on July 31. Suppose that we have a position that pays interest in the very edge between those two nodes, July 31. Should we assign this amount of interest to stage one or to stage two? This is a more tricky modeling choice but the important thing is that you decide and be consistent with that decision in all parts of the model. For example, if we decide that this interest payment belongs to stage one, we should not include it in marked-to-market and accrual valuations in the beginning of stage two. If the model decides to buy more of that position in stage two, the buy cash flow involved should discard the interest payment that was already received. To sum it up, one should be careful of what happens on the edge of nodes, to avoid double-counting or excluding relevant cash flows that could affect the model's solution.

Finally, we should always have in mind that contractual cash flows can happen on dates that are different from the decision date you specified for a node, and this can introduce distortions in your model. Let's suppose we are assuming that buys and sells happen at the beginning of the node, but a contractual cash flow happens at the end of it. If we assume that we have available to buy new assets, the full amount of cash that will be received later, we can eventually end up double counting the interest earned in that period. Let's say we receive an interest payment of 100 dollars at the end of the node. This payment of 100 dollars already includes the interest earned during that whole node along with (possibly) the amount earned and accrued in prior nodes. If we assume that we have the full 100 dollars available at the beginning of the node and use it to buy a new contract, we would additionally earn the interest due to that new contract during the time span of the current node, thus incorrectly amplifying our income results.

One possible solution to that would be to discount that cash flow to the decision date using risk free forward rates. Instead of receiving 100 at the end of the node, it would be as if the institution borrowed, let's say, 98 dollars on the decision date and bought that amount worth of other contracts, and then payed 100 dollars for that short-term borrowing at the cash flow date. That of course would imply an additional assumption that the institution can borrow in the short term at risk free rates.[2]

On the other hand, discounting contractual cash flows to decision dates could lead to discrepancies between model cash flow projections and projected cash flows calculated outside the model. In our example, the exogenous calculations would yield 10 dollars while the model would give us 98 dollars. If we need to reduce the impact of such an assumption we could change our decision date to the middle of node, or even reduce the size of the time step considered in a node.

2 The same argument would apply for a cash flow that is received before decision date. In this case, we would invest the cash flow received at risk free rates and use the proceedings to buy new contracts later on decision date.

**Code Snippet 6.18:** CashFlowsInterest Variable Declaration.

```
@variable(
    sp,
    CashFlowsInterest[a in ids(get_all_positions()), h in get_all_stages()]
)

for a in ids(get_all_positions()), h in get_all_stages()
    # grab position
    pos = get_position_by_id(a)
    # cash flow sign
    w = model_sign(pos)
    # amount of interest during this stage
    unit_interest_cf = get_unit_interest_cashflow(pos, stage)

    @constraint(
        sp,
        CashFlowsInterest[a,h] == w * unit_interest_cf * Quantity[a,h].out
    )
end
```

## 6.8 Income Variables

### 6.8.1 Income Auxiliary Variables

One of the most important variables we use in order to project income statements is the one that holds the income or loss earned due to a position held in a portfolio. The model variables we define to store that information are called `Income` variables.

Suppose we have a debt securities portfolio with a single position. We are in a node $t$ that starts in $t_1$, when the position has a book value of 1,000 dollars and ends at $t_2$ with a book value of 1,050 dollars. No contractual payments are done in node $t$. The income earned in node $t$ would be then 50 dollars, the difference between book value at $t_1$ and at $t_2$. That amount would be exactly the interest earned that was accrued and incorporated into the book value during that period.

$$\text{Income}(t) = \text{BookValue}(t_2) - \text{BookValue}(t_1) \tag{6.2}$$

Suppose now that an interest payment of 20 dollars was made during node $t$. When received, this interest is deducted from the accrued interest account. Nonetheless, it is earned interest so it should be accounted for in our income calculation. Instead of earning only 50 dollars, now we have earned $50 + 20 = 70$ dollars.

$$\begin{aligned}\text{Income}(t) = {} & (\text{BookValue}(t_2) - \text{BookValue}(t_1)) \\ & + \text{InterestReceived}(t)\end{aligned} \tag{6.3}$$

If a partial amortization of 100 dollars was also done, this payment reduces the principal amount calculated in $t_1$. Suppose that because of this amortization we have recalculated the book value in $t_2$ as 950 dollars. If we use Equation 6.3, we would end up with a loss instead of a gain: (950 – 1000 + 20) = –30 dollars. That is why we have to add amortization payments to restore the book value of $t_2$ to its initial notional and get an income of –30 + 100 = 70 dollars:

$$\begin{aligned}\text{Income}(t) = {} & (\text{BookValue}(t_2) - \text{BookValue}(t_1)) \\ & + \text{InterestReceived}(t) \\ & + \text{AmortizationReceived}(t)\end{aligned} \tag{6.4}$$

Imagine now that we have bought, at $t$, 500 dollars more worth of that debt security. Its book value in $t_2$ would then raise to 1,450 dollars and, using Equation 6.4, income would rise artificially to 1450 – 1000 + 20 + 100 = 570 dollars. So we have to deduct buy cash flows in order to accurately calculate an income of 570 – 500 = 70 dollars:

$$\begin{aligned}\text{Income}(t) = {} & (\text{BookValue}(t_2) - \text{BookValue}(t_1)) \\ & + \text{InterestReceived}(t) \\ & + \text{AmortizationReceived}(t) \\ & - \text{CashFlowsBuy}(t)\end{aligned} \tag{6.5}$$

The same argument would apply if selling (or in the special case of borrowings, prepaying) operations end up reducing our book value in $t_2$. To restore the income earned, we would need to sum them in our final income equation:

$$\begin{aligned}\text{Income}(t) = {} & (\text{BookValue}(t_2) - \text{BookValue}(t_1)) \\ & + \text{InterestReceived}(t) \\ & + \text{AmortizationReceived}(t) \\ & - \text{CashFlowsBuy}(t) \\ & + \text{CashFlowsSell}(t) \\ & + \text{CashFlowsPrepayment}(t)\end{aligned} \tag{6.6}$$

With the help of Equation 6.6, it is easy to understand the implementation of the dynamics of `Income` variables defined in Code Snippet 6.19. Because a typical asset has a negative buy cash flow, as discussed in Section 6.6, we must sum it to, instead of subtract it from, the variation of book values, as shown in line 13.

**Code Snippet 6.19:** Income Variable Declaration.

```
1  @variable(
2      sp,
3      Income[a in ids(get_all_positions()), h in get_all_stages()]
4  )
5
6  for a in ids(get_all_positions()), h in get_all_stages()
```

```
        @constraint(
            sp,
            Income[a,h] ==
                (BookValue[a,h].out - BookValue[a,h].in)
                + CashFlowsInterest[a,h]
                + CashFlowsAmortization[a,h]
                + CashFlowsBuy[a,h]
                + CashFlowsSell[a,h]
                + CashFlowsPrepayment[a,h]
        )
    end
```

These income variables are a per-position opening of the financial statements' income records shown in Table 3.2. We believe that this breakdown by position is very helpful for two reasons, the first being for debugging purposes. For example, if you have data issues in loading your financial contracts, it is likely that those issues would affect income statements' projections. So, it is useful resorting to income variables to spot the contract or group of contracts that are producing odd income numbers.

Secondly, different groups of contracts may have distinct income tax schemes and rates. For example, governments sometimes create tax-incentives to promote liquidity in a particular market or type of asset. By accounting for income separately, you can apply different taxing rules and have a more granular approach to income taxes in your model.

### 6.8.2 Unrealized Gains or Losses Variables

As covered in Section 3.5, available for sale is an intermediate classification between trading and held-to-maturity. Even though available for sale positions are fair valued in the balance sheet, their gains or losses are not directly recognized as income in financial statements. Instead, they are declared as unrealized gain or losses (UGL) and accumulated in a special shareholder's equity account. Once traded, these unrealized profits or losses are realized and thus recognized in income statements. At any moment $t$, the unrealized gain or loss of a marked-to-market contract will be:

$$\text{UGL}(t) = \text{FairValue}(t) - \text{AccrualValue}(t) \tag{6.7}$$

If fair value exceeds the amortized cost of that position, we say there is an unrealized profit to be realized whenever we trade that position. If market value is below the amortized cost, we have a negative UGL and thus an unrealized loss.

In our model we will have a variable called `UGL` to account for the unrealized profits or losses of positions as defined in Code Snippet 6.20. Although declared for all positions, we only need to account UGL variation for available-for-sale positions. In lines 11–16 we define this quantity as the evaluation of Equation 6.7 at the end of a node. All others positions can have zero UGL variations, as these numbers will not be needed anywhere.

**Code Snippet 6.20:** UGL Variable Declaration.

```
@variable(
    sp,
    UGL[a in ids(get_all_positions()), h in get_all_stages()],
    SDDP.State,
    initial_value = get_initial_ugl(a,h)
)

for a in ids(get_all_positions()), h in get_all_stages()
    pos = get_position_by_id(a)
    ac = get_accounting_classification(pos)
    if ac == "AFS"
        # UGL = FairValue - AccrualValue
        @constraint(
            sp,
            UGL[a].out == FairValue[a].out - AccrualValue[a].out
        )
    else
        @constraint(sp, UGL[a].out == 0.0)
    end
end
```

Available-for-sale contracts will have their fair value changes accumulated in an unrealized gains or losses special account in shareholder's equity. Simultaneously, the change in amortized cost will be declared as income and will also be incorporated to equity as retained earnings. To implement this special behavior, we need to fix the general implementation of income variables shown in Code Snippet 6.19. In the case of available-for-sale positions, income will not be based on the variation of book value, which is equal to fair value to those positions. It will be rather based on the variation of accrual value. In Code Snippet 6.21, we implement a new version of income definition which accounts for available-for-sale positions.

**Code Snippet 6.21:** Income Variable Declaration with Available For Sale Positions.

```
@variable(
    sp,
    Income[a in ids(get_all_positions()), h in get_all_stages()]
)

for a in ids(get_all_positions()), h in get_all_stages()
    pos = get_position_by_id(a)
    ac = get_accounting_classification(pos)
    if ac == "AFS"
        @constraint(
            sp,
            Income[a,h] ==
                (AccrualValue[a,h].out - AccrualValue[a,h].in)
                + CashFlowsInterest[a,h]
                + CashFlowsAmortization[a,h]
                + CashFlowsBuy[a,h]
                + CashFlowsSell[a,h]
                + CashFlowsPrepayment[a,h]
        )
    else
```

```
            @constraint(
                sp,
                Income[a,h] ==
                    (BookValue[a,h].out - BookValue[a,h].in)
                    + CashFlowsInterest[a,h]
                    + CashFlowsAmortization[a,h]
                    + CashFlowsBuy[a,h]
                    + CashFlowsSell[a,h]
                    + CashFlowsPrepayment[a,h]
            )
        end
    end
```

In the later Section 6.9.3 we will discuss in more details the additional constraints we need in order to make realized and unrealized incomes a part of the equity at the end of each period. That said, by equipping the model with the ability to differentiate and more realistically calculate the book value and income of positions considering their accounting criteria, we give the model the ability to optimize not only purchase decisions, but also the accounting assignment of new financial positions.

### 6.8.3 Income Statement Variables

This group of auxiliary variables is intended to help the representation of income statements. These variables do not concern specific contracts, and therefore do not have this dimension. A second aspect that deserves attention in the design of the auxiliary income statement variables relates to the hierarchical nature of this financial report, like we can see in the example presented in Section 3.2. To reach the final numbers, we must follow a bottom-up approach. That is, first we need to calculate the most granular items in the hierarchy, then go up by calculating the aggregations.

Obviously, there is an overhead in creating decision variables for aggregation lines, but for a number of reasons, we recommend creating decision variables for them as well. The first reason is to make sure that this part of the model is very similar to the official income statement that people are already used to. Secondly, it facilitates the design of constraints based on aggregate results, which is a relatively common thing. An example would be the case where a bank wants to ensure minimum net interest income on its asset. In this situation, it would be really desirable to have a variable that stores the amount of net interest income, since it would greatly simplify the mathematical equation corresponding to this constraint.

In Code Snippet 6.22, we illustrate the creation of income statement decision variables using as a template a subset of the rows of the income statement presented in Table 3.2.[3] In most cases, these variables are created free, meaning that they can assume

3 Although it is not usual in financial statements, we chose to include dividends as part of the income statement, because we will need to store dividend payments to be used later in some model constraints.

positive or negative values. In cases where we are sure of the sign of the variable, we recommend imposing this limit after the creation of the variable.

The indentation shown in lines 1–19 is not required and is only a visual helper to understand the structure of an income statement. If we think of it in a tree structure framework, we have rows that are leaves and have no elements bellow them, like “Interest Income/Loans.” We also have rows that are branches and have leaves or other branches bellow them. Think of “Interest Expenses,” which is the aggregation of expenses on deposits, short-term borrowings and, long-term debts.

**Code Snippet 6.22:** Income Statement Variable Declaration.

```
1   INCOME_STATEMENT_ROWS = [
2       "Interest Income",
3           "Interest Income/Loans",
4           "Interest Income/Trading Assets",
5       "Interest Expenses",
6           "Interest Expenses/Deposits",
7           "Interest Expenses/Short-term Borrowings",
8           "Interest Expenses/Long-term Debts",
9       "Non-Interest Income",
10          "Non-Interest Income/Service Fees",
11          "Non-Interest Income/Other Fees",
12      "Provision for Credit Losses",
13      "Non-Interest Expenses",
14          "Non-Interest Expenses/Administrative Expenses",
15          "Non-Interest Expenses/Other Expenses",
16      "Income Before Tax",
17      "Income Tax Expenses",
18      "Net Income",
19      "Dividends",
20      "Net Income After Dividends"
21  ]
22
23  @variable(sp, IncomeStatement[row in INCOME_STATEMENT_ROWS])
```

Now that we have defined a tree structure of income statement variable, we have to set the aggregation constraints. Their value will be a function of deeper branches and leaves from the income statement tree that will be populated later in Section 6.9.

We have to equate the constraints that guarantee that each branch will be the sum of all leaves below it. Notice that because we have signs in Code Snippet 6.23, we have implemented those constraints taking into account the tree structure proposed in this section.

**Code Snippet 6.23:** Income Statement Aggregation Constraints.

```
@constraint(
    sp,
    IncomeStatement["Interest Income"] ==
        IncomeStatement["Interest Income/Loans"] +
        IncomeStatement["Interest Income/Trading Assets"]
)

@constraint(
```

```
    sp,
    IncomeStatement["Interest Expenses"] ==
        IncomeStatement["Interest Expenses/Deposits"] +
        IncomeStatement["Interest Expenses/Short-term Borrowings"] +
        IncomeStatement["Interest Expenses/Long-term Debts"]
)

@constraint(
    sp,
    IncomeStatement["Non-Interest Income"] ==
        IncomeStatement["Non-Interest Income/Service Fees"] +
        IncomeStatement["Non-Interest Income/Other Fees"]
)

@constraint(
    sp,
    IncomeStatement["Non-Interest Expenses"] ==
        IncomeStatement["Non-Interest Expenses/Administrative Expenses"] +
        IncomeStatement["Non-Interest Expenses/Other Expenses"]
)

@constraint(
    sp,
    IncomeStatement["Income Before Tax"] ==
        IncomeStatement["Interest Income"] +
        IncomeStatement["Interest Expenses"] +
        IncomeStatement["Provision for Credit Losses"] +
        IncomeStatement["Non-Interest Income"] +
        IncomeStatement["Non-Interest Expenses"]
)

@constraint(
    sp,
    IncomeStatement["Net Income"] ==
        IncomeStatement["Income Before Tax"] +
        IncomeStatement["Income Tax Expenses"]
)

@constraint(
    sp,
    IncomeStatement["Net Income After Dividends"] ==
        IncomeStatement["Net Income"] +
        IncomeStatement["Dividends"]
)
```

## 6.9 Core Constraints

In this section, we will present the most fundamental constraints of a mathematical formulation of balance sheet projections. After inserting those constraints into your model, on top of the fundamental variables we described earlier in this chapter, your model will already be able to handle allocation decisions, roll over portfolios, and produce coherent accounting-compliant projection of financial statements.

### 6.9.1 Cash Flows Balance

A cash flows balance constraint is one of the cornerstones of a balance sheet model. Yet, its formulation is very concise: it states that the sum of all cash flows in a node must be zero. This constraint is responsible for disallowing the creation or destruction of money by the model. In other words, all inflow of cash must be allocated somewhere with a corresponding outflow of cash.

Imagine that an asset A pays interest in a specific node. This would represent a positive `CashFlowsInterest` value for contract A. To zero-out the sum of all cash flows, we would need a negative cash flow of the same size. So, the model could buy an appropriate quantity of a new asset B, incurring in a negative `CashFlowsBuy` that would exactly offset the interest payment.

In practice, many negative and positive cash flows are happening within a same node and the model will take decisions of buying, selling, prepaying contracts, paying expenses, and receiving fees, taking into consideration that no cash flow can be left without an use.

One important distinction we should do is the one between cash flows and cash. While the first represents a transfer of funds, the latter is considered a financial contract, within the model, that represents money or a cash account, in local or foreign currencies. If we receive an amortization payment due to an asset contract, this will be modeled as a cash flow. In order to balance it out we could buy other asset contracts. One possible decision would be to add those funds into a cash account. In that case, this cash flow would imply the buying of a cash position.

A cash flow balance constraint is implemented in Code Snippet 6.24. From lines 3–9 we are summing all decision and contractual cash flows for all positions registered in the model.

In line 10 we are also adding a variable called `NonContractCashFlows`, which is responsible for storing all cash flows that are unrelated to contracts. Good examples of negative non-contract cash flows could be payment of dividends, administrative expenses, and income taxes. Receiving fees from counterparts would represent positive non-contract cash flows.

**Code Snippet 6.24:** Cash Flows Balance Constraint.

```
1   @constraint(
2       sp,
3       sum(
4           CashFlowsBuy[a] +
5           CashFlowsSell[a] +
6           CashFlowsPrepayment[a] +
7           CashFlowsInterest[a] +
8           CashFlowsAmortization[a]
9           for a in ids(get_all_positions())
10      ) + NonContractCashFlows == 0.0
11  )
```

In Code Snippet 6.25, we define and populate the `NonContractsCashFlows` variable. Notice that most of the cash flows unrelated to contracts will be part of the income statement and thus will already be stored in the `IncomeStatement` variable.

**Code Snippet 6.25:** Non-Contract Cash Flows Variable.

```
@constraint(
    sp,
    NonContractCashFlows ==
        IncomeStatement["Non-Interest Income/Service Fees"] +
        IncomeStatement["Non-Interest Income/Other Fees"] +
        IncomeStatement["Non-Interest Expenses/Administrative Expenses"] +
        IncomeStatement["Non-Interest Expenses/Other Expenses"] +
        IncomeStatement["Income Tax Expenses"] +
        IncomeStatement["Dividends"]
)
```

On writing a cash flows balance constraint, one should be very careful about having a complete coverage of all variables that imply cash flows. For contractual cash flows, this can be achieved by iterating over all positions. For non-contract cash flows, it is usually a more tricky task. You have to look carefully so as not to leave anything that implies cash flows behind, because it could cause spillovers or inadvertent entry of money into the system.

Let's imagine we forgot to add the income tax expenses item in Code Snippet 6.25. In this case, it would be as if we have paid income taxes but spent no money in this task. As a result, we could end up with a larger asset if the model uses that money to buy new assets. Or with a smaller liability if the model uses the cash flow that was unaccounted for to borrow less money than actually required.

After implementing this fundamental constraint, your model will already be able to collect fees, pay taxes/expenses, and roll over all portfolios. The projections generated will be correct within a cash basis view. However, your balance sheet projections will still lack compliance to fundamental accounting equations. The following sessions will be dedicated to introducing those fundamentals into your model.

### 6.9.2 Income Statement Leaves

In Section 6.8.3, we defined `IncomeStatement` variables and set up the main aggregation constraints that populate branches of an income statement tree, such as "Net Income." Now it is time to discuss the constraints that set values for its main leaves, like "Interest Income/Loans" or "Income Tax Expenses."

Income Statement is a financial report that often uses accrual basis rather than cash basis for computing incomes and expenses. For fixed-income contracts, for example, that means that we should consider the interest earned in a node, regardless of coupon payments that may happen in that period. This quantity is already being calculated and stored in `Income` auxiliary variables, as defined in Section 6.8. So, we only need to assign each position to its related income statement row. In Code Snippet 6.26, we write a set of constraints that covers all financial contracts and populate "Interest Income" and "Interest Expenses" sections of an income statement. Here it is also important that no financial contract is left behind, or else we would not get an accurate net interest income measure.

**Code Snippet 6.26:** Contracts Income Constraints.

```

loans = ids(get_positions_by_balance_sheet_path("ASSETS/LOANS"))
@constraint(
    sp,
    IncomeStatement["Interest Income/Loans"] ==
        sum(Income[a] for a in loans)
)

investments = ids(
    get_positions_by_balance_sheet_path("ASSETS/INVESTMENTS")
)
@constraint(
    sp,
    IncomeStatement["Interest Income/Trading Assets"] ==
        sum(Income[a] for a in investments)
)

deposits = ids(get_positions_by_balance_sheet_path(
    "LIABILITIES/BORROWINGS/DEPOSITS"
))
@constraint(
    sp,
    IncomeStatement["Interest Expenses/Deposits"] ==
        sum(Income[a] for a in deposits)
)

st_borrowings = ids(get_positions_by_balance_sheet_path(
    "LIABILITIES/BORROWINGS/ST BORROWINGS"
))
@constraint(
    sp,
    IncomeStatement["Interest Expenses/Short-term Borrowings"] ==
        sum(Income[a] for a in st_borrowings)
)

lt_debt = ids(get_positions_by_balance_sheet_path(
    "LIABILITIES/BORROWINGS/LT DEBT"
))
@constraint(
    sp,
    IncomeStatement["Interest Expenses/Long-term Debt"] ==
        sum(Income[a] for a in lt_debt)
)
```

The item accounting for provision for credit losses in an income statement reports the addition or release of provisions in the provisions contra-asset account located in the balance sheet. This balance sheet item is populated with a pseudo-contract that has no cash flows, meaning that provisions/releases do not imply disbursement/receipt of cash. So, if we go back to Equation 6.6, we can infer that the `income` variable of provision pseudo-contracts will store only the change in the book value of its positions, which is exactly the release or provision that is reported in an income statement. Code Snippet 6.27 uses this finding to set the appropriate value of releases/provision in the income statement of a node.

**Code Snippet 6.27:** Provision for Credit Losses Income Statement Constraints.

```

provisions = ids(get_positions_by_balance_sheet_path(
    "ASSETS/PROVISIONS FOR CREDIT LOSSES"
))
@constraint(
    sp,
    IncomeStatement["Provision for Credit Losses"] ==
        sum(Income[a] for a in provisions)
)
```

The remaining items, regarding income and expenses that are not related to financial contracts, will generally be populated with the help of exogenous models or business assumptions.

Let's imagine we have an exogenous model to forecast administrative expenses. We could easily incorporate those projections in our model by fixing the expenses values, as seen in Code Snippet 6.28. The function `get_interest_expense(stage::Int)::Float64` returns the level of administrative expenses predicted by the exogenous model attributed to the time span of the node `stage`.

**Code Snippet 6.28:** Example of Exogenous Administrative Expenses Constraint.

```
@constraint(
    sp,
    IncomeStatement["Non-Interest Expenses/Administrative Expenses"] ==
        get_interest_expense(stage)
)
```

We can also use business assumptions to set income and expenses values to a function of other model variables. Let's imagine a simple assumption: income taxes are on average 25% of net income before taxes. This can be set with a simple constraint, implemented in Code Snippet 6.29.[4]

**Code Snippet 6.29:** Example of Income Taxes Constraint.

```
    @constraint(
    sp,
    IncomeStatement["Income Tax Expenses"] ==
        - 0.25 * IncomeStatement["Income Before Tax"]
)
```

4 Here we assume only profits as a result of income before tax.

As a final example of how to fix the values of income statement leaves, it is worth discussing the so-called transaction costs. Transaction costs in finance refer to the costs associated with buying or selling an investment. These costs can include commissions, fees, taxes, and other charges. Transaction costs can have a significant impact on the overall return of an investment, and should be taken into consideration when making investment decisions. Therefore, they must be mapped and considered in the optimization process.

In the snippet of code 6.30, we illustrate how this could be done using the control variables `CashFlowsBuy` and `CashFlowsSell`, which contain the value in dollars for which transaction costs were incurred for purchase and sale operations of assets or liabilities, respectively. We are going to account for the transaction costs in the line `"Non-Interest Expenses/Other Expenses."` In the example, we assume that each dollar traded in purchases or sales entails a cost of 0.01%. We must also highlight the adjustment to the sign of the `CashFlowsBuy` and `CashFlowsSell` variables through the helper function `model_sign(pos)`, so that they always have a positive sign and can be accounted for as an actual expense. In a more realistic implementation, this value would naturally be a function of the type of financial instrument, as well as the conditions under which it is being traded. This refinement could be easily represented by adapting the code below so that costs differ according to financial position.

**Code Snippet 6.30:** Example of Transaction Costs Constraint.

```
@constraint(
    sp,
    IncomeStatement["Non-Interest Expenses/Other Expenses"] == sum(
        0.0001 * (
            -model_sign(pos) * CashFlowsBuy[pos.id]
            + model_sign(pos) * CashFlowsSell[pos.id]
        )
        for pos in get_all_positions())
    )
)
```

There may also be fixed transaction costs in addition to those proportional to the size of the operation, although these tend to be less representative than the percentage ones. To represent them, it would be necessary to use integer variables to control whether the operation was carried out or not, which naturally can greatly increase the complexity of the mathematical problem due to the number of variables needed to track the purchases and sales of each existing financial position in the model. Therefore, these should only be added if their expected financial effect was in fact very material and if they cannot be approximated by continuous rather than binary variables.

In addition to making the profit calculation more accurate, transaction cost modeling also has an important positive effect on the smoothing of the model's results, as they help the model to execute as few operations and move the least amount of money as possible. We must remember that the only way the solver can evaluate the performance of the solution is evaluating the objective function. However, there may be infinite combinations for the values of the decision variables that lead to the same objective function value. Therefore, in the absence of transaction cost modeling, the solver is free to prescribe as a optimal solution one that contains a large number of buy and sell operations, many of them unnecessary. If the model considers transaction costs, this problem can be solved, since it will only prescribe buy and sell operations as they are necessary to meet the constraints and keep maximizing profits. In other words, unnecessary operations will penalize the objective function.

After implementing all items of all `IncomeStatement` variables, either with financial contract incomes or assumptions, you will already have an accurate projection of "Net Income After Dividends," which is the bottom line of an income statement. This quantity will be used in the next section to update an important component of the balance sheet.

### 6.9.3 Equity Accounts Update

The earnings or losses that remain at the end of an income statement should now be incorporated into a shareholder's equity account called "Retained Earnings." This account accumulates incomes or losses from period to period and is a reserve of earnings from which cash dividends are drawn out. At the same time, there is a "Capital Par Value" item in the balance sheet that accumulates capital transfers from shareholders to the institution. Also, as we discussed before, available-for-sale contracts have their unrealized gains or losses incorporated to an UGL equity account until that position is liquidated. Let's now discuss the mechanisms involved in implementing those equity events into our balance sheet projections, because they are a step we have to take before adding one of the most important model constraints, which will be described in next section.

Capital Transfers are events that involve transfer of funds, so a capital transfer must have a cash flow being accounted for in the model. If we populate this balance sheet item with a non-contract position that has buy cash flows, we can replicate the impact of a capital transfer in terms of balance sheet and cash flow representation. Then, each dollar transferred will be one dollar of buy cash flow entering the system and will also increase (in absolute value) capital par value by one dollar. So, in Code Snippet 6.31, we are creating a constraint to mimic a capitalization of 1,000 dollars into the balance sheet. In this case, we have a positive buy cash flow because buying a shareholder's equity position adds cash flow into the model.

**Code Snippet 6.31:** Example of Capital Transfer Constraint.

```
par_value = ids(get_positions_by_balance_sheet_path(
    "EQUITY/CAPITAL PAR VALUE"
))
@constraint(sp, sum(BuyCashFlow[a,h] for a in par_value, h in get_all_
     stages()) == 1000)
```

The case of booking earnings or losses in a balance sheet is quite different in nature, because this event does not involve cash flow exchanges of any kind. Remember that earnings are calculated in an accrual basis. This involves reporting interest earned rather than paid or received, and that earned interest is the quantity that is added to or subtracted from "Retained Earnings."

Because of that, we need to have booked in "Retained Earnings" pseudo-contract positions that do not possess buy or sell cash flows. If we do so, we can buy or sell this position in order to add or subtract from its booked value without adding or subtracting cash flows into the model. In Code Snippet 6.32, we plug "Net Income After Dividends" as the updater of retained earnings balance.

Equity positions have typically negative book value. Thus, an earning would make retained earnings more negative, while a loss would make it less negative. In other words, an earning would make the outgoing state of book values of retained earnings be more negative than its incoming state. This logic explains the minus sign we see in line 8.

**Code Snippet 6.32:** Retained Earnings Update Constraint.

```
1  ret_earnings = ids(get_positions_by_balance_sheet_path(
2      "EQUITY/RETAINED EARNINGS"
3  ))
4  @constraint(
5      sp,
6      sum(BookValue[a,h].out - BookValue[a,h].in
7          for a in ret_earnings, h in get_all_stages()) ==
8          -IncomeStatement["Net Income After Dividends"]
9  )
```

Cash dividends are already being considered in the variable "Net Income After Dividends," but their cash flow effects must also take part in the Cash Flows Balance constraint explained in Section 6.9.1. The good news is that dividends are already there, under the `NonContractsCashFlows` variable, as defined in Code Snippet 6.25.

Finally, the variation of fair value from available-for-sale positions must be incorporated into "Unrealized Gains or Losses" in equity. The constraint shown in Code Snippet 6.33 gathers the UGL variation of all available-for-sale assets and liabilities, and makes sure that this change is incorporated into equity's UGL account.

**Code Snippet 6.33:** UGL Update Constraint.

```
ugl = ids(get_positions_by_balance_sheet_path(
    "EQUITY/UGL"
))

assets = ids(get_positions_by_balance_sheet_path("ASSETS"))
liabilities = ids(get_positions_by_balance_sheet_path("LIABILITIES"))

@constraint(
    sp,
    sum(BookValue[a,h].out - BookValue[a,h].in
        for a in ugl, h in get_all_stages()) ==
```

```
        sum(UGL[a,h].out - UGL[a,h].in
            for a in set_union(assets, liabilities), h in get_all_stages()
            if get_accounting_classification(get_position_by_id(a)) == "AFS"
        )
    )
```

To sum it up, Table 6.1 shows us all equity events, their effects on the balance sheet, and the treatment given to their cash flows in our model implementation.

**Table 6.1:** Shareholder's equity events summary.

| Events | In Balance Sheet | Cash Flows |
|---|---|---|
| Capital Transfers | Adds to Capital Par Value | Buy cash flow |
| Cash Dividends | Draws from Retained Earnings | Non-contract cash flows |
| Realized Gains/Losses | Adds/draws from Retained Earnings | No cash flow |
| Unrealized Gains/Losses | Adds/draws from UGL | No cash flow |

### 6.9.4 Book Balance

The most fundamental accounting equation states that for any balance sheet assets must equal the sum of liabilities plus equity accounts (Equation 6.8). The double entry system guarantees that for every transaction there will be at least one debit and one credit, and they will even out as to keep the identity between assets, liabilities, and equity always true.

$$\text{Assets} = \text{Liabilities} + \text{Equity} \tag{6.8}$$

In Code Snippet 6.34 we synthetically implement this important accounting identity in the form of a *book balance* constraint on the outgoing state of each node. However concise, this constraint is applied over all book values of all contracts of the model. Because we have signed book values, we just need to sum everything and equal to zero.

**Code Snippet 6.34:** Book Balance Constraint.

```
@constraint(
    sp,
    sum(BookValue[a].out for a in ids(get_all_positions())) == 0
)
```

It is important to say that this is the constraint that guarantees the consistency of our balance sheet projections with the fundamental accounting equation. Nonetheless, this consistency was already achieved with the constraints we have defined so far, and this new one just enforces that everything was done in a right way. Let's understand why we can expect that this constraint will not be violated if we did right in the implementation of the code shown in previous sections.

If we consider that we start with a balanced state (i. e., respecting Equation 6.8 from the start), to keep the books balanced we need to guarantee that the variation of book value of equity equals the variation of assets minus the variation of liabilities, as described in Equation 6.9.

$$\begin{aligned}\Delta\text{Assets} &= \Delta\text{Liabilities} + \Delta\text{Equity}\\ \Delta\text{Equity} &= \Delta\text{Assets} - \Delta\text{Liabilities}\end{aligned} \tag{6.9}$$

From Equation 6.6, we can see that income of a position is the variation of book value plus all its event-driven and contractual cash flows. If we look at the income statement "Net Income After Dividends," it contains the income of all assets and liabilities contracts, plus all non-contract cash flows, as defined in Section 6.8.3.

But, because of the Cash Flows Balance constraint, described in Section 6.9.1, although a particular contract can have a positive or negative cash flow in a particular node, the sum of contract cash flows for all contracts plus non-contract cash flows must always be zero. That is why when we sum all income variables with all non-contract cash flows, the cash flows cancel out and the variation of book value is what is left. Again, because we have signed book values, what is left is in fact the variation of assets minus the variation of liabilities. This is set to be exactly the variation of the equity account "Retained Earnings," as seen in Code Snippet 6.32. To sum it up, in order to keep book balance, we need to make sure that all contracts and all non-contract cash flows are being considered in our income statement bottom line that will be accumulated in our retained earnings' account.

There are two exceptions for this rule. The first are, of course, capital transfers. These events push cash flows into the model, but they do not appear in as income in financial statements. The transferred amount is added to the "Capital Par Value" account, creating a positive equity variation. At the same time, as all cash flows must be allocated somewhere, the same amount of resources is used to grow assets and/or repay debts. Thus, capitalizations are also balanced in terms of book value, even though they do not use the retained earnings' account to achieve balance.

The second exception is available-for-sale assets and liabilities. As discussed previously, what is recognized as income for those contracts is based on amortized cost variation rather than book value changes. Because the variation of book value is calculated with fair value, this would in theory violate Equation 6.9. However, because the variation of their UGL is also booked in equity's UGL account, the total effect of these two bookings is similar to that of contracts with other accounting classifications. This is shown in Equation 6.10, where income and variation of UGL is calculated over a node $t$ that starts in $t_1$ and ends at $t_2$. Contractual and event-driven cash flows are collapsed into the quantity CashFlows.

$$\begin{aligned}\text{Income}(t) + \Delta\text{UGL} = {} & \text{AccrualValue}(t_2) - \text{AccrualValue}(t_1)\\ & + \text{CashFlows}\end{aligned}$$

$$
\begin{aligned}
&+ (\text{FairValue}(t_2) - \text{AccrualValue}(t_2)) \\
&- (\text{FairValue}(t_1) - \text{AccrualValue}(t_1)) \\
\text{Income}(t) + \Delta\text{UGL} &= \text{FairValue}(t_2) - \text{FairValue}(t_1) + \text{CashFlows} \\
&= \text{BookValue}(t_2) - \text{BookValue}(t_1) + \text{CashFlows} \qquad (6.10)
\end{aligned}
$$

Finally, we must reinforce that book balance constraints are very important and they must appear explicitly in your model as a way to guarantee to all model stakeholders that there is consistency in the balance sheets being projected.

We have now set up the minimum set of variables and constraints to represent all basic financial and accounting rules, and our model is capable of rolling over portfolios and producing balance sheets and income statements. But there is nothing yet saying why should we buy contract A over contract B when rolling over a portfolio. There is no directive yet to say if we should use capital transfers to prepay debts or to acquire new assets. The drivers for the model to take those decisions are what we call business constraints, which is the subject of the next chapter.

# 7 Building the Model: Business Rules

Each part of the model has its role in representing reality, but most of the hard work is done by constraints. If well organized and programmed, they lead to good and realistic solutions. A good set of constraints can also help us understand, maintain, and validate a model. The next sections will be entirely devoted to a class of equations called *business constraints*, which are created in order to enforce consistency between the model solution and business targets or limits.

Throughout this chapter, we will present different types of constraints, including constraints to control the dynamics and composition of assets and liabilities, constraints to represent limits and risk targets, as well as constraints designed to implement specific institutional policies. At the end of the section, we hope to have delivered a vast inventory covering the main constraints involved in the construction of a balance sheet optimization model.

Another important part of a mathematical balance sheet optimization model is the *objective function*, which can represent goals that an institution has set for itself or can help the model achieve certain desired properties.

In this chapter, we will discuss possible objective function choices considering, in particular, the fact that we are dealing with a multistage model. Additionally, we will discuss some important issues and tradeoffs associated with weighting the different terms that may compose the objective function.

## 7.1 Business Constraints

This section is intended to present a fairly vast menu of constraints that implement business rules. These constraints are the mathematical representation of policies and assumptions that an institution needs to consider when projecting its financial statements.

In practice, the large-scale balance sheet optimization model is built by successively adding different types of constraints. The bigger and more intricate an institution is, the higher the probability that a wider range and greater amount of constraints are necessary to ensure that the model accurately reflects reality.

While each of the constraints may seem simple, iterating over them can lead to problems that are difficult to debug. To illustrate this, consider the following case.

Let's imagine we have a business rule that imposes a loans portfolio growth of 2% per year. Now, suppose there are limits to the demand for loans, and these are a function of market conditions, for example. Although these two constraints are relatively simple to program, when combined they may imply infeasibility if the demand limits are such that they prevent us from reaching loan portfolio growth targets. But this is just a very trivial example.

https://doi.org/10.1515/9783110664669-007

In a large-scale balance sheet model, the relationship between two or more clashing constraints can be far more subtle and harder to spot on first glance. Therefore, it is important that the new constraints are added to the model one by one, and at each addition, the effect of the new constraint and the functioning of the pre-existing constraints are evaluated.

In any case, even if you follow this procedure carefully, there are still risks of some problems not being detected when changing the model.

Given the importance of the debugging process in the development of mathematical models, we will devote the entire Chapter 10 to this topic. But for now, in this chapter we will focus on enumerating and discussing some of the more typical classes of business constraints in a balance sheet optimization model.

### 7.1.1 Bank Growth or Shrinkage

Growth targets are very common and it might make sense to equip the model with this type of rule. Such targets may be formalized in the bank's business plan, but even if they are not, it may make sense to equip the model with this type of constraint so that projections are aligned with the institution's natural growth.

Alternatively, or additionally, we may be interested in putting a cap on the bank's growth. This cap would not come from planning goals, of course, but it could serve as a way to rule out solutions that are inconsistent with reality.

Imagine that our bank has a planned goal of growing its assets by 1% per year. On the other hand, we assume that a solution in which assets grow by more than 3% per year is an unrealistic solution.

Let's say that we have a model with yearly steps. These modeling choices can be implemented with constraints like the ones presented in Code Snippet 7.1. Basically, we should compare the book value of the loans portfolio at the beginning and at the end of a stage, requiring growth to stay within a desired range. In the example, we require the growth rate to be between 1% and 3% per year in each yearly step.

Obviously, in your implementation, it is wise to provide those limits through model inputs instead of hardcoding them.

**Code Snippet 7.1:** Minimal Growth Constraint.

```
loans_ids = ids(get_positions_by_balance_sheet_path("ASSETS/LOANS"))

@constraint(
sp,
    sum(BookValue[a, h].out for a in loans_ids, h in get_all_stages()) >=
    1.01 * sum(BookValue[a,h].in for a in loans_ids, h in get_all_stages())
)

@constraint(
sp,
    sum(BookValue[a,h].out for a in loans_ids, h in get_all_stages()) <=
```

```
        1.03 * sum(BookValue[a,h].in for a in loans_ids, h in get_all_stages())
    )
```

Despite limiting growth or even setting a growth target being legitimate constraints, they should be used with care. In the real world, a bank's growth is already constrained by less artificial constraints, such as borrowing demand constraints, funding market liquidity, risk limits, leverage limits, and even the bank's own operational capacity.

As much as possible, these constraints should be represented in the model. In this way, under a profit-maximizing objective function, for example, we decrease the chances of such limits hiding specification problems that could lead to an unbounded solution.

### 7.1.2 Leverage Ratio

The initial composition of assets, liabilities, and equity is completely given by decisions made in the past. However, as time passes and the market moves, the relative composition of the balance sheet accounts will passively change. Other events also have the potential to modify the balance sheet structure, such as amortizations, default, prepayments, capitalizations, etc.

Some of the most important relationships between balance sheet accounts are the financial ratios called *leverage ratios*. They indicate how an institutions' assets are being funded. In other words, they tell what is the composition between debts and equity. These ratios come in different flavors, but the most common definition of leverage ratio is the amount of debt divided by the amount of equity booked in a balance sheet, as shown in Equation 7.1. The idea is that the more debt a company holds, the higher the risk of defaulting in adverse scenarios.

$$\text{Leverage Ratio} = \frac{\text{Debt}}{\text{Equity}} \tag{7.1}$$

That said, an institution can have established leverage limits that can be expressed in terms of a maximum leverage ratio $L^*$. If $L^*$ is 1.5 for instance, it means that the company can have at maximum 50% more debt than the booked value of its equity, as shown in Equation 7.2.

$$\frac{\text{Debt}}{\text{Equity}} <= L^*$$
$$\text{Debt} <= L^* \times \text{Equity}, \quad \text{Equity} \geq 0 \tag{7.2}$$

The same inequality is then implemented in Code Snippet 7.2, using $L^* = 1.5$. One point of attention is that other constraints that regulate debt issues and capital changes (like dividends or even losses) can create states where there is no feasible solution without violating the leverage limit that was set. In that case, one possible solution is to relax the limit until the point where a feasible solution is found. Then you can investigate the conditions that occurred in the state that nearly violated the relaxed limit, and propose changes to overcome the infeasibility.

**Code Snippet 7.2:** Maximum Leverage Ratio Constraint.

```
liabilities = ids(get_positions_by_balance_sheet_path("LIABILITIES"))
equity = ids(get_positions_by_balance_sheet_path("EQUITY"))

@constraint(
    sp,
    sum(BookValue[a,h].out for a in liabilities, h in get_all_stages()) <=
        1.5 * sum(BookValue[a,h].in for a in equity, h in get_all_stages())
)
```

### 7.1.3 Portfolio Composition

A bank may have interest in ensuring that relative allocations between different business units remain within or are guided to a certain range. These bands may come from business targets or limits. They may also arise, for example, from regulatory requirements that control sector exposures.

We will illustrate the coding of this type of constraint by limiting the contribution of a set of sectors in the loan portfolio to a set of ranges. In Code Snippet 7.3, we assume that the loans' portfolio is segmented in two sectors named `PERSONAL` and `CORPORATE` and that we target an equally weighted portfolio, with a tolerance of 15 percentage points deviations from this target.

We also assume that the positions vector can be filtered using a function called `get_positions_by_tag_sector(sector::String)::Vector{Position}`. Hence, to obtain only the positions for the loans of a given sector, we just need to intersect the output of our helper functions `get_positions_by_tag_sector` and `get_positions_by_balance_sheet_path`. Finally, we use two inequality constraints to tell the model that the sum of the book values of each sector must lie in the desired percentage interval.

**Code Snippet 7.3:** Portfolio Composition Constraints.

```
all_loans = ids(get_positions_by_balance_sheet_path("ASSETS/LOANS"))

for sector in ["PERSONAL", "CORPORATE"]
    sector_ids = ids(get_positions_by_tag_sector(sector))
    loans_in_this_sector = intersect(loans_ids, sector_ids)

    @constraint(
        sp,
        sum(BookValue[a,h].out for a in loans_in_this_sector, h in get_all_stages()) <=
        (0.5 + 0.15) * sum(BookValue[a,h].in for a in all_loans, h in get_all_stages())
    )
    @constraint(
```

```
        sp,
        sum(BookValue[a,h].out for a in loans_in_this_sector, h in get_all_
            stages()) >=
        (0.5 - 0.15) * sum(BookValue[a,h].in for a in all_loans, h in get_
            all_stages())
    )
end
```

This is a easy way to indicate how the model should roll over this particular loans' portfolio. However, inside the percentage bands there is no clear indication of how the model should operate. Should it buy 65% of corporate and 35% of personal? Why not all the way around? Or should it produce an intermediate case? To solve these questions, we have to feed our model with more specific constraints and goals. Possible approaches will be discussed further in this chapter.

### 7.1.4 Investing Policies

Investment policies refer to the set of restrictions that will dictate the timing and characteristics of disbursements, particularly in bank loan portfolios.

Usually, the inputs for the construction of these blocks of constraints will come from planning teams, including disbursement targets and segmentation by division, sectors or product types. Rates, terms, and spreads also tend to be business assumptions defined by the business units, which are currently on the commercial front and, therefore, have more clarity on the volume and format of demand from their customers.

Therefore, for the mathematical model to properly consider such investment plans, two fundamental tasks must be fulfilled in the data preparation stage. The first is the structuring of business assumptions, and the second is the provision of a set of new positions in which the bank may or should invest, with characteristics and segmentation in line with the business plans.

Let's imagine our planning team expects disbursements of 100 million dollars for the next year. The `CORPORATE` segment will be 60% of that total, and the remainder will be granted to `PERSONAL`. They also assume that corporate loans are 3-month LIBOR deals with a long-term repayment schedule. Personal loans are fixed deals with a short-term repayment.

In practice, the 100 million dollars would be scattered through many different operations with different counterparts. But in the model, we should only break disbursements seldom as possible to separate all the dimensions we need to have in our reports and constraints. In that case, if we are only interested in separating corporate and personal segments, we could create two new positions: one with a 60 million dollars long-term LIBOR contract representing all corporate disbursements, the other with a 40 million short-term fixed contract that sums up all personal loans that will happen within the time span of the node.

The is_new getter should, of course, yield true when supplied with each one of those positions. We should also have another getter implemented called get_issue_date(p::Position)::Date, that returns the date of issue of the underlying contract. In this case, we assume that we set the date of issue to be the decision date of the node in which that position will be disbursed. As we should remember, in our example model the decision date is the beginning of the node.

In Code Snippet 7.4, we present a way to implement an investment policy in our model. Given all loans' positions, we must specify when to incorporate each new loan into the institution's portfolio. If and only if the decision date of this node coincides with the new position's date of issuance will we proceed to buy one unit of the underlying contract.

With this formulation, it is not possible to buy more of a contract that is already in our portfolio. The rolling over of this loan portfolio is totally determined with the business plans and assumptions, so these constraints will often collide with other constraints that try to regulate the composition of this portfolio, like the one described in Section 7.1.3, for example.

**Code Snippet 7.4:** Investing Policies Constraints.

```
decision_date = get_date_open(stage)
all_loans = ids(get_positions_by_balance_sheet_path("ASSETS/LOANS"))

for a in all_loans
    pos = get_position_by_id(a)
    if is_new(a)
        issue_date = get_issue_date(pos)
        if issue_date == decision_date
            # buy one unit
            @constraint(sp, sum(Buy[a,h] for h in get_all_stages()) == 1.0)
        else
            # do not buy
            @constraint(sp, sum(Buy[a,h] for h in get_all_stages()) == 0.0)
        end
    end
end
```

### 7.1.5 Price Elasticity

To increase its level of leverage, a bank may have to incur higher funding costs, whereas the higher the leverage, the higher the risk perception of lenders and depositors. On the other hand, to be able to lend more and increase its market share, a bank may need to decrease the spreads charged. In other words, in the debt and loan markets the law of supply and demand is also valid, and as far as possible such relations of demand elasticity in relation to price should be codified in the form of constraints.

To represent this, we need to work on two fronts. First, we need contracts with progressively higher (or lower) rates and then we need constraints to limit the volumes traded at each price.

Since the objective function will seek for profit maximization, the model will soon raise funds from lower rate contracts, moving to more expensive contracts only if necessary to attend other constraints or targets. The same is true on the asset side. To maximize profit, the model will lend using higher rate contracts, moving to lower rate contracts only if it is still profitable or needs to be met to meet other specific constraints.

Code Snippet 7.5 presents a possible way of coding a block of constraints that expresses the price elasticity of demand for loans. To facilitate understanding, we assume the existence of three levels of spreads, which are associated with operable market volumes. The higher the spread charged by the bank, the lower the demand for credit. Let's assume there is a helper function called `get_new_loans_by_spread_level(...)` which returns the set of new loans for each of the spread levels.

Furthermore, let's assume that the maximum volume that can be borrowed at each of the high, medium, and low spreads is 100, 200, 300 million per period. With this information in hand, just intersect the set of personal loans with the set relating to the spread to be charged and write a constraint limiting the maximum volume that can be dealt.

**Code Snippet 7.5:** Price Elasticity Constraint.

```

loans_high_spread = get_new_loans_by_spread_level("high")
loans_medium_spread = get_new_loans_by_spread_level("medium")
loans_low_spread = get_new_loans_by_spread_level("low")

@constraint(
    sp,
    sum(CashFlowsBuy[a,t] for a in loans_high_spread) <= 100e3
)

@constraint(
    sp,
    sum(CashFlowsBuy[a,t] for a in loans_medium_spread) <= 200e3
)

@constraint(
    sp,
    sum(CashFlowsBuy[a,t] for a in loans_low_spread) <= 300e3
)
```

### 7.1.6 Withdrawals and Prepayments

For commercial banks, deposits are an important source of fundraising. However, this type of funding source is known to be more unstable than conventional debts, particularly when we are dealing with so-called non-maturity deposits.

Understanding the profile of withdrawals in a deposit portfolio is critical to good risk management, and particularly liquidity and interest rate risks. Due to the sensitivity of banks to this source of funds and due to increasing regulation, banks have invested a lot of efforts in modeling conditional withdrawals rates and to establish more robust pricing and hedging strategies.

For a balance sheet optimization model to be able to consider the effects of deposit withdrawals, we need to equip it with constraints that emulate such a financial event appropriately over time and according to economic conditions.

A possible formulation is to represent withdrawal rate as part of the scenario, ideally keeping the proper correlations with the other economic variables such as inflation, interest rate and others that may help to explain withdrawal rates. The constraint can be implemented fixing the value of `CashFlowsPrepayment` variables, which will indirectly decrease the number of contracts in the portfolio with the respective cash outflow effect.

Code Snippet 7.6 illustrates the anatomy of such constraints, considering the withdrawal rate is expressed as a percentage of the book value at the beginning of the stage, and can be retrieved using the helper function `get_withdrawal_rate`.

It is also worth noting that, instead of creating a single constraint on the aggregate deposits portfolio balance, we chose to apply the rate position-by-position, which is important for two reasons. The first one is that, if we apply the withdrawal rate in aggregate form, the mathematical model is free to distribute the withdrawals unevenly across the portfolio, but this is not a decision we can make in practice.

Therefore, if we only have an aggregate rate of withdrawals, to guarantee the uniformity of its application we must create a constraint per position. The formulation presented also allows us to apply different withdrawal rates per position, if we have such information.

Finally, it is worth highlighting the signals embedded in the variables we used in the example. As we are dealing with a liability, the value of the `BookValue` variable will be negative by convention. Therefore, the sign of the `CashFlowsPrepayment` variable will also be negative by convention, which is correct considering that withdrawals imply cash outflows, which under our convention need to be negative in the equations.

**Code Snippet 7.6:** Withdrawals Rate Constraint.

```
deposits_ids = ids(
    get_positions_by_balance_sheet_path("LIABILITIES/DEPOSITS")
)
for a in deposits_ids
    withdrawal_rate = get_withdrawal_rate(a)
    @constraint(
        sp,
        sum(CashFlowsPrepayment[a,h] for h in get_all_stages()) ==
            withdrawal_rate * BookValue[a].in
    )
end
```

### 7.1.7 Prepayments

In the previous section, we discussed how to implement a block of constraints to consider the effect of deposit withdrawals, assuming that we have an appropriate withdrawal rate at each moment in time and in each economic scenario considered in the balance sheet projection. On the basis of such withdrawal rate, we set the variable value of `CashFlowsPrepayment` to indirectly reduce the warehouse stock.

This same modeling strategy can be used to consider the effects of prepayments on the loan portfolio, once we have prepayment rates as an assumption or even as part of the scenarios.

It is also important to point out that, in the absence of information about the payment rate, or if the modeler does not want to consider this effect in any model execution, care must be taken to set the value of prepayments at zero, in order to prevent misuses of such decision variables in an attempt to optimize the balance sheet. In practice, such variables are just a modeling device, not representing a decision per se.

### 7.1.8 Trading Volume Limits

For a number of reasons, the bank volume may be prevented from operating above a certain volume. In some cases, such constraints may have been defined by the institution itself, as part of an investment policy. Sometimes it can be part of a shareholders' agreement, which prevents the bank from selling the shares of a certain company for a determined period.

In other cases, volume constraints are necessary to represent the market's depth, preventing the model from producing solutions that in practice are not implementable due to liquidity reasons. Constraints on tradable limits also communicate with price and demand constraints. Ultimately, the latter communicates with the former, stating the threshold from which it is simply no longer possible to operate, even at a discount. For semantic reasons, we prefer to separate them in the model.

Finally, there may also be regulatory constraints on trading volumes in order to prevent fraudulent market manipulation. However, a bank may have good justifications for operating an atypical volume, such as authorization to make a large public offering or a large private deal. In Code Snippet 7.7, we present two variants of trading volume constraints.

In the first variant, we limit the volume of corporate bonds we can we can sell to represent the available market liquidity. We suppose positions can be retrieved using the helper function `get_positions_by_balance_sheet_path` and we hardcode the limits to simplify the examples. Naturally, in a real case we can have a more segmented structure and limits can come from a parameterized business assumption. In the second example, we limit the volume of debt issues to represent, for instance, an operational limitation.

The anatomy of both constraints is the same, but in the first we recur to `CashFlowsSell` variable, while in the second case we use `CashFlowsBuy` variable.

**Code Snippet 7.7:** Trading Volume Limits Constraint.

```

# cbonds selling limit
cbonds_ids = ids(
    get_positions_by_balance_sheet_path("ASSETS/INVESTMENTS/CORPORATE BONDS")
)
@constraint(
    sp,
    sum(CashFlowsSell[a,h]
        for a in cbonds_ids, h in get_all_stages()) <= 1_000_000_000
)

# debt issuance limit
debts_ids = ids(
    get_positions_by_balance_sheet_path("LIABILITIES/DEBTS")
)
@constraint(
    sp,
    sum(CashFlowsBuy[a,h]
        for a in cbonds_ids, h in get_all_stages()) <= 500_000_000
)
```

### 7.1.9 Liquidity Ratios

When it comes to balance sheet optimization, liquidity risk is an important factor to consider from both a regulatory and economic standpoint. Regulators require financial institutions to comply with liquidity regulations for the sake of financial stability. Meanwhile, from an economic point of view, it is important to make sure that a financial institution has enough liquidity to meet its short-term obligations and operate efficiently. If liquidity management is not done properly, it can lead to liquidity shortages, which can have dire consequences, such as a decrease in credit rating, a drop in share price, and even bankruptcy.

Therefore, when assessing liquidity risk, it is important to forecast bank cashflows under a stressed scenario and compare it with the current liquid assets portfolio to identify potential gaps. In a managerial analysis, the institution itself should define the analysis horizon and the parameterization and severity level of the stress scenario. For regulatory analyzes, the calculation rules tend to be more standardized.

In any case, the basic anatomy of a liquidity indicator consists of a ratio comparing the volume of available liquid assets and net cash outflows. Net cash outflows are the difference between projected cash outflows and inflows over a given time period. Cash outflows can include interest payments, debt amortizations, margin calls in derivative contracts, payments of administrative expenses, taxes, dividends, loan disbursements, etc. Inflows may include interest amortization receipts, service revenues, scheduled capitalizations, and new issues, although in stress scenarios this source of cash inflow is usually reduced or disregarded. Additionally, different weights may be given to the assets that make up the portfolio of liquid assets (known as haircuts) to take into account the fact that, in the event of a real need for liquidation, assets with different risk term profiles may be subject to different levels of discount.

To illustrate how to code a block of constraints to limit liquidity risk, let us assume that we have two functions to project cumulative cash inflows and outflows over a period of time. We will call these two functions `get_inflows(t)` and `get_outflows(t)`. We will also assume that we have a helper function `get_haircut()` that gives us the haircut associated with a particular financial position of our portfolio of liquid assets. We will analyze the cumulative gaps on a monthly basis over a total survival horizon of six months, which will require six constraints as shown in Code Snippet 7.8.

**Code Snippet 7.8:** Liquidity Ratios Constraints.

```


liquid_assets_ids = ids(
    get_positions_by_balance_sheet_path("ASSETS/INVESTMENTS")
)

for q in 1:6
    net_cf = get_outflows(q) - get_inflows(q)
    @constraint(
        sp,
        sum(get_haircut(a) * BookValue[a,h].out
            for a in liquid_assets_ids, h in get_all_stages()) >= net_cf
    )
end
```

It is important to note that liquidity ratios already make use of future cash flow projections. In our multistage balance sheet optimization model, the cash flow projections in each helper function are based on the current balance sheet state in each node. This takes into account not only the pre-defined assumptions, but also the solutions being considered in the problem-solving process. Furthermore, the model has a restriction to ensure the total consistency of cash flows, so that money is not created or destroyed without adhering to the law of double entries.

This may appear to be enough to guarantee the bank has enough liquidity to meet its objectives. However, the scenario used in liquidity risk management may not be the same as the one used for the balance sheet projection and optimization, particularly if a deterministic projection exercise is done for a low-risk baseline scenario. Therefore, the cash flow projections for calculating liquidity risk should not be confused with the cash consistency restrictions.

Even if the balance sheet optimization model takes into account multiple future scenarios, including cash stress scenarios, the cash flow scenarios used to manage liquidity risk could still be different. This is especially true if the institution is subject to regulatory limits that are based on standardized calculations and scenarios that are different from the ones the modeler thinks are realistic or in line with the bank's risk appetite.

To sum up, both the fundamental accounting constraints related to cash flow consistency and the constraints related to liquidity ratios are necessary to guarantee that the solution provided by the balance sheet optimization model is viable, as well as compliant with internal and regulatory limits for liquidity risk.

### 7.1.10 Capital Adequacy Ratios

Capital Adequacy Ratios (CARs) are a measure of a bank's financial strength and solvency from a regulatory perspective. They are calculated by dividing the bank's capital by its total risk-weighted assets (RWAs). CARs are important for banks as they help ensure that the bank has enough capital to cover unexpected losses that are not yet provisioned on the balance sheet.

CARs are an essential tool for ensuring the financial stability of both individual banks and the entire financial system. By setting minimum capital requirements for banks, CARs help protect the bank from insolvency and the financial system from systemic risk. Additionally, CARs encourage banks to maintain higher levels of capital, which helps reduce the risk of default and the possibility of a financial crisis. For this reason, constraints to represent the limits defined for the CARs are essential components in a balance sheet optimization model.

However, CAR calculations may vary across jurisdictions due to differences in the way jurisdictions calculate their risk-based capital requirements. For instance, some jurisdictions may use different risk weights for different asset classes or may use different models for calculating capital adequacy. Additionally, some jurisdictions may have different capital requirements for different types of financial institutions, such as banks, insurers, and pension funds.

Risk weighted assets may be based on linear formulas, but not always. In some cases, non-linear formulas may be used to take into account diversification effects or other calculation rules. The same is valid for capital calculations. To include the calculation of regulatory capital or RWAs in the balance sheet optimization model, we must evaluate the tradeoffs between calculation accuracy and model performance. Generally, we believe that linear approximations can provide a good cost benefit. However, some precautions must be taken when resorting to this type of modeling device.

We must ensure that the linear approximation is accurate enough to capture the nonlinearity of the function and monitor the odds that the linear approximation implies underestimation or overestimation of risks. To do this, we must use various methods to validate the linear approximation, such as Monte Carlo simulations or sensitivity analysis. In particular, we must consider the potential for nonlinear risk factors to interact with each other, and account for these interactions in the linear approximation. Lastly, we must ensure that the linear approximation is good enough for the range of values of interest, in addition to monitoring whether it remains valid over time.

In the code examples that follow, we won't focus on such calculation quirks. We'll be more interested in emphasizing the convenience of representing the different elements of the CAR calculation in specific auxiliary decision variables, to make it easier to specify regulatory constraints. This separation is especially desirable since the exact calculation or the approaches adopted can vary significantly between the different types of risk and their sub-parts.

In the code snippet below, let's assume that credit and market RWAs can be expressed using a simple linear function, where position balances are multiplied by weighting factors that can be retrieved by a helper functions called `get_credit_rwa_weight()` and `get_market_rwa_weight()`, respectively. The Total RWA is obtained by simply adding the RWAs for credit risk and market risk.

It is important to note that in the code example shown in Code Snippet 7.9, the control of the set of assets that must compose the calculation of credit and market RWAs is left to the helper functions, as long as they return the value zero for assets that do not concern the RWA in question. Because of this choice, the sums that define the RWAs are made around all the bank's assets, which can be retrieved through the already known helper function `get_positions_by_balance_sheet_path()`.

**Code Snippet 7.9:** Risk Weighted Assets Variables.

```

assets_ids = ids(
    get_positions_by_balance_sheet_path("ASSETS/")
)

@constraint(
    sp,
    MarketRWA ==
    sum(get_market_rwa_weight(a) * BookValue[a,h].out
        for a in assets_ids, h in get_all_stages())
)

@constraint(
    sp,
    CreditRWA ==
    sum(get_credit_rwa_weight(a) * BookValue[a,h].out
        for a in assets_ids, h in get_all_stages())
)

@constraint(
    sp, TotalRWA == MarketRWA + CreditRWA
)
```

Naturally, there may be other risks that may need to be added in the Total RWA calculation, but the modeling strategy may remain the same. We need to identify the calculation method and try to approximate it, as far as possible, through a linear function of the control or state variables of the mathematical model. Such variables need not concern only the balance sheet, but may also be related to the income statement or other financial statements.

Next, we need to define the auxiliary variables to store the different measures of regulatory capital. The most common are Tier 1 Capital, Tier 2 Capital, and Total Regulatory Capital.

Tier 1 capital mostly consists of shareholders' equity, retained earnings, and other disclosed reserves, while Tier 2 capital, also known as supplementary capital, is made up of undisclosed reserves, revaluation reserves, general provisions, hybrid instruments, and subordinated term debt. Finally, the total regulatory capital is the sum of Tier 1 and Tier 2 capitals.

In Code Snippet 7.10 we illustrate the calculation of regulatory capital measures. In the case of Tier 1 Capital, we consider share capital and retained earnings in the calculation. As for Tier 2 capital, we consider hybrid instruments and subordinated term debt, further assuming that they are separated into their own balance sheet paths.

**Code Snippet 7.10:** Regulatory Capital Variables.

```

tier1_ids = ids(
    union(
        get_positions_by_balance_sheet_path(""),
        get_positions_by_balance_sheet_path("")
    )
)

tier2_ids = ids(
    union(
        get_positions_by_balance_sheet_path(""),
        get_positions_by_balance_sheet_path("")
    )
)

@constraint(
    sp,
    Tier1Capital ==
    sum(BookValue[a,h].out
        for a in tier1_ids, h in get_all_stages())
)

@constraint(
    sp,
    Tier2Capital ==
    sum(BookValue[a,h].out
        for a in tier2_ids, h in get_all_stages())
)

@constraint(
    sp,
    TotalRegulatoryCapital ==
        Tier1Capital + Tier2Capital
)
```

Finally, having the total RWA and the different measures of capital, we can then equip the mathematical model with the regulatory limits for the CARs. In the example that follows, we create two limits, one for Tier 1 Capital and the other for Total Regulatory Capital, requiring that these be greater than or equal to 6% and 8%.

**Code Snippet 7.11:** Capital Adequacy Ratio Limits.

```

@constraint(
    sp, Tier1Capital >= 0.06 * TotalRWA
)

@constraint(
    sp, TotalRegulatoryCapital >= 0.08 * TotalRWA
)
```

### 7.1.11 Economic Capital

Economic capital is a measure of capital adequacy that is based on a probabilistic assessment of potential future losses. It is expressed as the difference between some given percentile of a loss distribution and the expected loss, and is sometimes referred to as "unexpected loss at the confidence level." It is this possibility for unexpected losses to occur that necessitates the holding of capital protection.

The higher the confidence level selected, the lower the probability of insolvency. Many banks using economic capital models selecte a confidence level targeting a given credit rating as a way of guaranteeing a certain level of security but also of implicitly transmitting information to the market about its financial soundness. The development and implementation of a well-functioning economic capital model is therefore essential for efficient bank management.

To represent the calculation of economic capital in a balance sheet optimization model, we must be able to represent basically two major quantities: expected losses and unexpected losses for different types of risk. Next, we must be able to aggregate these measures to form the total expected loss and the total unexpected loss to finally arrive at the calculation of the total economic capital necessary for the bank to be able to operate with the desired level of confidence.

Typically, expected losses and unexpected losses are calculated separately for different types of risks, and then aggregated taking into account the appropriate diversification effects. Expected losses represent a cost of doing business and are generally expected to be absorbed by operating income. In statistical terms, its calculation corresponds precisely to the calculation of the estimated average loss for a certain risk. Taking into account the linearity of the expectation, the total expected loss can be obtained by the simple sum of the expected losses of the individual risks.

In Code Snippet 7.12 we illustrate a simplified calculation of the expected loss for credit, market, and operational risks. For credit risk, we calculate the expected loss by multiplying the loan balance by its probability of default (PD) and by its LGD (Loss Given Default), parameters that we assume can be retrieved by the functions `get_loan_pd(pos)` and `get_loan_lgd(pos)`.

As for the market risk, we assume that the expected loss of each financial position can be obtained by a helper function called `get_market_el(pos)`. For assets for which we have no expectations of loss or gain, we can assume an expected loss of zero, for example. As for risk-free fixed income assets, we can assume an expected "gain" rather than a loss. But there may also be situations where it is prudent to attribute an expected loss if this is not already reflected in the market value of the position.

Finally, let's model the expected loss relative to operational risk in a very synthetic way, using a single multiplier in relation to total assets. To simplify the representation, let's hardcode such a multiplier at 0.1%. Of course, this formulation could be segmented by lines of business or in any other way that makes sense. Anyway, the anatomy of the constraint would be the same in the code presented in Code Snippet 7.12.

**Code Snippet 7.12:** Expected Losses Variables.

```

loans_ids = ids(get_positions_by_balance_sheet_path("ASSETS/LOANS"))
investments_ids = ids(get_positions_by_balance_sheet_path("ASSETS/INVESTMENTS"))
assets_ids = ids(get_positions_by_balance_sheet_path("ASSETS"))

@constraint(
    sp, CreditRiskExpectedLoss == sum(
        get_loan_pd(a) * get_loan_lgd(a) *
        BookValue[a,h].out
        for a in loans_ids, h in get_all_stages()
    )
)

@constraint(
    sp, MarketRiskExpectedLoss == sum(
        get_market_el(a) *
        BookValue[a,h].out
        for a in investments_ids, h in get_all_stages()
    )
)

@constraint(
    sp, OperationalRiskExpectedLoss ==
    0.001 *
    sum(
        BookValue[a,h].out
        for a in assets_ids, h in get_all_stages()
    )
)

@constraint(
    sp, TotalExpectedLoss ==
        CreditRiskExpectedLoss +
        MarketRiskExpectedLoss +
        OperationalRiskExpectedLoss
)
```

In turn, unexpected losses are related to some measure of risk such as VaR or CVaR. As the calculation of such measures is non-linear, the same considerations made for risk weighted assets calculations apply here. It is necessary to look for some representation that fits the chosen model type (for example, linear programming) and is at the same time safe, without unduly underestimating or overestimating the risks.

In the example in Code Snippet 7.13, we will not go into the merits of how such approximations can be made, as these are highly problem dependent. Let's assume that the auxiliary variables to store the VaR of the different types of risks have been created and defined through an appropriate constraint.

Regarding the aggregation of measures of different types of risk, the same considerations are valid. It is necessary to previously evaluate and define a way to represent the diversification effects appropriately in the chosen model type. We will use a very simple approach, where the diversification effect is represented by a positive number less than one, which will be used to multiply the simple sum of the different risks. Although quite simple, this approximation can already capture part of the diversification effect in a scenario where the relative contribution of risks is relatively stable.

**Code Snippet 7.13:** Value At Risk Variables.

```

@constraint(sp, CreditRiskVaR == ...)
@constraint(sp, MarketRiskVaR == ...)
@constraint(sp, OperationalRiskVaR == ...)

df = get_diversification_factor()

@constraint(sp, TotalVaR == df * (
        CreditRiskVaR +
        MarketRiskVaR +
        OperationalRiskVaR
    )
)
```

With the individual and total VaR measures in hand, the first thing we can do is create constraints to represent the internal risk limits, which is illustrated in Code Snippet 7.14. Such restrictions are fundamental to guarantee that the optimal solution will respect the individual and aggregated risk budgets.

**Code Snippet 7.14:** Value At Risk Limits.

```

@constraint(sp, TotalVaR <=
    get_total_var_limit())

@constraint(sp, CreditRiskVaR <= get_credit_var_limit())
@constraint(sp, MarketRiskVaR <= get_market_var_limit())
@constraint(sp, OperationalRiskVaR <= get_operational_var_limit())
```

Finally, we can define the total economic capital variable based on the difference between the total VaR and the total expected loss. In addition, we can create a constraint requiring that the total economic capital be greater than a capital measure defined by the institution. In this way, we have just equipped the model with the ability to seek solutions that respect the default probability target implicitly defined when choosing the confidence level for calculating the economic capital. This is illustrated in Code Snippet 7.15, where we use the entire equity balance as a cushion to support unexpected losses expressed by total economic capital.

**Code Snippet 7.15:** Total Economic Capital.

```

equity_ids = ids(
    get_positions_by_balance_sheet_path("EQUITY/")
)

@constraint(sp, TotalEconomicCapital ==
    TotalVaR - TotalExpectedLoss
)

@constraint(sp,
    sum(
        BookValue[a,h].out
        for a in equity_ids, h in get_all_stages()
    )
    >= TotalEconomicCapital
)
```

### 7.1.12 Open Currency Positions

For a bank to operate globally in an efficient manner, it is essential to explore investment and funding opportunities in different currencies. However, the risks associated with this type of strategy are high, especially for banks operating in highly volatile markets. Therefore, it is essential that the bank adopts policies and limits to control its open currency positions. To represent this type of constraint in the mathematical model, we need to know the foreign currencies exposure of each of the contracts in each of the decision nodes. Given the market scenario associated with each node, such information is static and can be computed and stored as one of the model coefficients.

In the examples that follow, we assume that such information can be retrieved by the helper function `get_fx_exposure(a, currency)`. Additionally, to make the implementation more readable, we will create auxiliary variables called `OpenCurrencyPosition`, which will be indexed by currency. To create such variables, we assume the existence of a helper function called `get_all_currencies()` that returns the name of all currencies. Code Snippet 7.16 shows how to create the variables and how to set their values.

**Code Snippet 7.16:** Open Currency Position Variables.

```

positions_ids = ids(get_all_positions())

@variable(OpenCurrencyPosition[c in get_all_currencies()])

for c in get_all_currencies()
    @constraint(sp, OpenCurrencyPosition[c] ==
        sum(
            get_fx_exposure(a, c) * Quantity[a,h].out
            for a in positions_ids, h in get_all_stages()
        )
    )
end
```

Typically, limits are set to absolute values as shown in the code snippet below. In Code Snippet 7.17, constraints are created for each currency requiring the sum of exposures in each currency to be less than a limit in module. It is important to note that the main loop of this block of constraints is around the list of currencies they are set for.

**Code Snippet 7.17:** Open Currency Position Limits.

```

for c in get_all_currencies()
    @constraint(sp, OpenCurrencyPosition[c] >=
        - get_fx_limit(c)
    )
    @constraint(sp, OpenCurrencyPosition[c] <=
        get_fx_limit(c)
    )
end
```

### 7.1.13 Interest Rate Risk Limits

According to the Basel Committee, interest rate risk in the banking book can be defined as the current or prospective risk to a bank's capital and to its earnings, arising from the impact of adverse movements in interest rates on its banking book, including assets, liabilities, and off-balance sheet items. To be properly managed, it is desirable that this risk be monitored from an economic and accounting perspective, since when interest rates change, the present value and timing of future cash flows change, which in turn changes the underlying value of banking book positions and hence its economic value (EVE). On the other hand, changes in interest rates also affect the bank's earnings by altering interest rate-sensitive income and expenses, affecting its net interest income (NII). As a result, regulators in major jurisdictions require that interest rate risk be managed and limited in terms of metrics such as ΔNII and ΔEVE, which measure, respectively, the sensitivity of earnings and market value of bank positions to interest rate fluctuations.

In order to represent this type of constraint, the first thing we need to do is have model coefficients with the values of such metrics for each of the positions in the banking book. More specifically, as such risk metrics are computed by scenarios, then the coefficients need to have this dimension. In the case of ΔNII, for example, we need two scenarios: a parallel up and a parallel down. As for ΔEVE, at least in the standardized calculation approach, in addition to the parallel shock scenarios we have four more scenarios: steepener, flattener, short rate up, short rate down. In addition to the scenario dimension, the calculation of these metrics is segmented according to the position's currency.

To implement this segmentation let's assume a few things. First, let's assume the existence of two helper functions called `get_delta_nii_scenario_names()` and `get_delta_eve_scenario_names()`, which return the list of ΔNII and ΔEVE calculation scenarios, respectively. Next, let's assume the existence of a function called `get_irrbb_currencies()`, which tells us the list of currencies for which the bank's interest rate risk metrics should be calculated. Finally, let's assume the existence of two more functions called `get_delta_nii(pos, currency, nii_scenario_name)` and `get_delta_eve(pos, currency, eve_scenario_name)` that give us the value of ΔNII and ΔEVE of a given position, currency, and calculation scenario.

Now, our task is to accumulate the individual interest rate risk in auxiliary variables indexed to the scenario name and currency. Code Snippet 7.18 shows how to do this. We highlight the suffix `SCENARIO_CURRENCY` used in the creation of these first variables related to IRRBB. As we carry out the aggregations, we will use similar variables but without the suffix.

**Code Snippet 7.18:** IRRBB Variables.

```

@variable(sp, dNII_SCENARIO_CURRENCY[
    s in get_delta_nii_scenario_names(),
    c in get_irrbb_currencies()
])

for s in get_delta_nii_scenario_names(), c in get_irrbb_currencies()
    @constraint(sp, dNII_SCENARIO_CURRENCY[s, c] == sum(
        get_delta_nii(pos, c, s) * Quantity[pos.id,h].out
        for pos in irrbb_positions, h in get_all_stages()
    ))
end

@variable(sp, dEVE_SCENARIO_CURRENCY[
    s in get_delta_nii_scenario_names(),
    c in get_irrbb_currencies()
])

for s in get_delta_eve_scenario_names(), c in get_irrbb_currencies()
    @constraint(sp, dEVE_SCENARIO_CURRENCY[s, c] == sum(
        get_delta_eve(pos, c, s) * Quantity[pos.id,h].out
        for pos in irrbb_positions, h in get_all_stages()
    ))
end
```

Next, we need to aggregate the results at the scenario level. That is, we need to drop the currency dimension. If regulation or internal methodologies allow risk netting between different currencies, a simple summation would do the job. If netting were not allowed, then additional modeling tricks may be required. In the most conservative rule of aggregation of results between currencies, no type of diversification is allowed, and currencies in which the interest rate shock implies gains instead of losses must be discarded in the aggregation.

To implement this, we need the auxiliary variable we suffix with CAPPED to express the minimum between the calculated value and zero. To fix the value of these variables, we use the constraints shown in Code Snippet 7.19.

**Code Snippet 7.19:** IRRBB Variables Aggregation.

```

# Variables for dNII and dEVE by scenario

@variable(sp, dNII[s for s in get_delta_nii_scenario_names()]
@variable(sp, dEVE[s for s in get_delta_eve_scenario_names()]

# Capping dNII and dEVE before aggregation

@variable(sp, dNII_SCENARIO_CURRENCY_CAPPED[
    s in get_delta_nii_scenario_names(),
    c in get_irrbb_currencies()
] <= 0.0)

for s in get_delta_nii_scenario_names(), c in get_irrbb_currencies()
    @constraint(sp, dNII_SCENARIO_CURRENCY_CAPPED[s,c] <= dNII_SCENARIO_CURRENCY[s,c])
end

@variable(sp, dEVE_SCENARIO_CURRENCY_CAPPED[
    s in get_delta_EVE_scenario_names(),
    c in get_irrbb_currencies()
] <= 0.0)

for s in get_delta_eve_scenario_names(), c in get_irrbb_currencies()
    @constraint(sp, dEVE_SCENARIO_CURRENCY_CAPPED[s,c] <= dEVE_SCENARIO_CURRENCY[s,c])
end

# dNII and dEVE aggregation by scenario

for s in get_delta_nii_scenario_names()
    @constraint(sp, dNII[s] == sum(
        dNII_SCENARIO_CURRENCY_CAPPED[s,c]
        for c in get_irrbb_currencies()
    ))
end

for s in get_delta_eve_scenario_names()
    @constraint(sp, dEVE[s] == sum(
        dEVE_SCENARIO_CURRENCY_CAPPED[s,c]
```

```
            for c in get_irrbb_currencies()
        ))
    end
```

In order for the code in Code Snippet 7.19 to work correctly, now we just need to maximize the CAPPED suffix variables in the objective function. In this way, if ΔNII or ΔEVE is positive for any scenario/currency pair, that is, it implies gains, these will be disregarded in the aggregation with the results of the other currencies within that scenario. This can be done by adding the term presented in Code Snippet 7.20.

**Code Snippet 7.20:** IRRBB Aggregation - Objective function Terms.

```

@stageobjective(sp,
    # ...
    # ...
    # ...
    W * (
        sum(dNII_SCENARIO_CURRENCY_CAPPED[s,c]
            for s in get_delta_nii_scenario_names(),
            c in get_irrbb_currencies()
        )
        + sum(dEVE_SCENARIO_CURRENCY_CAPPED[s,c]
            for s in get_delta_eve_scenario_names(),
            c in get_irrbb_currencies()
        )
    )
)
```

Finally, we can represent thresholds for Delta NII and Delta EVE, basically requiring that the value of these metrics is lower than stipulated in each of the scenarios, which therefore corresponds to a final aggregation step that requires Delta NII or Delta EVE to be taken as the worst case among the calculation scenarios. Code Snippet 7.21 shows how to do it, assuming we have the `get_delta_nii_limit()` and `get_delta_eve_limit()` helper functions, which give us the limits for the metrics in absolute values. As the variables `dNII[s]` and `dEVE[s]` will be negative by construction, in the constraint that represents the limits we need to adjust the signs for a correct comparison with the limits as returned by the helper functions.

**Code Snippet 7.21:** IRRBB Limits.

```

for s in get_delta_nii_scenario_names()
    @constraint(sp, -dNII[s] <= get_delta_nii_limit())
end

for s in get_delta_nii_scenario_names()
    @constraint(sp, -dEVE[s] <= get_delta_eve_limit())
end
```

### 7.1.14 Risk Targeting

So far, most of the constraints we have presented were expressed in terms of mathematical inequalities. Through them, we have guarantees that the optimal solution will respect, for example, the limits of risk, leverage, bank growth, or any other limit. However, we know that if our linear programming model have a feasible solution, this solution will invariably reside in one of the corners of the feasible region. In fact, navigating the corners of the feasible region in search of the optimal solution is exactly what the simplex method does.

Therefore, if the risk limits are very tight, eventually the optimal solution found by the mathematical solver will imply a total consumption of the risk limits. Although it is a feasible solution from a mathematical point of view, it is usually not desirable to operate permanently with full consumption of the available limits, being always on the verge of extrapolation. In practice, the limits are combined with consumption targets, in order to maintain a certain safety cushion against fluctuations in the risk factors involved.

To represent these consumption targets, we need to use equality constraints in which on the right side we have the consumption target accompanied by two slack variables, one to represent fluctuations above the target and the other to represent fluctuations below the target. Obviously, the utilization of such slack variables must be discouraged by penalizing it in the objective function. In an ideal situation, slack variables will not be used and the target will be perfectly achieved. In other cases, slack variables will be used, and we can inspect for deviations when analyzing the optimal solution.

Code Snippet 7.22 illustrates how we can specify a typical leverage target. We require the ratio between liabilities and equity to be around 2 using a equality and the positive slack variables `SlackLeverageTargetPos` and `SlackLeverageTargetNeg`, that should be minimized in the objective function. Combined with this constraint, we can have hard inferior and superior constraints on the leverage ratio, which will also limit the values of the leverage target slack variables.

**Code Snippet 7.22:** Risk Targeting Constraint.

```

liabilities_ids = ids(get_positions_by_balance_sheet_path("LIABILITIES"))
equity_ids = ids(get_positions_by_balance_sheet_path("EQUITY"))

@constraint(
    sp,
    sum(BookValue[a,h].out for a in liabilities_ids, h in get_all_stages()) ==
    2.0 * sum(BookValue[a,h].out for a in equity_ids, h in get_all_stages())
    + SlackLeverageTargetPos - SlackLeverageTargetNeg
)
```

This class of constraint on consumption targets can also be seen as a way of inducing the model to take directional positions for certain risks, especially in deterministic setups.

For stochastic formulations of the model, however, we do not recommend this type of approach. Ideally, market views should be embedded in the model formulation in the form of scenarios, not decisions. In other words, if the modeler believes that there is a 70% chance of interest rates rising, the underlying scenario graph should represent such a view. Combined with the other restrictions and, in particular, with the objective function, this approach tends to produce more coherent strategies than the mere imputation of directional bets through targets or locking of decision variables. We hope to clarify these reflections later in the book, when we come to work with an uncertain representation of the future.

### 7.1.15 Operational Losses

Operational risk can be defined as the possibility of losses resulting from failure, deficiency or inadequacy of internal processes, people and systems, or from external events. This definition includes legal risk, which is the risk associated with inadequacy or deficiency in contracts signed by the institution, as well as sanctions due to non-compliance with laws and compensation for damages to third parties arising from the activities carried out by the institution.

Despite the breadth of the concept and scope of this type of risk, to model the effect of operating losses we need to know whether the losses will have a cash effect or just an accounting effect, increasing, for example, the level of provisions for losses in this category.

In the first case, the model constraints should represent the cash outflow to represent, for example, a theft, or the decrease of the inflows due a failure in the interest collection process. Basically, we need to ensure that the cash outflows arising from the financial operating loss will be accumulated in the `NonContractCashFlows` variable, defined in Code Snippet 6.25.

When operational losses have no immediate cash effects, the constraints can be used to increase the provisioned balance by buying the appropriate pseudo-contract. An example of an operational event whose initial effects are only accounting is the increase in the probability of loss in a legal proceeding, which will usually be accounted for as an operational loss by increasing the provisioned balance.

It is worth noting that these formulations are also valid to represent recoveries instead of losses. In the case of recoveries with immediate cash effects, it is enough to alternate the cash flow sign, while in the case of strictly accounting recoveries, it is enough to sell the same pseudo-contracts instead of buying them.

### 7.1.16 Allowances for Credit Losses

The allowance for credit losses is a reserve for the estimated amount of loans that the bank will not collect from its borrowers. When a bank issues loans, there is a chance that some portion of the receivable will not be collected. Generally accepted accounting principles require the bank to set up an allowance for credit losses, containing an estimate of how much this bad debt may be. The main motivation for the existence of this requirement is that, without it, it is almost certain that a lender will overstate the amount of its receivable that will actually be collected.

Therefore, in order to project a bank's balance sheet, it is essential to specify how the account intended to accumulate allowances for credit losses will evolve over time. In our formulation, this counter account corresponds to the balance sheet line named "ASSETS/LOANS/ALLOWANCES FOR CREDIT LOSSES," which is associated with a pseudo-contract that can be bought or sold to increase or decrease the estimate of credit losses, respectively. It is worth noting that such purchases and sales have an accounting effect, but not a cash effect.

To represent the dynamics of this balance sheet row, it is necessary to equip the model with assumptions that indicate the level of provisioning that will be generated by the credit portfolios. Such assumptions can be informed in the form of credit quality scenarios in aggregate, or segmented by sectors, by rating or by another rule that makes sense for the bank.

In the code snippets below, we illustrate two possible approaches. In the first one, we assume that the bank's aggregate credit quality of loans portfolio will be 5%, that is, for each dollar we have invested in loans, we must provision five cents. In Code Snippet 7.23 we code this constraint basically using the `BookValue`, letting the solver decides if it's necessary to buy or sell the pseudo-contract associated with the balance sheet path related to credit allowances.

It's important to notice that since the allowances account is under the loans account in the example, the function `get_positions_by_balance_sheet_path("ASSETS/LOANS")` will also return the allowances pseudo-contracts. Hence, if we sum book values over this set of positions, we will obtain the a balance net from provisions. However our business assumption is expressed in terms of the gross loan portfolio balance. To obtain it, we need the function `setdiff` to remove the positions within `"ASSETS/LOANS"` that actually relate to provisions.

**Code Snippet 7.23:** Aggregate Allowances For Credit Losses Constraint.

```

loans_ids = ids(
    get_positions_by_balance_sheet_path("ASSETS/LOANS")
)

allowances_ids = ids(
    get_positions_by_balance_sheet_path(
        "ASSETS/LOANS/ALLOWANCES FOR CREDIT LOSSES"
```

```
    )
)

@constraint(
    sp,
    sum(BookValue[a,h].out for a in allowances_ids, h in get_all_stages()) ==
    0.05 * sum(BookValue[a,h].in
            for a in setdiff(loans_ids, allowances_ids), h in get_all_
                stages())
)
```

In the second approach, allowances are calculated by adding the individual contributions of each position booked in the loans' portfolio. In this case, the optimal decision may take into account the accounting tradeoffs between investing in operations of different credit qualities, something that is not possible in the aggregated approach. As shown in Code Snippet 7.24, the constraint anatomy is almost the same, but now we assume the existence of a helper function named `get_allowance_rate` that must receive at least the loan ID.

**Code Snippet 7.24:** Segmented Allowances For Credit Losses Constraint.

```

loans_ids = ids(
    get_positions_by_balance_sheet_path("ASSETS/LOANS")
)

allowances_ids = ids(
    get_positions_by_balance_sheet_path(
        "ASSETS/LOANS/ALLOWANCES FOR CREDIT LOSSES"
    )
)

@constraint(
    sp,
    sum(BookValue[a,h].out for a in allowances_ids, h in get_all_stages()) ==
    sum(get_allowance_rate(a) * BookValue[a,h].in
        for a in setdiff(loans_ids, allowances_ids), h in get_all_stages()
    )
)
```

### 7.1.17 Back-to-Back Hedging

By adding constraints to represent foreign exchange or interest rate risk limits, for example, we induce the model to eventually enter derivative positions when necessary. We do not specify when it should do this, nor the exact characteristics of derivatives. We leave it up to the model to choose the derivatives contracts to execute the hedging strategy in order to meet risk limits or targets.

However, in some situations, we may not be interested in optimizing, but rather executing a simpler and pre-approved strategy, such as a back-to-back hedging strategy. Under such a hedging policy, for instance, every time the bank issues a debt issue in a foreign currency, it also enters into a cross-currency swap operation with the same payment schedule, neutralizing all foreign exchange risks.

Paradoxically, although it is a simpler and non-optimized hedging policy, specifying it mathematically is more complex. To be able to represent it, for each potential new debt in foreign currency, there must be a swap with the same payment schedule. This is the simple part, and it can be solved in the data preparation phase, in which we will need, in addition to creating the new debt and new swap profiles, to tag them indicating that they form a pair.

In the model layer, we need to ensure that if the model chooses to raise funds using a particular debt instrument, it must enter the corresponding swap. This type of conditional rule implies the use of a binary variable that must be fed with the value 1 if the debt is issued. Subsequently, this flag can be used to determine whether or not we need to create a new constraint by setting the need for the model to also enter the swap identified with the same tag.

### 7.1.18 Freezing Short-Term Decisions

The most fundamental output of an optimization model is the optimal decisions to be made by its user. For a multistage balance sheet optimization model, this is still true. In particular this is true for the decisions prescribed for the present, since the decisions prescribed for the future stages are only optimal if they are conditioned to a state of nature that we do not know will take place.

However, in some model use cases we may be forced to disable the possibility of making new decisions at the root node. The most prominent of these cases are the regulatory stress tests. In such exercises, regulators are usually concerned with the effects of unexpected shocks under the premise that banks will not have time to rebalance their positions. In such situations, we need to add constraints to zero `Buy` and `Sell` decisions variables at the root node, as shown in Code Snippet 7.25.

**Code Snippet 7.25:** Freezing Short-Term Decisions Constraint.

```

all_positions_ids = ids(get_all_positions())

if t == 1
    for a in ids(get_all_positions()), h in get_all_stages()
        @constraint(sp, Buy[a,h] == 0.0)
        @constraint(sp, Sell[a,h] == 0.0)
    end
end
```

If the model step is quarterly, for example, then the initial balance sheet will suffer the full consequences of market shocks during such holding period. However, in the following steps the model will again be free to rebalance and recompose their financial positions, in particular their hedging positions.

In fact, holding periods are a recurring point of discussion between regulators and regulated. From our point of view, it makes sense to assume that the liquidity of the derivatives and debt markets will decline dramatically, but it seems too conservative to assume that it will completely evaporate.

Therefore, it may make sense for regulatory and internal stress testing exercises to consider a decrease in market liquidity and an increase in funding costs, or both, as this seems to better represent the market conditions to which the bank will be subject. In this way, each bank and, in our case, our mathematical model will be able to decide considering the tradeoffs associated with each type of decision, however adverse the market condition may be.

### 7.1.19 Financial Ratios

Financial ratios are quantitative measures used to assess the financial performance of a company. They are calculated by dividing one financial metric by another and are used to compare a company's performance to the industry average, to a competitor's or against itself in the past. These ratios are used to measure various aspects of a company's operations, such as profitability, liquidity, solvency, and efficiency.

They are essential in bank management because they provide an objective way to measure the performance of the bank, allowing for more informed decision-making, in addition to helping the bank identify areas of improvement. Having limits or targets for financial ratios is therefore an essential practice.

Some of the most recurrent financial ratios in bank management are ROA (return on assets), ROE (return on equity) and NIM (Net Interest Margin), in addition to the so-called CARs (Capital Adequacy Ratios), defined by regulators. However, from our point of view, the financial ratio that best encodes the banking optimization problem is the RAROC (risk-adjusted return on capital) (Guill, 2016).

It is a financial ratio that is used to measure the profitability of a bank's investments relative to the amount of economic capital it has invested. It is calculated by dividing the return of a bank's investments by its economic capital. The higher the RAROC, the more profitable the investments are relative to the amount of economic capital invested.

RAROC is superior to ROA (return on assets) and ROE (return on equity), for instance, in the context of bank management because it takes into account the risk associated with the investments. ROA and ROE measure the profitability of investments, but do not consider the risk of the investments. By incorporating the risk into the equation, RAROC provides a more accurate measure of profitability and a guide to a more optimal capital allocation. In addition, the use of risk-adjusted performance measures such as the RAROC can also help to avoid excessive risk-taking when also used to align employee incentives and compensation. It is no coincidence that financial management measures guided by a risk-adjusted return logic are one of the principles for sound compensation practices, according to the Financial Stability Board (FSB) (Board, 2009).

In the context of balance sheet optimization, constraints on RAROC or on other similar risk-adjusted return measures are of fundamental importance, as they will ensure that each new unit of risk incurred in taking new positions will require a change in the levels of capital appropriate to sustain the economic capital reserve that will ultimately guarantee the bank a level of protection against default according to its appetite.

A possible formulation of this type of constraint can be seen in Code Snippet 7.26, in which we use the auxiliary decision variables that express the bank's total economic capital and the decision variables that express the bank return in the period. Although quite synthetic, such a constraint will require something quite challenging since, combined, numerator and denominator of a RAROC calculation contain a summary of returns and risks of the entire bank's balance sheet, including all sorts of financial events and assumptions that are being taken into consideration. The trick to add financial ratio constraints into a linear model is to transform a non-linear ratio inequality like Equation 7.3 into a linear inequality like Equation 7.4 by multiplying both sides with the denominator variable.[1]

$$\text{RAROC} = \frac{\text{Return}}{\text{Capital}} \geq \text{Limit} \tag{7.3}$$

$$\text{Return} \geq \text{Limit} \times \text{Capital} \tag{7.4}$$

**Code Snippet 7.26:** Financial Ratios Constraints.

```
# RAROC
@constraint(
    sp,
    IncomeStatement["Net Income"] >= HURDLE_RATE * TotalVaR
)
```

It is worth noting that the formulation presented is just one of the many possible variants for calculating the RAROC. An interesting survey on the different ways of calculating RAROC accompanied by a discussion of whether the application of different methods for calculation generate significantly different results can be found in Lima et al. (2014).

### 7.1.20 Capitalizations

In some situations, it may be necessary to represent cash inflows from future capitalizations carried out by bank owners or from new public share offerings. This can be done by using equality constraints to fix the inflows associated with the purchase of the pseudo-contracts associated with the capital line of our reference balance sheet.

1 Provided that the denominator is strictly positive.

The payment schedules for such contracts will generate an instantaneous cash inflow at the time of purchase only, and will not generate any pre-defined repayment obligation. If the purchase of such pseudo-contracts is left free, the model can indefinitely inject money, which is clearly not realistic. Therefore, the purchase of such pseudo-contracts associated with capitalizations must be carefully controlled, directly or indirectly. This can be done through a strict capitalization schedule that should indicate the timing and volume of capitalizations.

Cash injections via capitalizations can also be indirectly controlled through the model constraints, such as liquidity and leverage targets, return on equity or risk-adjusted return targets, limits on bank growth rates, demand for credit, etc. The second approach seems more conceptually appropriate, but depends on a fairly comprehensive and correct specification of the listed constraints. Otherwise, the solver may be induced to misuse capitalizations. So, at least for a first round of implementation, we suggest starting by fixing capitalizations.

If you want to be a little bolder, you can allow capitalizations to a certain value using a inequality constraint. In this case, it is important to observe whether in the optimal solution this constraint is active. In other words, we must verify if the limit we imposed for capitalization is being completely consumed in a systematic way. This may indicate problems in the formulation of the aforementioned constraints.

Capitalizations can also be seen as an escape valve that can be activated as a last resort to solve problems in meeting some of the model's constraints. In other words, capitalizations can be seen as slack variables, whose use should be discouraged through the objective function. In the code snippets below, we show how to zero capitalizations. This constraint can easily be modified by toggling between equality and inequality and modifying the value on the right-hand side of the equation.

**Code Snippet 7.27:** Capitalization Costraints.

```

capital_ids = ids(get_positions_by_balance_sheet_path(
    "EQUITY/CAPITAL PAR VALUE"
))

@constraint(sp,
    sum(BuyCashFlow[a,h] for a in capital_ids, h in get_all_stages())
== 0)
```

## 7.2 Slack Variables

In the last section, we described a large number of mathematical constraints that we would like the bank to be able to comply with. However, in the real world it is not always necessary or possible to meet them all the time and in whatever state of the economy.

In the event of a sudden surge in the stock market, the desired balance sheet structure could be disrupted, resulting in exposure to this asset class beyond internal limits.

Conversely, if there were a steep drop in both the equity and credit markets, the bank could suffer heavy losses, depleting its equity and failing to meet the regulatory standards of capital adequacy ratios.

It is possible that in some scenarios one or more constraints are not met, culminating in an infeasibility. To work around this problem, we need to resort to so-called slack variables. They are a special type of decision variables used to flexibilize hard constraints, ensuring that a feasible solution will be found. Strictly speaking, they do not represent decisions that can be made, and therefore are artificial decision variables.

Let's illustrate the use of slack variables using a constraint that imposes a lower limit on the capital adequacy ratio, which is presented in Code Snippet 7.28. We define the slack variable `SlackTotalCapital`, which must be non-negative. Next, we add it to the constraint by adding it to the total regulatory capital, represented by the `TotalRegulatoryCapital` variable. Throughout the model resolution process, if it is not possible to meet the specified limit, the solver will use the slack variable to increase the value of the left side of the inequality until it is possible to respect the constraint.

**Code Snippet 7.28:** Flexibilizing Constraints Using Slack Variables.

```

@constraint(
    sp, TotalRegulatoryCapital + SlackTotalCapital
    >= 0.08 * TotalRWA
)
```

By default, we would like this constraint to be met at all times and in all scenarios. However, in some cases the bank may not be able to meet such a requirement, particularly in stress scenarios. To avoid unfeasibility, we add a slack variable to the constraint, and penalize its use in the objective function using a sufficiently high cost.

Thus, in scenarios where portfolio rebalancing is not sufficient to circumvent violations of the original constraint, the slack variable will be triggered, allowing a feasible solution to be found at the cost of decreasing the objective function value.

In analyzing the optimal solution, we will see that one or more slack variables may have been triggered, which may be interpreted as a constraint violation. In our example, we can interpret the solution as a limit extrapolation. We can analyze the state of the slack variables at different stages and scenarios, and, based on counting the number of times they were triggered, we can estimate the probability of limit extrapolations over a given time horizon. In addition, we can also estimate the degree of extrapolation by analyzing the exact values of the slack variables assumed in the optimal solution.

The introduction of slack variables to flexibilize constraints and avoid unfeasibility problems must be guided by the readability of the model and interpretation of the results. In the example shown, the value of the slack variable can be understood as the additional capital requirement to comply with the limit. When making such modeling choices, we must pay attention to the magnitude of the values that can be assumed by the slack variables, since this information is very important in the definition of slack variable weights in the objective function.

## 7.3 Objective Functions

A *objective function* in mathematical programming is a function that is used to measure the performance of the solution, being defined as a function of the decision variables. The goal of optimization process is to maximize or minimize such function. The objective function can be linear, quadratic or have other nonlinear formats, depending on the type of problem. In the context of bank balance sheet optimization, the objective function will typically be associated with return and risk indicators, such as ROA, ROE, and RAROC, among other financial indicators.

However, it may also make sense for a bank to have more *strategic* objectives, such as maximizing market share or customer satisfaction. For development banks, for example, it may make sense to have objective functions associated with the positive externalities generated by investments. These non-financial objectives, however, may require additional effort to be connected to the model's decision variables, which can be a very challenging task.

In real situations, it is necessary to equip the model with multiple goals at the same time. In these cases, we need to express the relative priorities and how we are going to handle the tradeoffs between the multiple objectives. Unfortunately, there is not yet a unique or simple approach that can be prescribed regardless of the problem nature.

As we know, to solve a multi-stage problem, we typically decompose it into subproblems and each of them will have its own objective function. Such objective functions may even be similar, but they are located at different points in time. For example, each subproblem may represent the profit maximization for a given year. However, in the process of solving the complete problem, the solutions of each subproblem will be combined together. Hence, it is important to consider that *relative importance* of profits obtained at different stages. A possible approach may be to multiply the objective function of each period by a discount factor to capture the time value of money. Other weighting schemes can make sense, being a modelers' responsibility to choose the most appropriate rule for each situation and for each term of the objective function.

In a stochastic model of multiple stages, we have another degree of freedom in defining the objective function, as we need to define the risk measure that will be used in the so-called *cost-to-go* function. By choosing the chosen risk measure and its confidence level, we can communicate to the model that we have a *time-varying risk appetite*. An example can help us provide more intuition on this matter.

Consider a multistage stochastic portfolio optimization model built for a pension fund. The problem faced by this type of institutional investor is characterized by a very long time horizon, which can be divided into the pre and post retirement phases. The optimization process must ensure that throughout the whole time horizon, all the relevant constraints are met. But these constraints vary over time according to the current actuarial profile. If most participants are still in the so-called contribution phase, then perhaps there is room for a more risky investment strategy. As time goes by and the pension fund needs to start disbursing more and more money to pay retirees' salaries, a more conservative investment strategy becomes more appropriate. To represent this dynamic, in the early stages of the model we can choose, for instance, a neutral-risky strategy, that can be expressed by the use of the expected value in the cost-to-go function. As soon as more money comes out than comes in we can choose to use CVaR with a 99% confidence level, as a way of expressing greater conservatism.

In the context of multistage optimization problems, the *temporal stability* of the results can also be one of the objectives. As we mentioned, although the process of solving the multistage problem optimization goes through the decomposition of the problem into more fundamental subproblems, the results of the optimization of such subproblems will be combined at the end of the process. Perhaps the weighting schemes or applying a discount factor are not enough to stabilize the results of the different periods, so that in the optimal solution we can have periods with very high profits and others very low. This volatility may be unacceptable for the managers or shareholders.

To work around this, we can opt for *max-min* objective functions, in which we seek to maximize the worst case, pushing the result of the most challenging subproblem as high as possible, at the expense of less expressive results in the other subproblems. Another way to approach this type of challenge is to add a term to the objective function asking the model to minimize the dispersion of the objective functions of the different subproblems. In this case, however, it may be necessary to abandon the linearity of the objective function, which is not necessarily a problem as long as you have a good solver.

Finally, it is worth noting that the objective function of a realistic balance sheet optimization model still contains several other *accessory terms*, which serve only to complement the functioning of one or more constraints. In some particular situations, these may even be the only terms present in the objective function, without this necessarily representing the absence of financial objectives. An example may also help to illustrate this type of situation.

Let's consider the case in which a bank has a profitability target as its objective, wanting neither more nor less. This desire can be encoded by means of a restriction equipped with slack variables that allow the bank to operate sometimes above and sometimes below the target. However, we are interested in reaching the target, and for that we need to discourage the use of such slack variables through their minimization in the objective function. The same concerns and cautions mentioned previously also apply to this type of objective function, but it may take a little more thought to formulate suitable and meaningful discounting or weighting schemes.

Now, let's take a look in some examples of code. In Code Snippet 7.29, we illustrate how to define the objective function for a subproblem using the macro `@stageobjective`. In the example, the objective function is expressed by the total value of the retained earnings account. As such an account stores the cumulative profits up to that point in time, then in a way there is redundancy in defining this objective function for each of the subproblems, while the cumulative profit of the second period contains that of the first, that of the third contains that of the second and first period, and so on.

**Code Snippet 7.29:** Maximizing Cumulated Retained Earnings.

```

retained_earnings_ids = ids(
    get_positions_by_balance_sheet_path(
    "EQUITY/RETAINED EARNINGS"
))

@stageobjective(sp,
    sum(BookValue[a,h].out
    for a in retained_earnings_ids, h in get_all_stages()
))
```

An alternative way of expressing profit optimization would be to analyze not the accumulated profits up to the period, but only the profits earned in the period related to the subproblem being optimized. For this, instead of expressing the objective function through the state variable `BookValue` at the end of the period, we must express profit as the change in the balance of such an account between the beginning and the end of the stage. This approach is presented in Code Snippet 7.30.

**Code Snippet 7.30:** Maximizing Variation Retained Earnings.

```

@stageobjective(sp,
    sum(BookValue[a,h].out - BookValue[a,h].in
    for a in retained_earnings_ids, h in get_all_stages()))
```

Now, to consider the due time value of money, we can weight the earnings of a period by a discount factor that brings all values to the same point in time, allowing them to be compared fairly. In the example presented in Code Snippet 7.31, we illustrate this weighting scheme using a hypothetical discount rate of 1% per period.

**Code Snippet 7.31:** Maximizing Present Value Of Stage Earnings.

```

@stageobjective(sp,
    (1 + 0.01)^(1/t) *
    sum(BookValue[a,h].out - BookValue[a,h].in
    for a in retained_earnings_ids, h in get_all_stages()))
```

To implement an objective function that seeks to minimize the dispersion of earnings, some extra modeling tricks would be needed. We'll give you some tips on how to do this. To implement this objective, we could, for example, minimize the earnings' variance in each period, or minimize the standard deviation of the present value of earnings. A possible approach would be to add a term in the objective function of the subproblem relative to the last stage expressing the calculation of the variance of earnings for each period. Or, to each subproblem, add a term expressing the calculation of earnings' variance up to that point in time.

However, to do this, we would need the earnings of each of the previous periods to be available in the current subproblem, which can only be achieved if we resort to a vector of state variables. Such a vector would be initialized with zeros in the root stage and continue updating the corresponding position with the earnings of the current subproblem, keeping the previously earnings fixed and zeroing the values related to future subproblems. Finally, when expressing the earnings' variance in the objective function of the subproblem of a certain stage, we must add to the summation only the variables related earnings of current and past stages.

It may have gone unnoticed that the sense of optimization did not appear in the given code examples, even though we mentioned the terms maximization and minimization in our considerations. Such parameterization needs to be done when creating the policy graph through the named parameter `sense`, as shown in Code Snippet 7.32. At this point, the parameters named `upper_bound` or `lower_bound` must also be highlighted. These must be provided in a mutually exclusive manner according to the direction of optimization. They work as additional information that will help the SDDP algorithm to build approximations of the objective functions of each period.

**Code Snippet 7.32:** Defining Objective Sense.

```
model = SDDP.LinearPolicyGraph(
    subproblem_builder;
    stages = 3,
    sense = :Min,
    lower_bound = 0.0,
    optimizer = Clp.Optimizer,
)
```

Finally, in a stochastic model, we also need to define the risk measure, and this must be done through the named parameter `risk_measure`, of the `SDDP.train` method. Such a function has multiple signatures, and this parameter can be provided in the form of a single element, in the form of a dictionary or as an anonymous function as shown in Code Snippet 7.33.

**Code Snippet 7.33:** Defining Risk Measure For Training.

```
# single risk measure
SDDP.train(
    model,
    risk_measure = SDDP.WorstCase(),
    iteration_limit = 10
)

# dict of risk measure
SDDP.train(
    model,
    risk_measure = Dict(
        1 => SDDP.Expectation(),
        2 => SDDP.WorstCase()
    ),
    iteration_limit = 10
)

# anonymous functions to define a risk measure
```

```
SDDP.train(
    model,
    risk_measure = (node_index) -> begin
        if node_index == 1
            return SDDP.Expectation()
        else
            return SDDP.WorstCase()
        end
    end,
    iteration_limit = 10
)
```

# 8 Running the Model

In Chapters 6 and 7, we learned how to describe our balance sheet optimization model using the Julia language and the SDDP package. Such a model consists of a set of variables that express the decisions that can be taken by the bank's managers, and all the restrictions that need to be respected so that the solution can be implemented in the real world. Our next step will be to show how to run the model and obtain optimal decisions, as well as financial statements projections conditioned to them. In other words, in this chapter we will focus on solving the mathematical model we just specified. To do this, we will discuss how to train the model to obtain the so-called optimal policy, show how to simulate it, and, finally, how to iterate through the results of this simulation to produce a variety of reports. We will also discuss the importance of equipping the solution with a battery of automated sanity checks to help us assess the integrity and quality of the solution obtained.

## 8.1 Training the Policy

Now that we have built a multi-stage policy graph, we need to run SDDP training routine to iteratively approximate the cost-to-go function and obtain a decision rule for our model. This can be achieved by passing our policy graph to `SDDP.train` function, as shown in lines 10–18 of Code Snippet 8.1.

**Code Snippet 8.1:** Training a Policy.

```
1   # creating a policy graph
2   model = SDDP.LinearPolicyGraph(
3       subproblem_builder; # model builder function
4       stages = 12,
5       sense = :Min,
6       upper_bound = 0.0,
7       optimizer = Clp.Optimizer
8   )
9
10  # training a policy
11  SDDP.train(
12      model;
13      iteration_limit=10,
14      time_limit=60.0,
15      print_level=1,
16      log_file="sddp-log.txt",
17      run_numerical_stability_report=true
18  )
```

`SDDP`'s training function, besides receiving a policy graph to be trained, has a lot of optional parameters. We will go through the most important of them regarding to our current formulation of a balance sheet model problem.

The first two optional parameters allow the user to create a stopping rule for the iterative process that is carried on while training a model. `iteration_limit` is an integer

https://doi.org/10.1515/9783110664669-008

that specifies the maximum number of iterations a training process can have. Alternatively, the `time_limit` parameter is supplied as the maximum number of seconds the process should take.

The next two parameters are related to log generation during the training phase. There is a `print_level` parameter that receives an integer and sets the level of detail training logs should have. Set this parameter to zero to perform a quiet execution. Supplying two, on the other hand, would result in a fairly detailed output. There is also an option to save logs into a file, whose path is supplied as a string to the parameter `log_file`.

The last important parameter is `run_numerical_stability_report`. When set to `true`, this parameter gives us information about the ranges of coefficients involved in our problem. As we will see later, these measures are very important to identify numerical issues that can arise when solving a mathematical optimization problem.

After running the training routine, we are given an output that looks like the one in the following box. Let's break down that log and explain the most important numbers that we should focus on in order to assess the status and quality of the training of our model.

```
--------------------------------------------------------------------------------
                      SDDP.jl (c) Oscar Dowson, 2017-21

Problem
  Nodes           : 12
  State variables : 360
  Scenarios       : 1.00000e+00
  Existing cuts   : false
  Subproblem structure                      : (min, max)
    Variables                               : (1153, 1153)
    VariableRef in MOI.LessThan{Float64}    : (1, 1)
    VariableRef in MOI.GreaterThan{Float64} : (217, 217)
    AffExpr in MOI.EqualTo{Float64}         : (742, 808)
Options
  Solver          : serial mode
  Risk measure    : SDDP.Expectation()
  Sampling scheme : SDDP.InSampleMonteCarlo

Numerical stability report
  Non-zero Matrix range     [1e+00, 1e+02]
  Non-zero Objective range  [1e+00, 1e+00]
  Non-zero Bounds range     [0e+00, 0e+00]
  Non-zero RHS range        [0e+00, 0e+00]
No problems detected

 Iteration    Simulation       Bound         Time (s)    Proc. ID   # Solves
        1    2.060716e+00   8.544249e-02   1.131900e+01          1         24
```

```
         2   2.159820e+00   1.061644e+00   1.167800e+01          1         48
         3   2.153405e+00   1.125148e+00   1.174100e+01          1         72
         4   2.252210e+00   2.060716e+00   1.180300e+01          1         96
         5   2.060716e+00   2.060716e+00   1.185300e+01          1        120
         6   2.060716e+00   2.060716e+00   1.191500e+01          1        144
         7   2.060716e+00   2.060716e+00   1.200900e+01          1        168
         8   2.060716e+00   2.060716e+00   1.207100e+01          1        192
         9   2.060716e+00   2.060716e+00   1.211800e+01          1        216
        10   2.060716e+00   2.060716e+00   1.216500e+01          1        240

Terminating training
  Status         : iteration_limit
  Total time (s) : 1.216500e+01
  Total solves   : 240
  Best bound     :  2.060716e+00
  Simulation CI  :  2.099045e+00 +- 4.152231e-02
------------------------------------------------------------------------------
```

The “Problem” section show us a description of the mathematical problem that arises from our model formulation. In this example, we have a 12-step problem with 360 state variables. Because our formulation is still deterministic we have only one scenario. In “Subproblem Structure” we are shown the minimum and maximum number of variables and constraints by type considering all 12 nodes. These numbers are calculated after the creation of additional variables and constraints that are required to run the SDDP algorithm.

“Numerical Stability Report” will be analyzed further in Chapter 10, when we discuss and troubleshoot numerical issues in a balance sheet mathematical formulation.

After that, we are presented with an iteration log, which is the main piece of information in a training output. For each iteration, we have an iteration identifier, the time in seconds it took and the number of subproblems solved so far. “Proc. ID” shows us which core process was used in an iteration in the case of a parallelized run.

“Simulation” is a stochastic cost of a single forward pass simulation. “Bounds,” on the other hand, should always be improving across training iterations. A minimization problem should monotonically increase bounds over each step, while a maximization problem should always have its bounds decreased. Observing a behavior different than that is an indication of problems in the formulation of a model.

The last section gives us information about how the training ended. In this example, it ended because the algorithm reached the supplied limit of 10 iterations in a total time of 12 seconds. At the end we have a confidence interval for the quality of the policy from the simulation column.

Other possible termination statuses that can be reported at the end of the training are *infeasible* and *unbounded*. In both cases, there probably are issues with the specification of the model, and those are preventing the solver to get an optimal solution for the underlying mathematical problem. Later in Section 10.1, we discuss and troubleshoot some of these specification problems and try to address a few possible strategies and solutions for them.

## 8.2 Simulating Optimal Policy

Once we have trained our policy adequately, we can perform simulations to access model results. The first letter in SDDP means that this technique is stochastic-oriented. However, we are still using a deterministic formulation, so one simulation will be enough to get all optimal decisions and states involved in our mathematical problem. In a stochastic setup, we can run thousands of simulations to assess the execution of the policy in different probabilistic scenarios.

In Code Snippet 8.2, we use the `SDDP.simulate` function on our trained policy to obtain simulated data. The second parameter is `number_replications`, which sets the number of simulations we want to generate from our model. The third input is a vector of symbols with the names of all model variables whose values we want to track in our simulations.

**Code Snippet 8.2:** Simulating a Policy.

```
# creating a policy graph
model = SDDP.LinearPolicyGraph(
    subproblem_builder; # model builder function
    stages = 3, sense = :Min, upper_bound = 0.0,
    optimizer = Clp.Optimizer
)

# training a policy
SDDP.train(model; iteration_limit=10)

# simulating a policy
number_replications = 1
variables = [:BookValue, :IncomeStatement, :Buy, :Sell]
sim = SDDP.simulate(model, number_replications, variables)
```

The output of a simulation function is a vector, with one position for each replication carried on by SDDP. Each element of this vector is also a vector, each entry being a different time step in the linear policy graph. Each entry of this inner vector contains a dictionary with all tracked variables and a few additional variables created by SDDP.

For example, if results from `SDDP.simulate` are stored in a variable called `sim`, we will have that `sim[1][3]` retrieves all simulated variables in the third node of the first replication.

We could then ask for `keys(sim[1][3])` to get the full list of variables stored in that dictionary. They would be of three kinds: model control variables, model state variables, and SDDP variables. We must apply different strategies to get simulated values for each one of these types of variables.

For a model control variables, like `Buys`, values are stored in a `SDDP.jl`-specific data structure called `DenseAxisArray`. Because we have declared two dimensions for each buy variable in Section 6.5, we must supply a position identifier `a` and a time of acquisition `h` in order to retrieve a specific buy value from the solution.

Imagine we have a position with the ID "Loan1" and we want to know how many units from that contract were bought at the third step of our model. Then, we need to ask for `sim[1][3][:Buy]["Loan1", 3]` in order to retrieve the desired quantity.

To access values from a model state variable, like `BookValues`, we would need to resort to a similar strategy. In this case, for each variable there is an incoming and an outgoing state, both being stored in the dictionary entry related to that variable. The entry `sim[1][3][:BookValue]` would also be a `DenseAxisArray`, but the specific variable `sim[1][3][:BookValue]["Loan1", 3]` would return an object of type `SDDP.State`.

These types of objects contain two fields: `in` and `out` with, respectively, the incoming and outgoing states calculated for that variable. So, in Code Snippet 8.3, we retrieve the two book value states from "Loans 1" at the third stage of the simulation. Both lines 4 and 7 will return the simulated results as floating point numbers.

**Code Snippet 8.3:** Example of Retrieving Values from State Variable.

```
1    sim = SDDP.simulate(model, 1, [:BookValue]) # BookValue => state variable
2
3    # incoming book value at node 3
4    sim[1][3][:BookValue]["Loan1", 3].in
5
6    # outgoing book value at node 3
7    sim[1][3][:BookValue]["Loan1", 3].out
```

Lastly, there a few entries in the simulation dictionary with specific SDDP data stored in special keys. `:node_index` is the index of the sampled node, `:noise_term` refers to the noise used in stochastic formulations. `:stage_objective` and `:bellman_term` are related to the objective function evaluated at that node.

## 8.3 Post-Run Routines

After running a model simulation and getting a results dictionary, it is a good practice to conduct a series of consistency checks before proceeding with the usage of those results to create management reports. Most of these checks can be implemented programatically as to speed up and error-proof the process of validating model results.

The first validation one should do is to check if the model had to resort to use *slack variables* in order to reach a feasible solution. By the term use we mean that the model produced a solution with non-zero values for slack variables. Of course, some slacks are intended to be used regularly and some are not. Slack variables related to matching or targeting constraints, like cash flow match hedging or risk targeting, are intended to be used normally and their values mean nothing more than the evaluated deviations from their target measures.

On the other hand, slacks that relax hard constraints are usually created for debugging purposes. Whenever the model has to use them, the solution produced should be used for debug only and should not be considered a valid solution.

Because a production model can have dozens or even hundreds of (activated or latent) slack variables, one can write a routine to check for their usage in the current solution. If this routine detects that a debugging slack was used, the user should be at least warned that the returned solution does not comply with the constraint that contains that non-zero slack variable. The importance of the violated constraint and the size of the violation will determine if it is reasonable or not to discard at once the results that were obtained.

A second step we should take is to analyze the *quality of the solution* returned by the model. This quality assessment can take many forms, but in general we should guarantee the adequacy of things that were not directly enforced as constraints but are expected to be reasonably derived from the current setup of the model.

Imagine that we have a model formulation in which the leverage ratio is not being constrained to an interval, or fixed to a target. Even so, we can calculate leverage ratios for each step to check if leverage projections are reasonable, i. e., within a range that is coherent with ratios that are expected in real world.

Other metrics that can be checked are the volume of trades executed by the model, to make sure that they are in line with liquidity and operational constraints encountered in each market by the institution, or if the general growth of balance sheet is far from institution's strategical goals. We should also look closer at income statement projections for unexpected behavior in profits or losses for each step, especially when profits are being maximized in our formulation. Objective function values should also be analyzed at least in terms of sign and order of magnitude.

This list is not, of course, intended to exhaust all the possible quality checks you should implement in your model, as this list will always be problem-dependent and will grow along with the degree of maturity the institution has in relation to its balance sheet model. We hope that by providing these few examples, we can help in creating a starting point for your post-run quality assurance process.

After assuring that we have a valid and reasonable solution, we can proceed with all *additional calculations* of metrics that were not included in the model, but are important and useful for management. There are different reasons why we should decide for formulating the model without that metric, as important as they may be: if these metrics are not used in any constraints, or because their non-linear nature cannot fit the current formulation, or if we add instead a simplified version of the metric for performance reasons.

Anyway, the actual precise metric can and should probably be calculated after the run of the model. To do that we can make use of parts of the solution data. Imagine that we control the risk of a portfolio using linear measures, but we are also interested in non-linear assessments of risk, for example, by using a Value at Risk (VaR) measure. After we have optimal portfolios being reported by the model, we can calculate the evolution of the VaR of these portfolios in order to report those numbers to management.

Lastly, we should also record and analyze *performance statistics* for the current run. They should include not only execution time, but also resource usage throughout the whole process. They should also be accounted in totals and also for each step of the execution if necessary. The final goal should be to compare with statistics generated in previous runs to detect the creation or solution of bottlenecks in the model execution routine.

## 8.4 Results Reporting Guidelines

Once we have concluded our result validation routines, it is time to derive management reports from the available simulated data.

In this section, we will briefly discuss a few guidelines that one should have in mind when designing a reporting process for a balance sheet model.

The first and most important step is to develop as much as possible an *automated reporting* routine. The amount of data that come from a balance sheet model is often enormous. Building reports from it will be certainly a repetitive and error-prone task. On top of that, in practice you will have to re-run and regenerate reports many times before incorporating feedback from all different model stakeholders, and before getting everything right in your model specification and input data. For all those reasons, it is very important to automate everything you can in order to save precious time and give agility to the process of generating balance sheet projections.

After your main reports are built successfully, you should also write *automated tests* to check the consistency of your reports. Even if you have already checked the solution dictionary, you should check reports to see if there are any errors in their assembly algorithms. It is important to check each report separately, but also the consistency across reports. For example, one could check if the sum of asset book values equals that of liabilities and equity for each balance sheet projection. At the same time, a leverage ratio report should consider as the total book value of liabilities and equity the same values that are reported in its correspondent balance sheet.

The third guideline in creating a reporting process is threefold: *reuse, reuse, and reuse*. Imagine that we are implementing a leverage ratio report. Instead of browsing the solution dictionary in order to calculate liabilities and equity book values, we could get these two quantities from an already assembled balance sheet report. In that way, we minimize the chance of incorrectly having two different numbers for the total book value of liabilities, for example. Whenever possible, the most complex reports must derive from simpler ones. This is often the best way to achieve consistency across all model reports.

The last thing you should have in mind is that you will always be *collecting feedback and adjusting* your balance sheet model. These comments, critiques, and observations will come from audit teams, validation teams, and specially from lower and upper management. Because a balance sheet model offers often a very complex and comprehensive view of an institution, you should expect leaving each result presentation with at least several incremental suggested enhancements that could be incorporated into your model. Of course the incorporation will depend on available resources and time, but the important lesson is that you should treat your model and reports as a living being in a continuous enhancement process.

The more automated the whole model process, from acquiring input data to creating final reports, the more capacity your team will have to incorporate suggestions and improve their balance sheet model efficiently.

## 8.5 Report Examples

In this section, we will provide examples of report generation code using simulated data from a balance sheet model represented by a trained SDDP policy. This list is, of course, not intended to be exhaustive, as there are myriad of ways to produce reports from a simulation dictionary populated with variables of interest in different stages and possibly under multiple scenarios.

For the first two report examples we will focus on extracting the right data from the simulated dictionaries stored in the `sim` variable, and organizing that information in a more informative and useful structure. In the last example, we will focus on creating a general report that is going to persist in disk as a comma-separated (CSV) file and will serve as raw data from which one can derive other reports through techniques such as table pivoting.

The main focus of interest when creating a balance sheet model is perhaps generating coherent and comprehensive projections of the balance sheet itself. In Code Snippet 8.4, we obtain *projected balance sheets* for each stage of the policy graph and store them in memory as dictionaries.

The problem of assembling a balance sheet from projected data is one of fetching the book value variable of every position and assigning it to the right balance sheet account (path). In line 2, we create an empty dictionary for each of the model stages. Then, in lines 3–5, we iterate over all positions and get their identifiers and balance sheet locations. Because book value variables are also indexed by the time of buying `h`, we also need to iterate over all possible buy stages. In line 7 we get the book value from the vector `sim` at time `i` of the first simulation. We are interested in projected values for each step, so we are reading the end-of-period (outgoing state) book values. Over line 8, we add the current value to the associated path at the dictionary of balances. Notice that the `get` function retrieves the current value for that path, or zero as a default value if the path is not yet registered in the dictionary. In lines 11–12 we just print the balances as a way to show that the data is correctly generated. An example of output is provided as comments in the final lines of the snippet.

**Code Snippet 8.4:** Obtaining Balance Sheet Projections.

```
for i in get_all_stages()
    balances = Dict()
    for pos in get_all_positions()
        a = pos.id
        path = pos.path
        for h in get_all_stages()
            val = sim[1][i][:BookValue][a,h].out # end-of-node book value
            balances[path] = get(balances, path, 0.0) + val
        end
    end
    println("[STEP #", i, "]")
    display(balances)
end

# [STEP #1]
# Dict{Any, Any} with 5 entries:
#   "LIABILITIES/BORROWINGS" => -90.1126
#   "EQUITY/RETAINED EARNINGS" => -3.01251
#   "EQUITY/UGL" => -1.98178
#   "EQUITY/PAR VALUE" => -5.0
#   "ASSETS/LOANS" => 100.107
# [STEP #2]
# Dict{Any, Any} with 5 entries:
#   "LIABILITIES/BORROWINGS" => -90.2265
#   "EQUITY/RETAINED EARNINGS" => -3.02517
#   "EQUITY/UGL" => -1.98886
#   "EQUITY/PAR VALUE" => -5.0
#   "ASSETS/LOANS" => 100.241
# (...)
```

Of course, the final goal must be to persist with incorporating that data in files or feed corporate databases or solutions with it. We will cover the first case in the last example we are going to show.

The second most important report we could generate from simulated data is one with *projected income statements*. In our balance sheet model, we have variables called `IncomeStatement` whose dimensions are exactly the items that should go into our report. Assembling projections of income statements, thus, can be achieved by iterating over all indexes of this auxiliary variable.

In Code Snippet 8.5, we also create dictionaries to hold in memory projections of income statements for each model stage. The implementation is indeed very similar to the one we have already seen on balance sheet reports. However, there is a different approach on iterating over the dimensions of the desired variable. In the first example, we assumed that we knew beforehand the space of possibles indexes for book value variables. That is why we iterated over all contracts and all possible buy stages. In this report, we are assuming we do not know what the items of an income statement are. In such a case, we need to draw out those dimension indexes dynamically from the simulation object itself.

In line 3, we iterate over all keys of an income statement variable at stage `i` of the first simulation. Each of these keys `k` are special objects that, aside from allowing us to retrieve their correspondent values in the simulated dictionary, have stored in them the actual values of the dimensions of a model variable.

These keys have a field `I` which holds the values of each variable dimension in a collection called `Tuple`. Like with a vector, we can get elements of a tuple using integer indexes. In line 4, we access the first element of the tuple of dimension values of a key `k`. We know that all income statement variables have only one dimension, that holds the name of the income statement item. We can get each of those names by using `k.I[1]`.

In order to get the variable value computed by the model, we just need to supply a key to the structure that holds income statement variable results, like we see in line 5. In line 6 we add this item to the dictionary of reports, and display it at the end of the keys iteration. In the commented lines at the end of the Code Snippet we can see a truncated output of the report assembly process.

**Code Snippet 8.5:** Obtaining Income Statement Projections.

```
1   for i in get_all_stages()
2       income_statement = Dict()
3       for k in keys(sim[1][i][:IncomeStatement])
4           item_name = k.I[1]
5           item_value = sim[1][i][:IncomeStatement][k]
6           income_statement[item_name] = item_value
7       end
8       println("[STEP #", i, "]")
9       display(income_statement)
10  end
11
12  # [STEP #1]
13  # Dict{Any, Any} with 17 entries:
14  #  "INTEREST INCOME" => 20.4358
15  #  "INTEREST EXPENSES" => -15.9326
16  #  "NON-INTEREST INCOME" => 2.0513
17  # (...)
```

The final report example is a more general report we call *solution report* that writes into a CSV file the results of a vector of tracked (and simulated) variables. In a more general implementation, we cannot assume that we know the index space of those variables: not only its possible values, but even the number of dimensions each variable has. We don't even know beforehand which variables of interest are control variables and which are state variables.

In the first line of Code Snippet 8.6, we define a vector of variables of interest whose values we want to track in our solution report. The first three variables have two-dimensional indexes, but the last one is a single-dimension variable. The first one is a state variable, while the last three are control variables.

In lines 3–8, we create an auxiliary function that prints into an input-output (IO) object[1] a group of information that is stored in a single line of the report. This includes

1 One example of IO object is a file in which we can read and/or write data.

the name of the variable, the values of its dimensions, and its value. It also includes a field with a state identifier in the case of state variables.

In line 10, we create a new text file called "SolutionReport.csv" and assign it to a variable called `f`. Headers are printed as the first line of the file, in lines 11–12. Then we iterate over all stages and variables. Then, from each key in the variable object, we gather the first and second dimension values in lines 16–17. By using the `get` function we are able to get an empty string as default value for variables that do not have a second dimension, like income statement variables.

In the next line we supply the key `k` in order to retrieve stored values. The types these values will have depend on the type of each variable. For control variables, stored values will be numbers. So, in lines 19–22 we pass that number to `print_result` along with an empty string as state. For state variables, we call the print function twice: for incoming and outgoing states of the variable. These calls will generate two entries in the report file, separating the two states with "in" and "out".

**Code Snippet 8.6:** Creating a Solution Report.

```
1  tracked_variables = [:BookValue, :Buy, :CashFlowsBuy, :IncomeStatement]
2
3  function print_result(io, variable, dimension1, dimension2, state, value)
4      println(
5          io, variable, ",", dimension1, ",", dimension2, ",",
6          state, ",", value
7      )
8  end
9
10 open("SolutionReport.csv", "w+") do f
11     # write header
12     println(f, "Variable,Dim1,Dim2,State,Value")
13     # write content
14     for i in get_all_stages(), variable in tracked_variables
15         for k in keys(sim[1][i][variable])
16             dim1 = get(k, 1, "")
17             dim2 = get(k, 2, "")
18             item_value = sim[1][i][variable][k]
19             if item_value isa Number
20                 # there is no state
21                 state = ""
22                 print_result(f, variable, dim1, dim2, state, item_value)
23             elseif item_value isa SDDP.State
24                 # one line for incoming state
25                 print_result(f, variable, dim1, dim2, "in", item_value.in)
26                 # other line for outgoing state
27                 print_result(f, variable, dim1, dim2, "out", item_value.out)
28             else
29                 error("invalid result type: $(typeof(item_value))")
30             end
31         end
32     end
33 end
```

The product of this snippet will be to create a CSV file to permanently store the results of the simulation. This file will contain basically the raw output coming from the model, and is not very useful as a management report. Nonetheless, such a general report can be useful for at least two reasons.

The first one is debugging. Because this report has the simulated data in its most granular level, one can inspect it in order to investigate possible problems the model might have. Imagine, for instance, that we encounter an unexpectedly large loss for the loans' portfolio in one of the income statement projections we built in the previous example. The first step of investigation could be to create a general report that tracks all simulated income variables. Then we could filter data related to the problematic step and to all loans, to try to spot those specific positions that are causing this unexpected behavior in results.

The second use we could do for a general report is that we can generate more informative reports from it simply by filtering and pivoting data. This can be done programatically, using Julia or another programming language, or with the help of specific software and data solutions. If your institution, for example, uses a data warehouse solution, this is probably the kind of report you should feed your corporate system with in order to generate automated management reports based on the projections coming from your balance sheet model.

# 9 Adding Uncertainty

So far, our mathematical model is completely deterministic, meaning the future path of risk factors is fully known. We refer to this as the "forward scenario," in which yield curves at each node are a series of forward curves calculated at the model's starting date. This scenario is useful for certain applications, particularly when forward rates can be traded through derivative contracts or other instruments that allow investors to protect against future interest rate changes.

However, following this type of static hedging strategy may not align with the bank's risk appetite. Furthermore, such a management policy is likely to be suboptimal in terms of risk-adjusted returns, while, by not considering the uncertainties in the evolution of risk factors, it does not allow diversification opportunities to be explored. This is especially relevant if we consider together the different asset classes that are typically present on a bank's balance sheets.

In practice, the state of the world will not evolve according to the forward scenario, although there is a probability that it will come true. But, there is also a certain probability that a scenario much more stressed than the forward scenario will take place. Unfortunately, the actual probabilities of each of these two illustrative scenarios occurring are unknown, but once we have a guess about their values, combined with their risk appetite, we have a chance to come up with a decision rule that is mathematically more consistent with our guesses than simply betting everything on the realization of the forward scenario.

In order to be able to represent future uncertainties, we sometimes need to resort to a different model architecture than the one we have used so far. Throughout this chapter, we will discuss how to do this, presenting some strategies for representing future uncertainties and their effect in obtaining decision rules from a balance sheet model.

## 9.1 Building Scenarios

In our balance sheet model, we must acknowledge that we can't predict the future with certainty, but we can have some ideas about what the future may look like. We assume that we can give some insight into possible future outcomes and the likelihood of each outcome occurring. The stochastic model is constructed with this uncertainty in mind.

A *scenario* is a set of values for economic and financial variables that affect a bank's balance sheet and income statement. These variables include GDP, inflation, interest rates, yield and spread curves, stock and foreign exchange rates, credit demand, prepayment and withdrawal levels, among many others. We also refer to these variables as *risk factors* because they have an impact on the values that appear on a bank's balance sheet and income statement.

In a stochastic setup, we typically have a collection of possible future scenarios, each with its own probability of occurring. These scenarios are important inputs to the

https://doi.org/10.1515/9783110664669-009

creation of model coefficients. Specifically, each node of the problem will have different coefficients in its internal mathematical model, depending on which scenario was chosen from the probabilistic distribution of scenarios in a specific forward pass. Each forward pass represents a possible trajectory of the economy in which the bank must optimize its balance sheet.

Determining the possible future scenarios and the likelihood of each scenario is a crucial task for a bank and can be quite challenging for the ALM modeler. Various methods, including mathematical, statistical, and econometric techniques, can be used to estimate these scenarios. The challenge of creating these scenarios for an ALM model primarily involves multivariate modeling. While there are many different multivariate models available, there is still no widely accepted method for addressing this issue in the literature or industry.

It's important to remember that the model is essentially a tool for organizing information, including the market views of bank managers. For medium and long-term financial simulation, incorporating people's opinions becomes even more crucial, as historical data may not be as valuable as a fundamental analysis in such time horizons. After all, in three or five years, presidents change, new technologies emerge, new wars break out, new competitors enter the market, and so on. It may not be possible to account for all these possibilities in a traditional econometric model in time, but it is likely that managers will want to consider such scenarios in their decision-making. In summary, we believe that one of the most important attributes of a good scenario generator is the ability to incorporate such opinions on possible future states and their probabilities.

In practice, we believe that incorporating scenarios into decision-making significantly improves the robustness of our decisions. Furthermore, since we are developing a model that aims to optimize an entire bank, it's important to overcome skepticism. One way to do this is by allowing users to see themselves as decision makers. This can be achieved by creating a scenario generator that is more interpretable and less complex.

It is also important to note that having too many risk factors can lead to a highly complex and computationally intensive model that may be difficult or even impossible to solve. This can make it difficult for the bank's management to make informed decisions and can also lead to a less efficient use of resources.

Therefore, it is important for banks to strike a balance between considering all relevant risk factors and keeping the model manageable. This can be achieved by carefully selecting which risk factors to include in the model and by using dimensionality reduction techniques to simplify the model. By doing so, banks can ensure that the optimization model is both accurate and efficient, and that the management can make informed decisions based on the model's output.

However, important as this is, we will not be focused here on presenting those methods, but rather we will assume that we have the means of obtaining future scenarios and probabilities, and storing them in a data structure that is accessible to Julia. This way we can focus on the implementation of the problem and not the scenario generation.

## 9.2 A Simple Stochastic Model

In this session, we will be presenting an implementation of a simple stochastic version of the balance sheet model, which has been previously presented in this book. The incorporation of stochastic elements in the model allows for the analysis of potential risks and uncertainties in financial projections. The session will begin with a review of the basic principles of the original balance sheet model, followed by an explanation of the modifications necessary to make it stochastic.

In Figure 9.1, we can see a visual representation of a linear policy graph. To a balance sheet model that uses such a policy architecture we can add *random variables*, on top of state and control variables we have been discussing in previous implementations. We can also make model coefficients be influenced by the realization of such variables drawn out from their probability distributions $\Omega$.

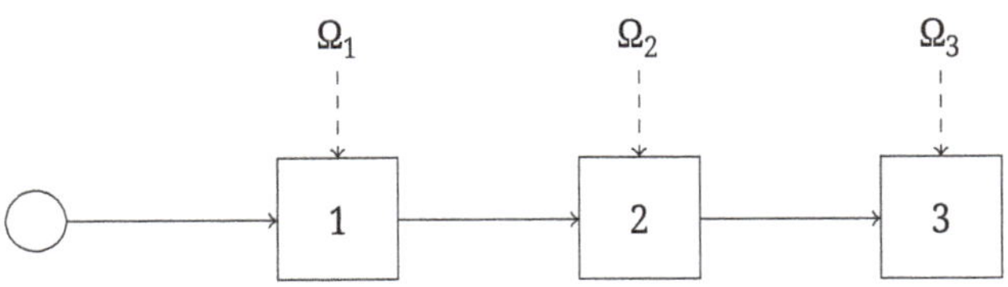


**Figure 9.1:** Linear policy graph example with three stages.

Let's take a look at a simple example where we have one risk factor and two different scenarios: $S_1$, where the risk-free rate is 0.5%, and $S_2$, with a risk-free rate of 1.0%. In this example, we'll imagine that in each of the three stages represented in Figure 4.1, the probability of being in scenario $S_1$ is 20%, 30%, and 40% respectively.

Imagine we have a balance sheet with a valuation constraint, like the `FairValue` variable discussed in Section 6.6.2. At each model step there will be a collection of constraints that calculates the marked-to-market value of each position. Then the group of constraints that represent the dynamics of these variable (Code Snippet 6.9) could be rewritten more succinctly, as we show in Code Snippet 9.1. This JuMP syntax allows us to define a group of constraints in a single call to the `@constraint` macro, creating a *container* (an array) of constraints. It also allow us to give a name to each constraint and refer later to each of them by its name. In this example we are giving a name `FairValueConstraint[a,h]` for each position ID $a$ and stage of buying $h$.

**Code Snippet 9.1:** FairValue State Variable Dynamics – Container Version.

```

s = get_scenario_at_close(stage)
@constraint(
    sp,
    FairValueConstraint[a = ids(get_all_positions()), h = get_all_stages()],
    FairValue[a,h].out ==
```

```
7            model_sign(get_position_by_id(a)) *
8            price(get_position_by_id(a), s) *
9            Quantity[a,h].out
10    )
```

We should pay special attention to line 8, where we are pricing each position $a$ with a deterministic stage-scenario $s$. In an ALM model with stochastic scenarios, we would like to draw this scenario from a probabilistic distribution of scenarios and then use it to create a fair value constraint. Then each forward pass will have a different coefficient for the `Quantity[a,h].out` variable, depending on which scenario is being considered in the pricing function.

We call *model parameterization* the notion of using sampled random noises to modify a subproblem. This sample is in SDDP related drawn from a vector of discrete *realizations* and each respective *probability*. These modifications can be one of: changing the right-hand side constant of a constraint, changing a stage objective definition, or rewriting variable coefficients in a constraint.

In our example we will use the latter to build different fair value constraints, based on the sampled scenario.

In Code Snippet 9.2 we start by defining in lines 2–8 the vectors that contains our example data. The possible realizations of risk-free rates `RF_RATES` is constant over time and can be represented as a vector. The `PROBABILITIES` of each scenario being true is varying over time and can be represented as a vector of vectors. We then use the JuMP container syntax to create a vector of named fair value constraints, over all positions and buying stages.

In this stage we do not know yet what the sampled scenario will be, so we only define the structure of the constraint, meaning that each `FairValue` variable will be a linear function of its `Quantity`. We use a unit coefficient to represent this relationship in line 14.

Then we use the `SDDP.parameterize` function to override those unit coefficients with a scenario-dependent measure. We have to supply as arguments, along with the subproblem, two things: a vector of scenario and its stage-specific vector of probabilities. After that, the sampled quantity (either 0.5% or 1.0%) is available in the variable we called `S`. Although in this simple example we are sampling a single floating-point number, in a multivariate stochastic model we can sample from a vector of vector, or even a vector of a custom data structure we build to store the full amount of data each scenario contains.

Inside each parameterization we can then proceed to build a scenario data structure using the sampled measures (line 20). Then, for each position and buying stage, we proceed to change the fair-value constraint coefficient associated to the `Quantity.out` variable to a new measure that depends on its price under the sample scenario `s` that was built.[1]

1 The function `model_sign` is, like seen before, a function that returns +1 for assets and asset-like positions, and −1 otherwise.

Notice that we need to put a minus sign before the coefficient in line 26, because JuMP always stores constraints in the canonical format. More specifically, the constraint stated in line 14 becomes `FairValue[a,h].out - 1.0 * Quantity[a,h].out == 0.0` in the canonical form.

**Code Snippet 9.2:** FairValue State Variable Parameterization.

```
1
2    # example data
3    RF_RATES = [0.5/100, 1.0/100]
4    PROBABILITIES = [
5        [0.2, 0.8],
6        [0.3, 0.7],
7        [0.4, 0.6]
8    ]
9
10   # creating constraint container with unit coefficients
11   @constraint(
12       sp,
13       FairValueConstraint[a = ids(get_all_positions()), h = get_all_stages()],
14       FairValue[a,h].out == 1.0 * Quantity[a,h].out
15   )
16
17   # parameterizing coefficients, based on sampled scenario S
18   stage_probabilities = PROBABILITIES[stage]
19   SDDP.parameterize(sp, RF_RATES, stage_probabilities) do S
20       s = build_scenario(stage, S)
21       for a in ids(get_all_positions()), h in get_all_stages()
22           JuMP.set_normalized_coefficient(
23               sp,
24               FairValueConstraint[a,h],
25               Quantity[a,h].out,
26               - model_sign(get_position_by_id(a)) * price(get_position_by_id(a), s)
27           )
28       end
29   end
```

It is important to say that there can only be one call to `SDDP.parameterize` inside each model builder function. That is why it is important, in a stochastic setup, to separate all constraints that have scenario-dependent coefficients to apply this procedure to the whole block of constraints in a single call.

The `SDDP.jl` package also allow us, inside a parameterization function, to change the right-hand side of constraints, or to redefine completely a stage objective function.

Imagine that in our model we now have a trading-volume limit for a specific group of positions, like the ones discussed in Section 7.1.8. Imagine also that this trading volume limit, which is uncertain, has a baseline of 1 billion US dollars, but there is a probability of 20% of it being 800 million. It can also be enlarged to 1.3 billion, with a likelihood of 15%.

In Code Snippet 9.3, we define a trading volume limit constraint in lines 14–15 as the sum of 1 billion plus a noise `EPS` that was created in line 7. The noise realizations and their associated probabilities are defined as vectors in lines 3–4. We then use the

`JuMP.fix` function to fix the `EPS` variable to the sampled value that was chosen in the `SDDP.parameterize` block.

**Code Snippet 9.3:** Trading Volume Limit Parameterization.

```

# example data
LIMIT_NOISES = [-200_000_000, 0, 300_000_000]
PROBABILITIES = [ 0.2, 0.65, 0.15]

# defining volume limit noise variable
@variable(sp, EPS)
# cbonds selling limit
cbonds_ids = ids(
    get_positions_by_balance_sheet_path("ASSETS/INVESTMENTS/CORPORATE BONDS")
)
@constraint(
    sp,
    sum(CashFlowsSell[a,h]
        for a in cbonds_ids, h in get_all_stages()) <= 1_000_000_000 + EPS
)

# parameterizing noise, based on sampled scenario epsilon_value
SDDP.parameterize(sp, LIMIT_NOISES, PROBABILITIES) do epsilon_value
    JuMP.fix(sp, EPS, epsilon_value)
end
```

Suppose now that we can estimate a joint probability distribution of risk-free rates and trading volume limit noises and extract discrete representative scenarios from it, like the example in Table 9.1. In this table, the base scenario 3 has a likelihood of 40% with a risk-free rate of 1.0% and a zero trading volume limit noise.

**Table 9.1:** Multivariate scenario example.

| Scenario | Probability | Risk-free Rate | Trading Volume Noise |
|---:|---:|---:|---:|
| 1 | 10% | 0.5% | −300,000,000 |
| 2 | 20% | 0.7% | −100,000,000 |
| 3 | 40% | 1.0% | 0 |
| 4 | 20% | 1.2% | 100,000,000 |
| 5 | 10% | 1.3% | 200,000,000 |

Then we need to resort to a more complex data structure to store the information contained in each scenario. In Code Snippet 9.4, we use named tuples in lines 3–9 to store risk-free rates and trading volume limit noises in a vector of scenarios. After creating fair value constraints and defining a variable to hold noise values (omitted in lines 12–15), we can parameterize our subproblem and replace coefficients and variables with their scenario-dependent values.

In line 20, we build a scenario based on the `rf_rate` field of the named tuple, to be later utilized in the pricing function that determines fair value constraint coefficients. The noise `EPS` used as a constant in the trading volume limit constraint is fixed in line 31, by accessing the `volume_noise` field of the sampled scenario.

**Code Snippet 9.4:** Multivariate Example Parameterization.

```
1
2    # example data
3    SCENARIOS = [
4        (rf_rate = 0.5/100, volume_noise = -300_000_000),
5        (rf_rate = 0.7/100, volume_noise = -100_000_000),
6        (rf_rate = 1.0/100, volume_noise = 0),
7        (rf_rate = 1.2/100, volume_noise = 100_000_000),
8        (rf_rate = 1.3/100, volume_noise = 200_000_000)
9    ]
10   PROBABILITIES = [0.1, 0.2, 0.4, 0.2, 0.1]
11
12   # creating constraint container with unit coefficients
13   # (...)
14   # defining volume limit noise variable EPS
15   # (...)
16
17   # parameterizing noise, based on sampled scenario epsilon_value
18   SDDP.parameterize(sp, LIMIT_NOISES, PROBABILITIES) do SCENARIO
19       # changing fair value constraints coefficients
20       s = build_scenario(stage, SCENARIO.rf_rate)
21       for a in ids(get_all_positions()), h in get_all_stages()
22           JuMP.set_normalized_coefficient(
23               sp,
24               FairValueConstraint[a,h],
25               Quantity[a,h].out,
26               - model_sign(get_position_by_id(a)) * price(get_position_by_id(a), s)
27           )
28       end
29
30       # fixing volume noise
31       JuMP.fix(sp, EPS, SCENARIO.volume_noise)
32   end
```

In short, by utilizing model parameterization in a linear policy graph, we can easily make our model stochastic by using discrete representative scenarios to change the coefficient matrix and right hand side constants of each subproblem. However, when creating long-term scenarios for financial and economic series, it is often beneficial to take into account that the economy operates in different regimes. In the following section, we will examine how to incorporate regime-switching uncertainty into our balance sheet model, to produce more realistic long-term scenarios.

## 9.3 Markov-Switching Uncertainty

A Markov-switching model is a type of econometric model that is used to analyze time series data that exhibit regime-switching behavior. The model assumes that the underlying data generating process is a Markov process, meaning that the probability of being in a particular state at a given time depends only on the state at the previous time. The model also assumes that there are multiple regimes, or states, that the data can switch between, and that the probability of switching between these regimes is governed by a Markov process. Markov switching models are commonly used to analyze economic and financial time series data, such as interest rates, exchange rates, and stock prices.

In Figure 9.2, we have a Markovian policy graph of a three-stage model that has two Markovian States: Good or Bad. Each of the six possible combinations of stage and state has a scenario probability distribution Ω. The arrows in this graph represent transitions, and three of them will be required in a full forward pass.

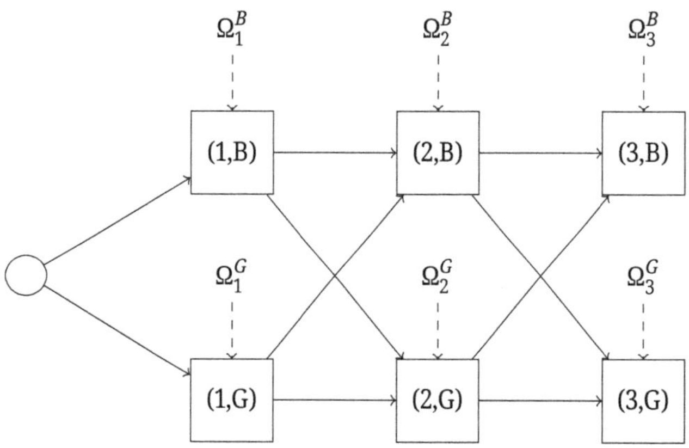


**Figure 9.2:** Markovian policy graph example with three stages and two states.

Transitions in this model are governed by a set of *transition matrices*. These matrices describe the probability of transitioning from one state to another in a discrete time Markov process. Each element in the matrix, denoted by $P_{i,j}$, represents the probability of transitioning from state $i$ to state $j$. The sum of each row in the matrix must equal 1, since the probability of being in one of the states at any given time must equal 1. The number of rows is related to the number of initial states, while each column represents a possible final Markov state.

In our example, three transition matrices will be required: one $1 \times 2$ matrix to select the state in the first step of the model, and two $2 \times 2$ matrices to represent transitions to the second and third steps. For example, if we assume that good state is represented by 1 and bad state equals 2, then Equation 9.1 tells us that there is a 90% probability of being in a good state in the first step.

Given that we are in good state in the first step, the first row of Equation 9.2 means that we have a 70% probability of remaining in a good state in the second step, and a 30%

chance of going into a bad state. If we were in a bad state, there would be a probability of 80% of remaining in a bad state, as shown in the second row of the same matrix.

$$T_1 = \begin{bmatrix} 0.9 & 0.1 \end{bmatrix} \tag{9.1}$$

$$T_2 = \begin{bmatrix} 0.7 & 0.3 \\ 0.2 & 0.8 \end{bmatrix} \tag{9.2}$$

$$T_3 = \begin{bmatrix} 0.6 & 0.4 \\ 0.5 & 0.5 \end{bmatrix} \tag{9.3}$$

Let's first imagine that at each Markov state we know for sure what scenario will take place. To build upon the example introduced in Section 9.2, we can suppose that in a good state we will have a risk-free rate of 1.0% and a 1 billion dollars trading volume limit. In a bad state, rates will drop to 0.5% and trading limits will shrink to 700 million dollars.

In Code Snippet 9.5, we are creating a `SDDP.MarkovianPolicyGraph` that implements this example. Lines 2–6 creates the vector of transition matrices using example data. Notice that in line 3 we use the `transpose` function to transform a vector into a $1 \times 2$ matrix. These matrices are then passed to the Markovian policy graph constructor in line 14.

**Code Snippet 9.5:** Markovian Policy Model Example.

```
1
2   TRANSITION_MATRICES = [
3       transpose([0.9, 0.1]),
4       [0.7 0.3; 0.2 0.8],
5       [0.6 0.4; 0.5 0.5]
6   ]
7
8   STATES = [
9       (rf_rate = 1.0/100, trading_limit = 1_000_000), # good
10      (rf_rate = 0.5/100, trading_limit = 700_000) # bad
11  ]
12
13  model = SDDP.MarkovianPolicyGraph(
14       transition_matrices = TRANSITION_MATRICES,
15       sense = :Min,
16       lower_bound = 0,
17       optimizer = Clp.Optimizer
18
19  ) do sp, node_index
20
21      stage, state = node_index
22
23      s = build_scenario(stage, STATES[state].rf_rate)
24      for a in for a in ids(get_all_positions()), h in get_all_stages()
25          @constraint(
26              sp,
27              FairValue[a,h].out == model_sign(get_position_by_id(a)) *
28                                    price(get_position_by_id(a), s) *
```

```
29                                  Quantity[a,h].out
30          )
31      end
32
33      # cbonds selling limit
34      cbonds_ids = ids(
35          get_positions_by_balance_sheet_path("ASSETS/INVESTMENTS/CORPORATE BONDS")
36      )
37      @constraint(
38          sp,
39          sum(
40              CashFlowsSell[a,h]
41              for a in cbonds_ids, h in get_all_stages()
42          ) <= STATES[state].trading_limit
43      )
44
45      # rest of the model implementation
46      # (...)
47
48  end
```

The model builder function is condensed into the do block, using this compact syntax available to build a model. The two parameters of the builder function are: `sp`, the mathematical model that represents a subproblem to which we will append constraints and an objective function; and `node_index`, which will be a tuple representing the stage and Markov state we are in. For example, if we are building the inner model of the second stage in a good scenario, `node_index` will be the tuple `(2,1)`. We can then unpack their values into two variables, as shown in line 21.

In the body of the model builder function we can retrieve the risk-free rate to build a scenario (line 23), which will then be used to create constraint coefficients, like the one fair value constraints (lines 24–30). We can also use the trading volume limit value to build a limit constraint, like that defined in lines 37–43.

Then we could train and simulate this Markovian balance sheet model using the same `SDDP.train` and `SDDP.simulate` functions we have discussed in Section 8.2. The main difference would be that in a stochastic setup we do need to simulate a number of different replications in order to understand how the policy works under different paths of states.

In Code Snippet 9.6, we simulate ten different replications (i. e., stochastic forward passes) of a Markovian policy in line 15. Then we iterate over the simulation to print all the paths that were generated based on the samples from the transition matrices. In line 21, we access the `:node_index` field of the inner dictionary to gather this information from each stage of each simulation. The results are printed as comments in the end of the Code Listing. We can see that in the first forward pass we started in a good Markov state, which was maintained in the second stage, finishing in a bad state in the last step. Other simulations, of course, followed different paths based on the sampled values from the transition probabilities.

**Code Snippet 9.6:** Simulating a Markovian Policy.

```
# creating a policy graph
model = SDDP.MarkovianPolicyGraph(
    transition_matrices = TRANSITION_MATRICES, # previously built matrices
    subproblem_builder; # model builder function
    stages = 3, sense = :Min, upper_bound = 0.0,
    optimizer = Clp.Optimizer
)

# training a policy
SDDP.train(model; iteration_limit=100)

# simulating a policy
number_replications = 10
variables = [:BookValue]
sim = SDDP.simulate(model, number_replications, variables)

# printing simulated states
for sim_id in 1:length(sim)
    println("Simulation $sim_id:")
    for stage in 1:length(sim[sim_id])
        println(sim[sim_id][stage][:node_index])
    end
end

# Simulation 1:
# (1,1)
# (2,1)
# (3,2)
# Simulation 2:
# (1,1)
# (2,2)
# (3,2)
# Simulation 3:
# (1,1)
# (2,2)
# (3,1)
# (...) (truncated output)
```

So far, in this Markovian setup, all the uncertainty is related to the states the economy will be in on each step of the model. We can go further and define different scenario probability distributions for each Markov state. In Table 9.2, we can see an example of state-dependent multivariate scenarios for risk-free rates and trading volume limits. We could relate this Table to Figure 9.2 by saying that the first three lines are defining the probability distributions $\Omega_1^G = \Omega_2^G = \Omega_3^G$. The last three lines are defining the common probability distributions for all stages that fall into a bad state ($\Omega_1^B = \Omega_2^B = \Omega_3^B$).

In Code Snippet 9.7, we define a vector of names for the two Markov states. Then we create dictionaries to store vectors of scenarios and their respective probability vectors for each state. After creating an `SDDP.MarkovianPolicyGraph` we can have access to the sampled state at each stage, by inspecting the `node_index` parameter of the model builder function. We can unpack the stage and state ids into two separate variables, as

**Table 9.2:** Example of state-dependent scenario probability distributions.

| State | Scenario | Probability | Risk-free Rate | Trading Volume Noise |
|---|---|---|---|---|
| Good | 1 | 20% | 0.5% | −200,000,000 |
| Good | 2 | 70% | 1.0% | 0 |
| Good | 3 | 10% | 1.2% | 100,000,000 |
| Bad | 1 | 10% | 0.9% | −300,000,000 |
| Bad | 2 | 60% | 1.2% | −100,000,000 |
| Bad | 3 | 30% | 1.5% | −50,000,000 |

shown in line 31. The actual state name (`:Good` or `:Bad`) is retrieved from the `MARKOV_STATES` vector in the following line.

With the state name we can retrieve the state scenario realizations and their respective probabilities from the dictionaries we have defined in the beginning of the code. This information will be supplied to `SDDP.parameterize` so that SDDP can sample realizations of each state-dependent probabilistic distribution of scenarios. Of course, we can then proceed to fetch the actual scenario data by its field names in the named tuple. This information will be later used to parameterize the subproblem, i. e., replace coefficients and right-hand side constants.

Another possible use case of model parameterization is to have objective functions that depend on the state. Imagine that in a good state we want to maximize average profit, but in a bad state we want to protect ourselves from a specific risk factor, or penalize more undercapitalizations. By using the `if` statement implemented in lines 47–51 we can re-weight a multi-objective function or even rewrite completely the objective function depending on which Markov state we are in.

**Code Snippet 9.7:** Markovian Example With State-Dependent Scenario Distribution.

```
1
2  TRANSITION_MATRICES = [
3      transpose([0.9, 0.1]),
4      [0.7 0.3; 0.2 0.8],
5      [0.6 0.4; 0.5 0.5]
6  ]
7
8  MARKOV_STATES = [:Good, :Bad]
9  SCENARIOS = Dict(
10     :Good => [
11         (rf_rate = 0.5/100, volume_noise = -200_000_000),
12         (rf_rate = 1.0/100, volume_noise = 0),
13         (rf_rate = 1.2/100, volume_noise = 100_000_000)
14     ],
15     :Bad => [
16         (rf_rate = 0.9/100, volume_noise = -300_000_000),
17         (rf_rate = 1.2/100, volume_noise = -100_000_000),
18         (rf_rate = 1.5/100, volume_noise = -50_000_000)
19     ]
20 )
```

```
21    PROBABILITIES = Dict(:Good => [0.2, 0.7, 0.1], :Bad => [0.1, 0.6, 0.3])
22
23    model = SDDP.MarkovianPolicyGraph(
24        transition_matrices = TRANSITION_MATRICES,
25        sense = :Min,
26        lower_bound = 0,
27        optimizer = Clp.Optimizer
28
29    ) do sp, node_index
30
31       stage, state_id = node_index
32       state = MARKOV_STATES[state_id]
33
34       # model implementation here
35       # (...)
36
37       SDDP.parameterize(sp, SCENARIOS[state], PROBABILITIES[state]) do S
38           # retrieve risk-free rate
39           rf_rate = S.rf_rate
40           # retrieve trading volume limit noise
41           noise = S.volume_noise
42
43           # implement parameterization here
44           # (...)
45
46           # implement state dependent objective function
47           if state ==:Good
48               @stageobjective(sp, ...)
49           else
50               @stageobjective(sp, ...)
51           end
52
53       end
54
55       # rest of the model implementation
56       # (...)
57
58    end
```

The simulation of this Markovian policy is done in Code Snippet 9.8. As before, we use `SDDP.train` to train the policy with 1,000 iterations, and `SDDP.simulate` to run a simulation with 10 replications (forward passes). Using two `for` loops to iterate over all replications and all stages, we can access each sampled state and by accessing the `:node_index` entry in the output dictionary. In this example, the second element of the index tuple will be 1 for `:Good` and 2 for `:Bad`. In line 37 we use this information to retrieve the state name from the `MARKOV_STATES` vector. The sampled scenario is stored under the `:noise_term` entry for the same dictionary. It contains the original scenario tuple that was sampled in each `SDDP.parameterize` of the forward passes. At the end of the Code Snippet we can see the printed output representing each forward pass that was conducted in the simulated policy executions.

**Code Snippet 9.8:** Simulating a Markovian Policy With State-Dependent Scenario Distribution.

```

MARKOV_STATES = [:Good, :Bad]
SCENARIOS = Dict(
    :Good => [
        (rf_rate = 0.5/100, volume_noise = -200_000_000),
        (rf_rate = 1.0/100, volume_noise = 0),
        (rf_rate = 1.2/100, volume_noise = 100_000_000)
    ],
    :Bad => [
        (rf_rate = 0.9/100, volume_noise = -300_000_000),
        (rf_rate = 1.2/100, volume_noise = -100_000_000),
        (rf_rate = 1.5/100, volume_noise = -50_000_000)
    ]
)

# creating a policy graph
model = SDDP.MarkovianPolicyGraph(
    transition_matrices = TRANSITION_MATRICES, # previously built matrices
    subproblem_builder; # model builder function
    stages = 3, sense = :Min, upper_bound = 0.0,
    optimizer = Clp.Optimizer
)

# training a policy
SDDP.train(model; iteration_limit=100)

# simulating a policy
number_replications = 10
variables = [:BookValue]
sim = SDDP.simulate(model, number_replications, variables)

# printing simulated states
for sim_id in 1:length(sim)
    println("Simulation $sim_id:")
    for stage in 1:length(sim[sim_id])
        node_index = sim[sim_id][stage][:node_index]
        state = MARKOV_STATES[node_index[2]]
        noise = sim[sim_id][stage][:noise_term]
        println("$state: $noise")
    end
end

# Simulation 1:
# Good: (rf_rate = 0.01, volume_noise = 0)
# Good: (rf_rate = 0.012, volume_noise = 100000000)
# Bad: (rf_rate = 0.012, volume_noise = -100000000)
# Simulation 2:
# Good: (rf_rate = 0.005, volume_noise = -200000000)
# Bad: (rf_rate = 0.012, volume_noise = -100000000)
# Bad: (rf_rate = 0.009, volume_noise = -300000000)
# Simulation 3:
# Bad: (rf_rate = 0.012, volume_noise = -100000000)
# Bad: (rf_rate = 0.012, volume_noise = -100000000)
# Good: (rf_rate = 0.01, volume_noise = 0)
# (...) (truncated output)
```

To summarize, simulating a balance sheet model requires thorough testing and preparation for various potential scenarios. This includes training the model with multiple scenarios and testing it against a wide range of possible future outcomes. This chapter covered ways to incorporate probability and uncertainty into the model, both in the constraints and objectives of linear policy graphs and in regime-switching Markovian policy graphs.

By incorporating uncertainty and potential variations into the model, it can better account for changes in market conditions, economic fluctuations, and unforeseen events that may affect a bank's financial performance. This leads to a more reliable balance sheet model that can better inform decision-making and risk management.

# 10 Troubleshooting Strategies

Debugging is a crucial step in the creation of any computer program. Even for small and straightforward programs, it's likely that your initial attempt to code a solution will have bugs when run. The process of identifying and fixing issues within a program is called debugging or troubleshooting. This chapter will focus mainly on techniques for debugging problems caused by mistakes in the mathematical specifications of a model. While these techniques can be applied generally, we will use examples from the development of balance sheet optimization models to illustrate them.

## 10.1 Optimal, Infeasible, and Unbounded

Before we begin to discuss the problem-solving techniques that we may need throughout the development of our mathematical model of balance optimization, we need to define the possible statuses of completing a process of attempting to solve a mathematical model.

The first of these is the *optimal status*, and to come across it is already great news, but it is not enough to be a reason for celebration, unfortunately. The optimal status only indicates that the mathematical solver was able to find at least one feasible solution for the mathematical model. That is, the solver found values for the decision variables in order to maximize the objective function while respecting all the restrictions of the model. However, it does not exclude the possibility that the model is poorly specified or incomplete. Therefore, additional validations are needed to ensure that the solution makes sense. Such validations may consist of checking the values of balance sheet accounts, the income statement, risk measures, etc. Here, validations rules different from those already required by the specification of the mathematical model are especially useful, which of course will already be met by the optimal solution. However, a certain amount of skepticism does not hurt, and validating compliance with restrictions is also important, as there will always be a risk of poor specification, especially in constraints that are conditioned to specific stages or states, or any conditional piece of the source code, etc.

The second termination status in a mathematical model resolution process is *unbounded status*. The term unbounded refers to the objective function, and it means that the solver was able to find at least one combination of values for the decision variables that brought the value of the objective function to infinite in maximization problems (or minus infinite in minimization problems). In a mathematical model for balance optimization, it is easy to see how this type of problem can happen. A bank is nothing more than an intermediary, which raises funds and lends them by adding a spread to remunerate its costs, risks, and to guarantee some profit. If a bank can finance itself infinitely and lend an indefinitely high volume, it can make infinite profits. However, in practice this is not possible for a number of reasons. One of them is the existing limits for supply

https://doi.org/10.1515/9783110664669-010

and demand for credit, which naturally must be considered as model constraints. Another reason is the existence of limits on leverage, concentration, and risks that may not have been correctly considered. An important aspect about unbounded status is that it can occur for a purely numerical reason, and not for a problem of poor specification of constraints. This can happen if the weights that multiply the terms of the objective function are too high, so that when they are multiplied by the profit or other objectives, they take the objective function to values above the representation limit of the computer or the solver. In an unbounded solution, the mathematical solver does not give us the value of the decision variables, and therefore its debugging needs a different strategy than the one used when we have the optimal status.

The third possible termination status is an *infeasible status*, and it is certainly the most challenging of the three. It indicates that the mathematical solver was unable to find a combination of values for the decision variables that respects all constraints. In the simplest cases of infeasibility, good mathematical solvers are able to indicate at least one constraint that cannot be met. In many cases, this indication is provided very quickly already in the preprocessing stage, in which the solver tries to reduce the model by eliminating redundant variables and constraints before calling the solution method. Although it is already an important input for the debugging process, this tip provided by the solver can lead the modeler to look for the problem in incorrect parts of the model. This can happen because, in most cases, constraints work in a coordinated way with each other, and the error in one of them can imply infeasibility problems in others. In other words, the tip provided by the solver does not always point to the root cause of infeasibility. In fact, it is precisely at this point that debugging problems in mathematical programming models becomes substantially different from debugging general computer problems. The solving process runs in a practically atomic way, its step-by-step execution. So, the use of break-points, the inspection of the value of variables during the execution, etc. are not available strategies for troubleshooting. Therefore, the success in the process of debugging infeasibilities will depend strongly on the skill and experience of the modeler, who must seek to know the possible relationships between the different model constraints.

## 10.2 Unit Tests

As mentioned, our work is not done when the termination status of the solver is optimal. Thereafter, we need to validate the optimal solution that was calculated by the solver. A good strategy to do this is to develop a set of *unit tests* to be performed on the solution provided. Ideally, these tests should be completely automated, so that they can be easily repeated with each run of the model. The more comprehensive the set of tests, the more sure the modeler will be about the quality of the solution obtained. However, to prioritize the process of implementing automated tests, it is worth following a top-down strategy, in which the highest level accounts of the balance sheet, the income statement, and the capital and risk reports are subjected to basic tests of sanity about their order of magnitude, sign, and accounting consistency.

Typical tests consist of validating compliance with the main constraints of the model, such as equity between assets and liabilities and the total fund-balance constraint, which requires that the sum of all cash flows is always equal to zero. Sanity tests of capital adequacy ratios are also quite useful, since the bank's capital, expressed in the numerator, is the result of the dynamics of the entire balance sheet with scenarios, strategy, and accounting rules, while the risk, expressed in the denominator, synthesizes the profile of the optimal portfolio of assets and liabilities produced by the model. If the capital adequacy ratio shows reasonable values and signs, however, there is still room for problems, since if the model is poorly formulated, it can correct an error with another in an attempt to respect a hard constraint defined on capital ratios.

Unit tests can also be very useful to explore the misuse of slack variables, whether they are used as a part of the model, or just a problem-solving device. In summary, a wide range of unit tests is essential not only to validate the quality of the solution, but also to greatly speed up the process of developing and debugging problems, especially in cases of large models, where each execution can take several hours.

## 10.3 Disabling Constraints

When faced with an infeasible termination status, then the model is probably having difficulty respecting one or more constraints. Depending on the complexity of the problem, it is likely that the solver will be able to indicate exactly which constraint is being violated, which can greatly speed up the solution process. In complex cases, the infeasibility may be due to a non-trivial combination of model constraints, so that the solver cannot even objectively indicate where the problem is. It will be up to the modeler to try and trace the constraints that are possibly the source of the infeasibility.

For example, let's imagine we have a constraint that limits debt issuing running alongside a minimum liquidity constraint. Depending on input data, it can be the case that the new debts limit for a certain period is not enough to achieve a minimum liquidity portfolio. In that case, disabling either of the constraints will make the problem feasible again. In other words, none of the two constraints is responsible alone for the infeasibility state we have reached, but rather it is the combination of both that causes the issue.

Having chosen the investigation targets, we can disable the suspicious constraints and check if in this way the solver is able to find a viable solution. When choosing research targets, it is interesting that the modeler follows the opposite path to that of the implementations, starting with the last constraints that were added or changed in the model. To try and isolate the problem as much as possible, initially it is advisable that the modeler disable the restrictions one at a time, and not several at the same time, although this may be necessary in the debugging of more complex unfeasibilities.

When we find the constraint problematic, we can think about partially disabling it, for example only after a certain stage of time. In this way, the modeler will be able to identify if there is a generalized problem in the definition of the constraint, or if it only fails in specific situations. If the model works well up to stage 5, for example, it may be that the infeasibility is related to specific events that only occur from that stage, such as expiring contracts, mandatory purchases or sales, or any other assumptions that are used only from the stage up to which the model works correctly. If the problem occurs due to specific contracts, it may be legitimate or it may be the result of problems in modeling the contract coefficients.

In the process of debugging infeasibility problems, the full or partial disabling of restrictions is certainly the most effective technique, although this method is often quite manual and dependent on the modeler's knowledge. On the other hand, it is precisely during the process of debugging complex unfeasibilities that we have the opportunity to think deeply about the balance sheet and the bank's *modus operandi*, and in some cases it may even be possible to have new insights about the model or the institution itself. Therefore, we should not be saddened by the termination status being infeasible, as it probably has a lot to teach us about how the bank works.

In the example of a conflict between new debt issuance limits and a minimum liquidity policy, it is the infeasibility that gives us the opportunity to re-discuss those policies and calibrate those limits in order to avoid having conflicts between these two valid and noble objectives.

## 10.4 Temporary Slack Variables

Disabling constraints that are candidates of causing infeasibility problems is an effective mechanism for testing such a hypothesis. Typically, this can be achieved by simply commenting on the source code corresponding to the constraint, which will completely neutralize its influence on the model. An intermediate debugging alternative is the introduction of temporary slack variables into supposedly problematic constraints. In multistage stochastic optimization models, it is interesting to index slack variables in time and scenario, as this will allow the modeler to detect the root causes of infeasibility points more precisely. As with any slack variable, in order for them to influence the model properly, their use will need to be penalized in the objective function, with potentially high weights, so that they are only triggered when it is really necessary to avoid an infeasible solution.

In Code Snippet 10.1, we add two temporary slack variables to a total book value constraint. We create them as two non-negative variables. While `TotalBookValueSlackPositive` is intended to cover a positive book value gap, `TotalBookValueSlackNegative` is deducted from the total sum of book values in line 18, and is responsible for covering negative gaps in the total sum of book values.

In lines 22–26, we simulate the objective function penalty terms that disincentivize the usage of these slack variables in a solution. This means that the model will always try to use them as little as possible in order to reach a feasible state. This also implies that no optimal solution will use both slacks at the same time. Notice that we are assuming a maximization problem, and that is why we use negative coefficients for those slack variables in the objective function. If we had a minimization problem, they would obviously need positive coefficients to have the same effect.

**Code Snippet 10.1:** Adding a Temporary Slack Variable to a Model.

```
1
2    # original total book value constraint
3    # constraint(
4    #  sp,
5    # sum(BookValue[a,h] for a in get_all_positions(), h in get_all_stages()) == 0.0
6    # )
7    #
8
9    # slack variables
10   @variable(sp, TotalBookValueSlackPositive >= 0)
11   @variable(sp, TotalBookValueSlackNegative >= 0)
12
13   # new total book value constraint
14   @constraint(
15       sp,
16       sum(
17           BookValue[a,h] for a in get_all_positions(), h in get_all_stages()
18       ) + TotalBookValueSlackPositive - TotalBookValueSlackNegative == 0.0
19   )
20
21   # new penalty term added to objective function (if maximizing)
22   @stageobjective(
23   # (...)
24       - 100 * TotalBookValueSlackPositive
25       - 100 * TotalBookValueSlackNegative
26   # (...)
27   )
```

Although more laborious than disabling constraints completely, the temporary slack variables are more powerful in the debugging process while allowing, in addition to identifying problematic constraints, to estimate the extent of infeasibility by inspecting the values assumed by the slack variables. In some cases, the modeler may even conclude that problematic constraints cannot be met unconditionally in all time stages and scenarios, so that the slack variables used for debugging have to be incorporated into the model definitively.

## 10.5 Limiting Objective Function

In cases of unbounded termination status, disabling constraints partially or fully will not help in solving the problem. In fact, what we need is just the opposite. That is, we need to add constraints to the model in order to prevent the objective function from growing indefinitely. A hypothetical situation in which this could happen would be one in which the bank can borrow indefinitely and lend all resources at a rate higher than that of borrowing. Obviously, such a model would not be realistic, since in the real world the bank will be subject to a series of constraints regarding incremental funding costs, restrictions on demand for credit, leverage limits, and risk limits.

Provided they are well formulated and coded, such constraints are likely to be able to prevent unbounded termination status from occurring. However, once this occurs, it can be difficult to identify which of these restrictions is missing or simply badly coded. In these cases, an interesting strategy is to limit the value that can be assumed by the objective function using a constant high enough to allow the villains to appear. Typically, the root cause of the problem will be exposed by the disproportionate growth of the balance of specific accounts in liabilities and assets that are not properly controlled by the leverage and risk constraints.

However, in some cases the termination status may occur not due to problems in the restrictions, but simply due to the order of magnitude of the objective function, which in large models can be composed of a series of terms, each weighted by different weights to give a sense of priority, but that when misconfigured can lead the solver to conclude that the model is unbounded, when in fact it is a problem of scale of the objective function coefficients. These cases can be identified when, after limiting the objective function, we do not observe erroneous behavior in the balance sheet accounts.

## 10.6 Inspecting Contract Sets

Throughout the model, mathematical expressions are always expressed by summation over sets of contracts. As we saw in Chapter 5, we can and need to segment financial contracts under different criteria, including currency, index, account classification, portfolio etc. When poorly specified, such sets will lead to errors in the formulation of restrictions and the objective function. In extreme cases, badly specified sets can lead to infeasibility problems, but the most problematic situations are those in which the solver is able to find an optimal solution but which, however, is not a correct solution. The poor definition of contract sets is a trivial problem close to the other challenges involved in the construction of a large sized model, but once it occurs it does so in a mysterious way and it may take time for the modeler to suspect that this could be the root cause of the problem.

Thus, the most recommended option is that these risks are mitigated through an analysis, preferably automatic, of coverage and consistency of the sets of contracts. The coverage analysis aims to ensure that all contracts are covered by the sets, so that none of them is inadvertently left out of the calculations. Consistency analyses may consist of assessing whether a contract does not belong to two mutually exclusive sets, so that they contribute in a duplicate way to the calculation of profits or risk measures, for example.

In the first case, the model will probably have difficulties in respecting the equality restriction between assets and liabilities, since the variation in the contract value will be accounted for twice in profit. In the second case, infeasibility problems may not occur, but the risk will be overestimated, leading the model to overrebalance its portfolios to decrease it. That is, the model will make an error to correct another. Depending on the materiality of the contracts, this bug may simply go unnoticed.

As a final warning, it is important to emphasize that although contract sets are very simple components in the general architecture of the model, they are relatively dynamic, and it is common to need to change and create new sets to accommodate new modeling needs. It is extremely dangerous and unproductive to underestimate the risks arising from its bad specification, and it is essential to have routines to test the coverage and correction of the sets, both in the development phase and in the phase and debugging.

## 10.7 Inspecting Coefficient Matrices

In our approach to the problem, the coefficients of the mathematical model play a crucial role in representing the payment schedule and overall evolution of the contract value over time and in different scenarios. These coefficients express the changes in contract balance, cash flows, market value, and other essential quantities necessary for modeling. They also indicate the contract's maturity, the point at which it reaches a zero value.

Additionally, the model is equipped with coefficients to simplify the modeling of the income statement, which is vital for ensuring accounting consistency. Even if all the model's equations are written correctly, errors in the coefficient preparation phase can cause the model to fail. Common mistakes include incorrect signals, non-zero coefficients for expired contracts, and coefficients with excessively high values.

Overall, these issues are relatively straightforward to identify and fix. These errors often prevent the model from satisfying the equity constraints between assets and liabilities or the constraint that requires total cash flow to be zero. This is particularly significant because these constraints apply to all modeled contracts. Therefore, it can be challenging to pinpoint which contracts have poorly modeled coefficients. The process of debugging and correcting the coefficients may need to be done for all contracts, but this is precisely what is expected in the automated unit testing phase. In other words, it's better to prevent these issues by catching them early on.

## 10.8 Analyzing LP Files

The process of debugging a problem typically begins with analyzing the code written in a high-level programming language. In this case, we are using Julia and its extension, the JuMP package. To refresh your memory, JuMP adds additional functions and macros to Julia, allowing us to efficiently describe optimization models that closely mirror the mathematical equations defining the problem. The Julia/JuMP problem description is the only representation of the problem that we will work with directly.

However, in certain situations, it may be beneficial to export the model definition to other formats to aid in the debugging process. Two popular formats supported by major commercial mathematical solvers are LP and MPS. These are plain text files that describe the decision variables, constraints, and objective function of the model.

The main difference between representing the model in Julia/JuMP and LP or MPS formats is that the latter presents the definitions in an expanded format. This means that instead of a loop creating multiple restrictions by time and scenario, each restriction will be listed separately. The sums involving the variables that make up a set of contracts will be broken down into their individual terms, and the coefficients can be seen as actual numbers rather than variables. This expansion makes LP and MPS files less visually appealing to the modeler and they can potentially be large depending on the number of contracts, stages, and states required by the model. However, with practice in handling and reading these files, certain modeling problems can become quickly evident, particularly in the coefficients.

Exporting the model to these formats can also be useful if the modeler wants to test its resolution using another solver that does not have direct integration with Julia/JuMP. These files can also be used for interaction with software vendors, if you have a support contract to help you with debugging or fine-tuning the model by selecting scale, tolerance, and the best algorithm parameters.

## 10.9 Changing Solver Tolerance

Solving mathematical programming models is a demanding process of numerical computation, during which the various equality and inequality restrictions are tested multiple times.

While computers are capable of representing numbers with high precision, it's not always practical to use all that potential when designing an algorithm. In many cases, it's sufficient to use only three decimal places instead of 16 or 32. Mathematical solvers are general-purpose software and do not have information about the desired level of precision from the modeler. Therefore, they have default settings to dictate the degree of precision used to test the model's constraints.

If the formulation does not have scale problems, meaning it does not have vastly different coefficient sizes, the default precision of the solvers will not cause issues. However, in medium to large Asset-Liability Management (ALM) models, scale problems can easily occur due to the wide variety of constraints required. Some can be expressed in billions of dollars, such as risk limits, while others can be less than one, such as leverage limits. While it is possible to re-scale these numbers, it harms the readability and maintainability of the model since the equations have moved away from representing the business rules and become focused on numerical calculation issues.

A scale problem may be suspected when constraints are properly formulated and coefficients are correct, but the mathematical solver still reports a problem of infeasibility. A simple way to test this is by slightly changing the values on the right-hand side and checking if the infeasibility is eliminated. In this case, we are not changing the solver's accuracy, but the model coefficients in a localized way.

In more complex cases where the problem's origin is uncertain, we can adjust the solver's overall tolerance level to be less strict on the equality and inequality tests. This should be done with caution, particularly for problems with restrictions written at different scales. For example, 0.1 may not be significant in a constraint that limits the sales of a particular asset, but it can be crucial in a constraint that limits the bank's leverage.

When used correctly, fine-tuning the model's tolerance level can not only help solve numerical infeasibility problems but also speed up the solution process, saving a lot of time.

## 10.10 Fine-Tuning Your Solver

In addition to adjusting tolerance parameters, there are typically many other ways to fine-tune the performance of the mathematical programming solving routine. These options vary depending on the nature of the problem, the type of mathematical programming problem, and the solver software being used.

Linear Programming (LP) solvers are used to solve optimization problems where the objective function and constraints are all linear. Some common parameters used in LP solvers include:

- **Tolerance**: this parameter sets the level of precision required for the solution. A lower tolerance will result in a more accurate solution but may take longer to compute.
- **Maximum number of iterations**: this parameter sets the maximum number of iterations that the solver will perform before stopping.
- **Algorithm**: this parameter selects the algorithm used by the solver. Common choices include simplex method, Interior Point Method (IPM), and barrier method.
- **Pivot strategy**: this parameter controls the order in which the solver selects the pivot variable and pivot row/column during the simplex method.
- **Scaling**: this parameter controls the use of scaling techniques to improve the numerical stability of the problem.
- **Presolve**: this parameter controls the use of presolve techniques to simplify the problem before solving it.
- **Dual simplex**: this parameter controls the use of the dual simplex algorithm to improve the solution during the solving process.

These are just some examples. Depending on the solver, there might be other parameters specific to that solver.

Mixed Integer Linear Programming (MILP) solvers are used to solve optimization problems where some of the variables are restricted to be integers. Some common parameters used in MILP solvers include:

- **Branching strategy**: this parameter controls the order in which the solver explores the solution space. The most common strategies are depth-first and best-first.
- **Node selection strategy**: this parameter controls which node to explore next.
- **Cut generation**: this parameter controls the use of cutting planes to improve the linear relaxation of the problem.
- **Heuristics**: this parameter controls the use of heuristics to guide the search for feasible solutions.
- **Time limit**: this parameter limits the amount of time that the solver is allowed to run before stopping.
- **Integer tolerance**: This parameter controls the level of precision required for the integer variables.
- **Presolve**: this parameter controls the use of presolve techniques to simplify the problem before solving it.
- **Feasibility pump**: this parameter controls the use of the feasibility pump algorithm to improve the solution during the solving process.

## 10.11 Using Different Solvers

In most cases, when there are problems with solving a model, it is the modeler's mistake rather than an issue with the mathematical solver. High-end commercial software, which is developed and thoroughly tested by large teams of researchers, has a much lower chance of having bugs compared to new, untested software like yours. Therefore, before suspecting a bug in the mathematical solver, it is important to thoroughly search for any issues in your own code.

Nonetheless, it can be beneficial to test the model resolution using different solvers if multiple options are available. Even though these software serve the same purpose, each solver may approach the problem differently. The basic algorithms may be similar, but these software are equipped with various heuristic layers to accelerate the search for a solution, whether in the pre-processing phase or during the resolution itself.

Due to these variations, different solvers may perform better depending on the specific problem being solved. For example, solver A may be faster than solver B, but solver B may be more effective at identifying infeasibility issues. Testing the model on multiple solvers can greatly improve the efficiency of the development and debugging process.

One of the great benefits of using Julia/JuMP is the ease with which you can switch between solvers by simply changing one line of code, especially if the solvers in question have an integration with Julia. Fortunately, major commercial solvers such as Gurobi,

Cplex, Xpress, and others have integrations with the JuMP package. If you need to test the resolution of the model on a solver that is not compatible with JuMP, you can always choose to export the model to LP or MPS formats and then solve them using the alternative solver.

# 11 Conclusions

Throughout this book, we have tried to provide a comprehensive survey of the most varied challenges associated with implementing a balance sheet optimization model, from high-level simple modeling guidelines to code snippets to implement accounting rules and constraints to represent risk limits. We hope that the journey has been pleasant, at least most of the time, and that we have contributed to helping the reader broaden their vision on the subject and pave the way for those who wish to carry this banner forward in their work environments.

However, we are convinced that the material presented is just a snapshot and that the topic of balance sheet optimization is a living topic, as are the different areas of knowledge involved in this task. In particular, the dynamism of the economy, financial markets, regulation and technology, that continually change the way people and corporations function, deserve to be highlighted. Given the incredible complexity of the world and the increasing speed of technological change, it is to be expected that banks and financial institutions will continue to undergo profound transformations in their most different layers of operation.

Whenever we need to change, we need time to understand the new situation, to make decisions, and for the decisions to have the desired effect. For organizations, the same is true, just as it is true that time is money. If a bank or organization of any nature needs more and more time to correct its ways, more and more money will be needed. In extreme cases, some of them may simply go bankrupt in an attempt to adapt to new contexts. Therefore, for a bank to be able to truly protect itself against future turmoils, it must be able to formulate its decision problem in an increasingly realistic way in terms of the set of decisions that can be taken, when they can be taken, and, mainly, in terms of an increasing number and variety of possible futures that may occur.

This modeling refinement comes at a price, that is partially associated with the number of people needed to carry on with the arduous task of modeling the different aspects of the balance sheets dynamics. But not all banks seem to have agreed to the importance of having an integrated optimization model. And even among those who already understand the need, many still haven't allocated enough resources to face the challenges. Many others have already started to venture out, but still limit model use to meeting specific regulatory demands, or annual planning exercises, which prevents them from reaping all the benefits that can indeed be obtained through a system of this nature.

And speaking of regulators, it also seems to us that they could be more effective if they themselves had their own balance sheet simulation models, which could be used to coordinate systemic stress tests more efficiently, for which they would only need to receive inputs from the institutions, and not the simulation results. We are not suggesting that the current approach based on delegating to financial institutions the execution of simulations must be abandoned. The current approach is essential and has a disciplinary character, since it encourages and enforces financial managers to carry out and incorporate regulatory exercises and their results into management. But we believe that

https://doi.org/10.1515/9783110664669-011

this mode of operation could perhaps be complemented with a more proactive posture by supervisors. Having their own balance sheet simulation/optimization model – which can be conditioned to the banks' inputs – would enable them to do the calculations themselves instead of saying how it has to be done.

Another part of the price we will have to pay to take the balance sheet optimization discipline one step further concerns computing power. As we try to represent more granularly the functioning of banks and their ecosystem, larger models will become, demanding much and much more computing capacity. In order to be able to abandon the simplifications that we still need to make today when building a balance sheet optimization model, we will need more computational power. Part of this need may be partially met at some point in the near future by the thriving and promising quantum computing. (Sutor, 2019)

Such technology can leverage mathematical optimization in the near future by allowing for more efficient and accurate calculations of complex optimization problems, and in particular for combinatorial optimization problems, where the computational explosion is an even bigger bottleneck. Quantum computing could also help to improve the performance and accuracy of non-linear models, which is especially useful for banks, while economics, individual risks, diversification effects, customer behavior, and that of companies' counterparts can be represented much more realistically.

However, the potential increase in computing power that can come from technological advances will not necessarily be accessible to all institutions at the same time and to the same extent. And even if they are, this probably won't be a silver bullet. Mathematical optimization will continue to be a very challenging task from a theoretical and computational point of view, so that the progress coming from quantum computing, although substantial, will be smaller in relative terms when compared to what can be obtained in other areas of computing. The need for advances in areas like algorithms, mathematical modeling, statistics, and machine learning will not be eliminated. In the context of optimizing balance sheets and the economy in general, we believe that advances will come from an increasing convergence of these areas of knowledge. One example would be the advances in the field of *Optimization with Constraint Learning*, (Fajemisin et al., 2021) which tries to capture complex underlying relationships between decisions, contextual variables, and outcomes using machine learning and embed them in a traditional optimization model. Such techniques would certainly be of help when representing non-linear risk measures in a linear balance sheet model framework.

Nor can we start to underestimate the need to understand the most fundamental areas such as accounting, financial calculations, and regulation, since these are and will remain the cornerstones of the model. If misplaced, the damage can be even greater, as it will be amplified by incredible computational power. In addition, these areas of knowledge make up the language through which technicians can communicate with non-technicians. Any small difficulty in this interaction is extremely harmful, since it can make room for poorly formulated models, and misinterpreted results, putting to waste all the effort to develop such complex models.

Finally, from a more philosophical point of view, we believe that the financial system has an important role in the development of the world, although many times these have been corrupted by people of low character. In this sense, we believe that all efforts to make the system more efficient are extremely valid and desirable. We believe that the knowledge presented in this work – optimizing banks – fits into this category. They can be used not only to increase the profits of individual organizations, but to improve the efficiency of the financial system, on which countless people and families of the most varied ethnicities and social conditions across the globe depend. After all, as highlighted by Nobel laureate Robert Schiller, finance is not merely about making money. It's about achieving our deep goals and protecting the fruits of our labor. It's about stewardship and, therefore, about achieving the good society.

# Appendix A Introduction to Julia, JuMP, and SDDP

## A.1 Considerations

Throughout this book, we present code snippets for an ALM model written in Julia programming language. More specifically, we use Julia version 1.6 syntax along with the packages `SDDP.jl` version 0.4.6 and `JuMP.jl` version 1.1.1. In this appendix we will be giving a brief introduction to Julia syntax and to those two important mathematical modeling packages, to help you in case you are not familiar with these tools. Julia download instructions can be found at https://julialang.org/downloads/.

We prefer and have been using Julia to run mathematical programming models for a long time because it delivers C-like performance with a clean high-level syntax and a nice package ecosystem.

We believe that scripting languages, like Python, are also great for mathematical programming. Nonetheless, you have to be very careful to create efficient code to compute model coefficients, as this part of the process is usually more computational-intensive for ALM models than it is for other more classical applications of mathematical programming.

We also believe that traditional compiled languages, like C and C++, are also great choices to do mathematical programming because of their performance. On the other hand, code written in those languages can often end up being harder to be maintained and to be understood by someone who is not familiar with its syntax.

With all that said, we hope that you also find Julia's syntax very clear and easily translatable to your preferred programming language.

## A.2 Julia Basics

After installing Julia, you just need to execute `julia` to get into Julia's interactive mode (also called REPL).

```
> julia

   _       _ _(_)_     |  Documentation: https://docs.julialang.org
  (_)     | (_) (_)    |
   _ _   _| |_  __ _   |  Type "?" for help, "]?" for Pkg help.
  | | | | | | |/ _` |  |
  | | |_| | | | (_| |  |  Version 1.6.4 (2021-11-19)
 _/ |\__'_|_|_|\__'_|  |  Official https://julialang.org/ release
|__/                   |
```

https://doi.org/10.1515/9783110664669-012

You can then run a simple command to test your REPL:

```
julia> 1+1
2
```

You can then proceed to create an integer variable x and a floating point number y and do some basic math operations.

```
julia> x = 2
2

julia> y = 3.5
3.5

julia> x + y # addition
5.5

julia> x - y # subtraction
-1.5

julia> x * y # multiplication
7.0

julia> x / y # division
0.5714285714285714

julia> x ^ y # exponentiation
11.313708498984761
```

All functions that can be applied to scalar values can also be applied to vectors and matrices. We just need to prepend a dot sign to the operator in order to apply it element-wise in the set of numbers.

```
julia> X = [1,2,3] # vector of integers
3-element Vector{Int64}:
1
2
3
```

```
julia> Y = [1.5, 2.5, 3.5] # vector of floating point numbers
3-element Vector{Float64}:
1.5
2.5
3.5

julia> X .+ Y
3-element Vector{Float64}:
2.5
4.5
6.5

julia> X .- Y
3-element Vector{Float64}:
-0.5
-0.5
-0.5

julia> X .* Y
3-element Vector{Float64}:
1.5
5.0
10.5

julia> X ./ Y
3-element Vector{Float64}:
0.6666666666666666
0.8
0.8571428571428571

julia> X .^ Y
3-element Vector{Float64}:
1.0
5.656854249492381
46.76537180435969
```

We can also define a matrix by using spaces between elements and semicolons separating rows.

```
julia> A = [1 2 3; 4 5 6; 7 8 9]
3x3 Matrix{Int64}:
1  2  3
4  5  6
7  8  9

julia> B = [1 0 0; 0 1 0; 0 0 1]
3x3 Matrix{Int64}:
1  0  0
0  1  0
0  0  1

julia> A .+ B
3x3 Matrix{Int64}:
2  2   3
4  6   6
7  8  10
```

There is a very useful syntax to define arrays and matrices with iterations over an existing collection. In this example we create a vector of integers with the number of letters of each element in a string vector, with the use of the `length` function.

```
julia> fruits = ["apple", "banana", "watermelon"]
3-element Vector{String}:
"apple"
"banana"
"watermelon"

julia> [length(f) for f in fruits]
3-element Vector{Int64}:
5
6
10
```

Then we create a matrix with the logarithm of each element contained in another matrix. This can be done by iterating over each element of the matrix and applying the `log` function.

```
julia> A = [1 2 3; 4 5 6; 7 8 9]
3x3 Matrix{Int64}:
1  2  3
4  5  6
7  8  9

julia> [log(x) for x in A]
3x3 Matrix{Float64}:
0.0       0.693147  1.09861
1.38629   1.60944   1.79176
1.94591   2.07944   2.19722
```

Finally, we can get or set elements and subsets of a vector (or matrix) by using their indices between brackets. These indices are integers between 1 (first element) and the length of that dimension (which can be referred to with the keyword `end`).

```
julia> A = [1 2 3; 4 5 6]
2x3 Matrix{Int64}:
1  2  3
4  5  6

julia> A[2,3] # row 2, column 3
6

julia> A[1,3] = 0 # row 1, column 3 becomes 0
0

julia> A
2x3 Matrix{Int64}:
1  2  0
4  5  6

julia> x = [10,20,30,40]
4-element Vector{Int64}:
10
20
30
40
```

```
julia> x[end] = 50
50

julia> x
4-element Vector{Int64}:
10
20
30
50
```

There is a special kind of collection that stores key-value pairs, called a dictionary. We can use keys as indexes to retrieve or to set values. There is also a special iterator to iterate simultaneously over keys and values of a dictionary. Please notice that the information in a dictionary is not stored in any particular order.

```
julia> d = Dict("A" => 1, "B" => 2)
Dict{String, Int64} with 2 entries:
"B" => 2
"A" => 1

julia> d["A"]
1

julia> d["C"] = 3 # setting new value
3

julia> d
Dict{String, Int64} with 3 entries:
"B" => 2
"A" => 1
"C" => 3

julia> for (k, v) in d
            println("for $k we have a value of $v")
       end
# for B we have a value of 2
# for A we have a value of 1
# for C we have a value of 3
```

## A.3 Julia Packages

As in many other programming languages, Julia's basic functionalities can be extended by importing packages, i. e., pieces of code that help you implement specific tasks. Packages can be imported with the `using` command. When it is the first time you use a package, it can be necessary to install it by using `add` function that is part of the preinstalled `Pkg` package.

In this example we are using the preinstalled package `Dates` to create two dates and query the number of actual days between them.

```
julia> using Dates

julia> d1 = Date(2022,1,1) # Jan 1st
2022-01-01

julia> d2 = Date(2022,2,1) # Feb 1st
2022-02-01

julia> d2-d1
31 days
```

Finally, we are installing the `JuMP` package and using it.

```
julia> using Pkg

julia> Pkg.add("JuMP")

julia> using JuMP
```

## A.4 JuMP Basics

In the words of its creators, the Julia package called `JuMP` (Dunning et al., 2017) is a "modeling language and collection of supporting packages for mathematical optimization in Julia. `JuMP` makes it easy to formulate and solve a range of problem classes, including linear programs, integer programs, conic programs, semidefinite programs, and constrained nonlinear programs."

It is a fast, user-friendly, and solver-independent library that helps you create and solve mathematical optimization problems with an easy-to-understand syntax.

Let's solve the following linear problem, using `Clp` as solver:

$$\begin{aligned} \text{maximize} \quad & 50x + 120y \\ \text{subject to} \quad & 100x + 200y \leq 10000 \\ & 10x + 30y \leq 1200 \\ & x + y \leq 110 \\ & x, y \leq 0 \end{aligned}$$

First we load all required packages and create a new model, passing the `Clp` optimizer to its constructor function. Notice that it is an empty model, i. e., a feasibility problem without variables.

```
julia> using JuMP

julia> using Clp

julia> model = JuMP.Model(Clp.Optimizer)
A JuMP Model
Feasibility problem with:
Variables: 0
Model mode: AUTOMATIC
CachingOptimizer state: EMPTY_OPTIMIZER
Solver name: Clp
```

Then we can add the two variables x and y with the `@variable` macro, and set the maximization objective function by using `@objective`. Notice that we can set non-negativity constraints while creating variables.

```
julia> @variable(model, x >= 0)
julia> @variable(model, y >= 0)

julia> @objective(model, Max, 50x + 120y)
50 x + 120 y
```

Now it is time to add the other constraints, by using the `@constraint` macro.

```
julia> @constraint(model, 100x + 200y <= 10000)
100 x + 200 y <= 10000.0

julia> @constraint(model, 10x + 30y <= 1200)
10 x + 30 y <= 1200.0

julia> @constraint(model, x + y <= 110)
x + y <= 110.0
```

A print of the model object allows us to check if the problem is well-defined. The function `optimize!` calls `Clp` solver to run the optimization routine.

```
julia> print(model)
Max 50 x + 120 y
Subject to
100 x + 200 y <= 10000.0
10 x + 30 y <= 1200.0
x + y <= 110.0
x >= 0.0
y >= 0.0

julia> optimize!(model)
Coin0506I Presolve 3 (0) rows, 2 (0) columns and 6 (0) elements
Clp0006I 0  Obj 0 Dual inf 170 (2)
Clp0006I 3  Obj 5400
Clp0000I Optimal - objective value 5400
Clp0032I Optimal objective 5400 - 3 iterations time 0.012
```

By using the `termination_status` function we can check if an optimal solution was found. You can get the optimal values for the variables with the help of the `value` function.

```
julia> termination_status(model)
OPTIMAL::TerminationStatusCode = 1

julia> value(x)
60.0
```

```
julia> value(y)
20.0
```

When we have bigger models, it is common to organize variables in arrays. Let's illustrate that procedure with a simple 0-1 knapsack problem. Imagine we have one unit of different fruits. Each fruit has a weight and a price, and we want to carry as much worth of fruits in our knapsack as possible, subject to the knapsack's maximum weight capacity.

First we need to load JuMP and Cbc solver, create two dictionaries with weights and prices, and also define a total weight limit.

```
julia> using JuMP

julia> using Cbc

julia> WEIGHTS = Dict(
"apple" => 150,
"orange" => 200,
"watermelon" => 800,
"kiwi" => 80
)
Dict{String, Int64} with 4 entries:
"orange"     => 200
"kiwi"       => 80
"apple"      => 150
"watermelon" => 800

julia> PRICES = Dict(
"apple" => 5,
"orange" => 6,
"watermelon" => 12,
"kiwi" => 7
)
Dict{String, Int64} with 4 entries:
"orange"     => 6
"kiwi"       => 7
"apple"      => 5
"watermelon" => 12
```

```
julia> FRUITS = keys(WEIGHTS)
KeySet for a Dict{String, Int64} with 4 entries. Keys:
"orange"
"kiwi"
"apple"
"watermelon"

julia> WEIGHT_LIMIT = 1000
1000
```

Now we can create an empty model and define binary variables x for each fruit, to store whether it will be in our knapsack or not. Notice that with a single `@variable` we are actually defining four variables, one for each fruit.

```
julia> model = JuMP.Model(Cbc.Optimizer)
A JuMP Model
Feasibility problem with:
Variables: 0
Model mode: AUTOMATIC
CachingOptimizer state: EMPTY_OPTIMIZER
Solver name: COIN Branch-and-Cut (Cbc)

julia> @variable(model, x[f in FRUITS], Bin)
1-dimensional DenseAxisArray{VariableRef,1,...} with index sets:
Dimension 1, ["orange", "kiwi", "apple", "watermelon"]
And data, a 4-element Vector{VariableRef}:
x[orange]
x[kiwi]
x[apple]
x[watermelon]
```

Then we can define the objective function as the maximum sum of prices of each fruit in our bag. We do that easily using Julia's `for` iterator to browse over all fruits.

```
julia> @objective(model, Max, sum(PRICES[f] * x[f] for f in FRUITS))
6 x[orange] + 7 x[kiwi] + 5 x[apple] + 12 x[watermelon]
```

Finally, we can add our total weight constraint and print the resulting model.

```
julia> @constraint(
        model,
        sum(WEIGHTS[f] * x[f] for f in FRUITS) <= WEIGHT_LIMIT
)
200 x[orange] + 80 x[kiwi] + 150 x[apple] + 800 x[watermelon] <= 1000

julia> println(model)
Max 6 x[orange] + 7 x[kiwi] + 5 x[apple] + 12 x[watermelon]
Subject to
200 x[orange] + 80 x[kiwi] + 150 x[apple] + 800 x[watermelon] <= 1000
x[orange] binary
x[kiwi] binary
x[apple] binary
x[watermelon] binary
```

After optimizing the model, we can see that we have an optimal solution that yields us a total price of 19.

```
julia> optimize!(model)
Welcome to the CBC MILP Solver
Version: 2.10.5
Build Date: Jan  1 1970
(truncated output)
Result - Optimal solution found

Objective value:                19.00000000
Enumerated nodes:               0
Total iterations:               0
Time (CPU seconds):             0.08
Time (Wallclock seconds):       0.08

Total time (CPU seconds):       0.08   (Wallclock seconds):   0.08

julia> println(termination_status(model))
OPTIMAL
```

```
julia> objective_value(model)
19.0
```

We can iterate over all fruits to see that one watermelon and one kiwi were allocated in the bag.

```
julia> for f in FRUITS
                  println(f, ": ", value(x[f]))
              end
orange: 0.0
kiwi: 1.0
apple: 0.0
watermelon: 1.0
```

Finally we can evaluate the total weight of the bag by summing the product of weight and x, to get a total weight of 880.

```
julia> sum(WEIGHTS[f] * value(x[f]) for f in FRUITS)
880.0
```

## A.5 SDDP Basics

SDDP (Dowson and Kapelevich, 2021) is a package for solving large multistage convex stochastic programming problems using stochastic dual dynamic programming. In this kind of problem, an agent takes decision over multiple time steps, and there is uncertainty in the variables observed by this agent. In each of these steps (stages) the agent incurs a cost (or a gain) when taking that decision, which is also referred to as the *stage objective*, which will be the object of the minimization or maximization process.

In each node (place of decision), there are three types of variables. The most important are the *state variables*, which allow information to flow from node to node. It always comes into a node with the income state, is updated during the decision making, and goes out to the next node with its outgoing state. In the context of a portfolio, for instance, the quantity invested in a financial asset could be a state variable. The initial quantity (incoming state) goes into a node, the agent takes a decision to buy, sell or maintain the investment, and an updated quantity is sent to the next node as an outgoing state, in which a new decision will be taken.

The other type of variable are *control variables*, which usually store actions and auxiliary data. In the previous example, the quantity sold could be a control variable. Control variables only exist in the scope of a particular node, and their value cannot be carried across nodes.

Finally, we can also have *random variables*, which add uncertainty into the model. This could be, for example, the return of the financial asset to be observed in a particular node. In practice, this value is stochastic and drawn from a given distribution.

One important concept in stochastic dual dynamic programming is a *policy graph*, which is the way multiples nodes are connected together. The most simple policy is the *linear policy graph*, in which each node is connected to a subsequent node, and a decision is taken step by step throughout the nodes.

Let's solve a simple production planning example using the SDDP framework. Imagine we face a demand of 60, 90, and 75 items for the next three months, during which we can produce a maximum of 100 items to supply the demand or to keep it in inventory for the next periods. Our warehouse capacity is 50 items, and we start with a inventory of 20 items. We want to fulfill all the demand in the next three periods, incurring a production cost of 30, 10, and 20 dollars respectively for months 1, 2, and 3. The cost of holding an item in inventory is 5 dollars per month. Code Snippet A.1 gives us a full implementation of the Julia code that solves this problem using `SDDP` package and `GLPK` free solver.

From lines 6–14 we define problem data as global variables, to be used in the `subproblem_builder` function, which is responsible for creating mathematical models for each of the three stages (subproblems) of the whole problem. Two parameters are required for a linear policy graph subproblem builder function: a `JuMP.Model` (named `sp` in this example) and the integer representing the stage that is being created. In our example, this function will be called three times by the `SDDP` library when building the whole problem: passing the value 1 to create the first stage, 2 to build the second, and so on.

Inside each subproblem we define a inventory state variable (line 19) as a non-negative integer variable. We also use the parameter `initial_value` to set the incoming state at stage 1 to `INITIAL_INVENTORY`. We also add two non-negative integer control variables to represent production output and market demand in each subproblem.

In the heart of our model is the state variable dynamics constraint (line 26). It says how we update our inventory state variable given its incoming state and the decision that was made in this node. From lines 27–30 lie the other constraints, that set a ceiling for production and inventory and define the demanded quantity for a particular stage by reading the appropriate position in the `DEMAND` vector.

Finally we set the stage objective to be minimized as the production cost plus warehouse costs.

**Code Snippet A.1:** Production Planning SDDP Implementation.

```

using SDDP
using JuMP
using GLPK

# PROBLEM DATA
# Stage-dependent data
PRODUCTION_COST = [30, 10, 20]
INVENTORY_HOLDING_COST = [5, 5, 5]
DEMAND = [60, 90, 75]
# Constants
MAXIMUM_PRODUCTION = 100
INITIAL_INVENTORY = 20
MAXIMUM_INVENTORY = 50

function subproblem_builder(sp::JuMP.Model, stage::Int)

    # State variables
    @variable(sp, inventory >= 0, SDDP.State, Int, initial_value = INITIAL_INVENTORY)

    # Control variables
    @variable(sp, production >= 0, Int)
    @variable(sp, demand >= 0, Int)

    # State variable Dynamics
    @constraint(sp, inventory.out == inventory.in + production - demand)
    # Constraints
    @constraint(sp, inventory.out <= MAXIMUM_INVENTORY)
    @constraint(sp, production <= MAXIMUM_PRODUCTION)
    @constraint(sp, demand == DEMAND[stage])

    # Stage objective
    @stageobjective(
        sp,
        PRODUCTION_COST[stage] * production + INVENTORY_HOLDING_COST[stage] * inventory.out
    )

end

model = SDDP.LinearPolicyGraph(
    subproblem_builder;
    stages = 3,
    sense = :Min,
    lower_bound = 0.0,
    optimizer = GLPK.Optimizer
)

SDDP.train(model, iteration_limit = 100)

SIMULATED_VARIABLES = [:inventory, :production, :demand]
NUMBER_OF_SIMULATIONS = 1
sim = SDDP.simulate(model, NUMBER_OF_SIMULATIONS, SIMULATED_VARIABLES)

```

```
54 for stage in 1:length(sim[1])
55     println("")
56     println("STAGE $stage")
57     for k in SIMULATED_VARIABLES
58         println(name(k), ": ", sim[1][stage][k])
59     end
60 end
61
62 #
63 # STAGE 1
64 # inventory: SDDP.State{Float64}(20.0, 0.0)
65 # production: 40.0
66 # demand: 60.0
67 #
68 # STAGE 2
69 # inventory: SDDP.State{Float64}(0.0, 10.0)
70 # production: 100.0
71 # demand: 90.0
72 #
73 # STAGE 3
74 # inventory: SDDP.State{Float64}(10.0, 0.0)
75 # production: 65.0
76 # demand: 75.0
```

From lines 40–46, we create a linear policy graph with 3 stages and set the optimization sense to minimize the stage objective function. An important parameter for the SDDP algorithm is the lower bound of the stage objective (or upper bound for maximization), that we have set to the theoretical minimum cost of 0 (no production nor stock). Finally we set the optimizer to be used in the optimization routine as GLKP. Now that we have a policy graph, we initiate the training process of the SDDP algorithm (line 48), which use cuts to approximate the Bellman Function of the problem (for more details see Dowson and Kapelevich (2021)). The criteria that we use to interrupt the training is 100 iterations.

Now that our model is trained we can simulate the policy to get the optimization results. Because our problem will typically have a lot of variables, we can set the variables of interest (*tracked variables*) as a parameter of the simulation function. As there is no uncertainty in this example, we only need to simulate once.

From `SDDP.simulate` we get a vector of simulations (in our case the only simulation will be hosted at `sim[1]`). Each simulation is also a vector with one dictionary for each stage of the problem. Each dictionary has one entry for each tracked variable. So, for example, if we want to get the production level at the second stage of the first simulation, the code would be `sim[1][2][:production]`.

From lines 54–60 we iterate over all stages and tracked variables printing the output represented in commented lines 62–76. Because we have the highest production cost at stage 1, the optimal solution is to end stage 1 with no inventory. As stage 2 has the minimum production cost, it is optimal to produce at full capacity at stage 2 (maximum of 100 units), leaving an inventory of 10 units to stage 3.

Now let's introduce a stochastic demand to our problem. Imagine that our total demand is comprised of the expected demand, given in our last example, plus an unexpected term which is stochastic and can be one of –10, –5, 0, 5 or 10 units, each with equal probability. That said, the expected demand of 60 units in stage 1 would have realizations of 50, 55, 60, 65 or 70 units, each scenario with 1/5 of probability. In Code Snippet A.2 we can see the implementation of this stochastic demand optimization problem.

**Code Snippet A.2:** Production Planning SDDP with Stochastic Demand.

```

using SDDP
using JuMP
using GLPK
using Statistics

# PROBLEM DATA
# Stage-dependent data
PRODUCTION_COST = [30, 10, 20]
INVENTORY_HOLDING_COST = [5, 5, 5]
EXPECTED_DEMAND = [60, 90, 75]
# Stochastic model
UNEXPECTED_DEMAND = [-10, -5, 0, 5, 10]
PROBABILITIES = [1/5, 1/5, 1/5, 1/5, 1/5]
# Constants
MAXIMUM_PRODUCTION = 100
INITIAL_INVENTORY = 20
MAXIMUM_INVENTORY = 50

function subproblem_builder(sp::JuMP.Model, stage::Int)

    # State variables
    @variable(sp, inventory >= 0, SDDP.State, Int, initial_value = INITIAL_
        INVENTORY)

    # Control variables
    @variable(sp, production >= 0, Int)
    @variable(sp, demand >= 0, Int)

    # Stochastic variables
    @variable(sp, EPSILON, Int)
    SDDP.parameterize(sp, UNEXPECTED_DEMAND, PROBABILITIES) do x
        JuMP.fix(EPSILON, x)
    end

    # State variable Dynamics
    @constraint(sp, inventory.out == inventory.in + production - demand)
    # Constraints
    @constraint(sp, inventory.out <= MAXIMUM_INVENTORY)
    @constraint(sp, production <= MAXIMUM_PRODUCTION)
    @constraint(sp, demand == EXPECTED_DEMAND[stage] + EPSILON)

    # Stage objective
    @stageobjective(
        sp,
        PRODUCTION_COST[stage] * production + INVENTORY_HOLDING_COST[stage]
            * inventory.out
    )

```

```
48  end
49
50  model = SDDP.LinearPolicyGraph(
51      subproblem_builder;
52      stages = 3,
53      sense = :Min,
54      lower_bound = 0.0,
55      optimizer = GLPK.Optimizer
56  )
57
58  SDDP.train(model, iteration_limit = 100)
59
60  SIMULATED_VARIABLES = [:inventory, :production, :demand]
61  NUMBER_OF_SIMULATIONS = 1000
62  sim = SDDP.simulate(model, NUMBER_OF_SIMULATIONS, SIMULATED_VARIABLES)
63
64  for i in 1:3
65      production_vector = [s[i][:production] for s in sim]
66      inventory_vector = [s[i][:inventory].out for s in sim]
67      cost_vector = (PRODUCTION_COST[i] .* production_vector) .+ (INVENTORY_
            HOLDING_COST[i] .* inventory_vector)
68
69      mu = round(mean(cost_vector), digits = 2)
70      ci = round(1.96 * std(cost_vector) / sqrt(length(sim)), digits = 2)
71
72      println("Cost at stage $i: ", mu, " +- ", ci)
73
74  end
75
76  # Cost at stage 1: 1197.3 +- 12.95
77  # Cost at stage 2: 1050.97 +- 2.17
78  # Cost at stage 3: 1297.8 +- 12.35
```

In lines 11–14 we define the data necessary for generating scenarios of demanded units. In the subproblem builder function we have now a stochastic variable `EPSILON` being defined and populated in lines 29–33. We use the function `parameterize` to fix the value of EPSILON equal to the value x drawn from the discrete distribution in each simulation.

The total demand is now being defined as the expected demand plus the stochastic part `EPSILON` (line 40). With that setup we are running 1,000 simulations in line 62.

With the help of the `Statistics` package, we are calculating confidence intervals for the total cost in each of the three stages (lines 64–74). The results are shown as comments in lines 76–78. Notice the creation of production and inventory levels vectors in lines 65 and 66, and the vectorized syntax involved in the creation of the cost vector (line 67).

# Bibliography

Bardaeva, P. (2021). *Bank Asset Liability Management Best Practice*. De Gruyter, Berlin, Boston.

Bellman, R. (1957). *Dynamic Programming*. Dover Publications.

Bertsimas, D. and Tsitsiklis, J. (1997). *Introduction to linear optimization*. Athena Scientific.

Bezanson, J., Edelman, A., Karpinski, S., and Shah, V. B. (2017). Julia: A fresh approach to numerical computing. *SIAM Review*, 59(1):65–98.

Birge, J. R. (2022). George Bernard Dantzig: The pioneer of linear optimization. *Production and Operations Management*, 31(5):1909–1911.

Black, F. and Scholes, M. (1973). The pricing of options and corporate liabilities. *Journal of Political Economy*, 81(3):637–654.

Board, F. S. (2009). Principles for sound compensation practices. https://www.fsb.org/wp-content/uploads/r_0904b.pdf. [Online, accessed 01-February-2023].

Choudhry, M. (2018). *The Moorad Choudhry Anthology*.

Dowson, O. and Kapelevich, L. (2021). SDDP.jl: a Julia package for stochastic dual dynamic programming. *INFORMS Journal on Computing*, 33:27–33.

Dunning, I., Huchette, J., and Lubin, M. (2017). JuMP: A modeling language for mathematical optimization. *SIAM Review*, 59(2):295–320.

Dupire, B. (1994). Pricing with a smile. *Risk*, 7:18–20.

Fajemisin, A., Maragno, D., and Hertog, D. d. (2021). Optimization with constraint learning: A framework and survey.

Gatheral, J., Jaisson, T., and Rosenbaum, M. (2018). Volatility is rough. *Quantitative Finance*, 18(6):933–949.

Guill, G. D. (2016). Bankers trust and the birth of modern risk management. *Journal of Applied Corporate Finance*, 28(1):19–29.

Heston, S. L. (1993). A closed-form solution for options with stochastic volatility with applications to bond and currency options. *Review of Financial Studies*, 6(2):327–343.

Knuth, D. E. (1997). *The Art of Computer Programming, Vol. 1: Fundamental Algorithms*. Addison-Wesley, Reading, Mass., third edition.

Lima, F. G., De Castro Junior, S. C., Júnior, T. P., and Gaio, L. E. (2014). Performance of the different RAROC models and their relation with the creation of economic value. a study of the largest banks operating in Brazil. *Contaduría y Administración*, 59(4):87–104.

Markowitz, H. (1952). Portfolio selection. *The Journal of Finance*, 7(1):77–91.

Nemhauser, G. L. and Wolsey, L. A. (1988). *Integer and Combinatorial Optimization*. Wiley-Interscience, USA.

Pereira, M. (1989). Optimal stochastic operations scheduling of large hydroelectric systems. *International Journal of Electrical Power Energy Systems*, 11(3):161–169.

Pereira, M. V. and Pinto, L. M. (1991). Multi-stage stochastic optimization applied to energy planning. *Mathematical programming*, 52(1):359–375.

Sutor, R. (2019). *Dancing with Qubits: How Quantum Computing Works and how it Can Change the World*. Expert Insight. Packt Publishing.

Williams, H. (2013). *Model Building in Mathematical Programming*. Wiley.

https://doi.org/10.1515/9783110664669-013

# List of Figures



https://doi.org/10.1515/9783110664669-014

# List of Tables




https://doi.org/10.1515/9783110664669-015

# List of Code Snippets



https://doi.org/10.1515/9783110664669-016

# About the Authors

**Diogo Gobira** is a skilled finance professional and entrepreneur with a strong background in quantitative risk management and mathematical finance. He holds a Master of Science degree in Mathematical Finance from the Institute for Pure and Applied Mathematics (IMPA), and has worked as a Market Risk and Quantitative Modelling Manager at BNDES (Brazilian National Development Bank). Diogo is proficient in a range of technical areas, including programming, databases, derivatives pricing, portfolio optimization, integrated risk management, IRRBB, FTP, stress testing, and balance sheet optimization. Diogo is also a co-founder of Financial Risk Academy, a company specializing in the development of balance sheet optimization models and advanced training and consulting in quantitative finance.

**Lucas Processi** is an engineer and financial expert with a passion for market risk management and pricing of financial instruments. With a Bachelor's degree in Production Engineering from the Federal Fluminense University (UFF) and a Master's degree in Economics and Finance from the Getulio Vargas Foundation (FGV), Lucas is a market risk manager at the Brazilian National Development Bank (BNDES) and one of the founders of the Financial Risk Academy, where he shares his expertise in quantitative finance and programming with students and professionals alike. Additionally, his experience in the banking industry has enabled him to be a consultant in robo-advisors development, mathematical programming, ALM, and balance sheet optimization.

https://doi.org/10.1515/9783110664669-017

## About the Series Editor

**Moorad Choudhry** is an independent non-executive director at Recognise Bank Limited, a non-executive director at the Loughborough Building Society and a non-executive director at the Wandle Housing Association. He is Honorary Professor at University of Kent Business School. He was latterly Treasurer, Corporate Banking Division at The Royal Bank of Scotland.

Moorad is a Fellow of the Chartered Institute for Securities & Investment, a Fellow of the London Institute of Banking and Finance, a Fellow of the Global Association of Risk Professionals, a Fellow of the Institute of Directors and a Freeman of The Worshipful Company of International Bankers. He is author of *The Principles of Banking* (John Wiley & Sons 2012, 2022).

Moorad was educated at Claremont Fan Court school, University of Westminster and University of Reading. He obtained his MBA from Henley Business School and his PhD from Birkbeck, University of London. He was born in Bangladesh and lives in Surrey, England.

https://doi.org/10.1515/9783110787429-013

https://doi.org/10.1515/9783110664669-018

# Index



https://doi.org/10.1515/9783110664669-019

## The Moorad Choudhry Global Banking Series

*Principles of Green Banking: Managing Environmental Risk and Sustainability*
by Suborna Barua

*Reverse Stress Testing in Banking: A Comprehensive Guide*
by Michael Eichhorn, Tiziano Bellini, and Daniel Mayenberger (eds.)

*Bank Asset Liability Management Best Practice: Yesterday, Today and Tomorrow*
by Polina Bardaeva

*Random Walks in Fixed Income and Foreign Exchange: Unexpected Discoveries in Issuance, Investment and Hedging of Yield Curve Instruments*
by Jessica James, Michael Leister, and Christoph Rieger

*Banking Associations: Their Role and Impact in a Time of Market Change*
by Sladjana Sredojevic and Milan Brkovic

*Inflation-Linked Bonds and Derivatives: Investing, Hedging and Valuation Principles for Practitioners*
by Jessica James, Michael Leister, and Christoph Rieger

*Banking in the Age of the Platform Economy: Digital Acceleration Through Strategies of Interdependence*
by Giorgio Bou-Daher

*ALM Modeling and Balance Sheet Optimization: A Mathematical Approach to Banking*
by Diogo Gobira and Lucas Processi

www.degruyter.com

www.ingramcontent.com/pod-product-compliance
Lightning Source LLC
Chambersburg PA
CBHW080937240926
51849CB00004BA/480
*9783110664225*